WHAT COULD I SAY?

A HANDBOOK FOR HELPERS

WHAT COULD I SAY?

PETER HICKS

Inter-Varsity Press

INTER-VARSITY PRESS
38 De Montfort Street, Leicester LE1 7GP, England

First published 2000

British Library Cataloguing in Publication Data
A catalogue record for this book is available from the British Library.

ISBN 0–85111–538–1

Set in Garamond
Typeset in Great Britain by Avocet Typeset, Brill, Aylesbury, Bucks
Printed and bound in Great Britain by Creative Print and Design
(Wales), Ebbw Vale

Inter-Varsity Press is the book-publishing division of the Universities and Colleges Christian Fellowship (formerly the Inter-Varsity Fellowship), a student movement linking Christian Unions in universities and colleges throughout Great Britain, and a member movement of the International Fellowship of Evangelical Students. For more information about local and national activities write to UCCF, 38 De Montfort Street, Leicester LE1 7GP.

CONTENTS

People in long, dark valleys need extra patience, love and support ... 31

Beware of the seven evil spirits ... 33

The people of God are a fantastic support ... 34

Watch out for one of the devil's nastiest tricks ... 35

Give them the whole will of God ... 36

Make the most of the Bible ... 37

Prayer is the key ... 39

PART 2
·······

PLEASE START HERE

They didn't have counsellors or pastoral workers in Bible times. But they had a tremendous way of helping and caring for those who were hurting or in need.

They all cared for each other.

In Old Testament days if you were in trouble it was your family or small local community that helped you. If special wisdom or counsel was needed you would probably turn to the head of the family, or to the elders in the community.

In the New Testament the local church took over much of the caring role of the family. Here hurting or troubled individuals found support, security, practical help, love, and wise counsel. And it wasn't just the church leaders who did the helping. Everyone did it. It was a key part of the ministry of the body.

Our society tends to assume that caring and helping are the responsibility of the professionals and experts. In our churches, too, we're increasingly turning to trained counsellors for professional help. Undoubtedly there's a place for this, but it doesn't mean that all the rest of us can therefore do nothing. There's still tons for us to do.

Sometimes when people need help they need a trained counsellor. But most times they don't. My guess is that the proportion is about one in ten. That is, 90% of the time they need the kind of love and support and listening ear and so on that any Christian should be able to give. It's only 10% of the time, or less, that they need a trained counsellor.

On the day I'm writing this, I've been involved in trying to help two individuals. One has just been bereaved; the other is facing a marriage break-up. Both urgently need understanding and love and support and prayer. But neither, at the moment, needs professional counselling. I've offered the possibility of marriage counselling to the second person, but his response is: 'At the moment I just want someone to talk to.' If something should go wrong in the grieving process the first person may one day need specialized help; but at the moment what she needs is the caring, understanding support that every Christian ought to be able to give.

Two issues arise from this. First, all Christians, and especially those who find themselves confronted with hurting or needy people, need to do what they can to make their caring and helping as effective as possible. We all know from experience that it's pretty easy to make things worse by saying or doing the wrong thing. But, equally, being aware of some basic principles and a bit of background information can often make our help much more effective.

Secondly, if 10% of the time the people we are trying to help need a trained counsellor, it's vital we are able to spot when this is so. We'll do neither them nor ourselves any good if we fail to do this, and try to plough on on our own.

This book sets out to cover these two points. It's not a training manual for professional counsellors. I happen to have the privilege of being involved in running a training course for professional counsellors, and I'm aware that there are plenty of such books around already.

But this is a book for the 90%. Its aim is to help caring Christians do what the New Testament calls us to do as parts of the body of Jesus Christ together in the local church, and at the same time to spot when people need the kind of help that only trained counsellors can give.

As far as possible I've tried to avoid using technical terms, or assuming knowledge of technical issues. But if you should come across something that needs further explanation, check the index for additional material elsewhere in the book.

USING THIS BOOK

The first part of the book outlines some general principles which are foundational in our helping and caring for people. Much of it you'll already know, but we all need to be reminded of these things, and to check that we are putting them into practice. So it's worth reading through those pages more than once, and even using them as an aid to a periodic check-up to make sure that there's nothing in us that gets in the way of the effectiveness of our caring.

The second part of the book lists in alphabetical order a broad range of issues we may encounter. This is primarily designed for easy reference as and when issues arise. Not every issue is listed. That would require a very large volume. But often issues overlap, or material that is relevant to one issue is also applicable to another, so, if you find the topic you're looking up is not in the second section, have a look for it in the index. For example, though there are no sections specifically on amputation or burglary, the index will refer you to the articles on bereavement and trauma, both of which contain relevant material.

The lengths of the articles vary. Most start with a general introduction and then give background information that we need to know in order to understand and help the person involved. This kind of information is important, since it helps us to begin to see where the person is at, why they feel as they do, and so on. Keeping such information in mind can help us avoid making obvious mistakes, and should help us to express an understanding and accepting attitude.

The articles then move on to more practical material. This is not meant to be a set of instructions that you have to follow. Clearly, every situation is unique, and it is quite impossible to prescribe just what should be done and said in every given situation. So what is written here is no more than suggestions of what could be helpful, and of the kind of things you might say. The thing here is to read them through, all the time keeping the specific situation or individual very much in mind, and seeking the wisdom and guidance of God in just how to apply the material in that situation.

This is especially true of the 'What could I say?' sections. In most cases there is plenty of material here – far too much to say all at once! Each paragraph starts with a basic suggestion, written in italics, and then goes on to amplify it. Perhaps, as you read the section through, just one or two of the suggestions will stand out as particularly applicable in the current situation; obviously, they will need to be presented in your own words, and shared with the person in a sensitive way that is relevant and helpful to them at that time.

Sometimes an article will contain some practical exercises, such as the 'Five sheets of paper' exercise that can be used to help people struggling with low self-esteem, or the 'Marriage check-up'. Where they're relevant, these can be used as they stand. But you may well feel it right to adapt them for a specific situation.

The articles tend to assume that the person you are seeking to help is a Christian or at least sympathetic to a Christian approach. But a fair bit of the material can be adapted and used should you find yourself involved with someone who rejects Christianity.

If, when you look up an article, you begin to feel you are a bit out of your depth, do be willing to admit it, both to yourself and to the person you are trying to help. Assure them that you are still willing to stand by them and offer general support and Christian love, but encourage them to get specific help from someone who has the particular knowledge or skills to help them (see 'A note on resources', on p. 304). The same applies if, part-way through the process of helping someone, you find that issues are arising that you don't feel you can cope with, or if you feel that you've done all that you can and yet the person needs further specific help. Never be afraid to admit your own limits, and to stick within them. But, of course, if you do encourage the person to get more specific help from someone else, don't just drop them and leave it all to the expert. Continue to offer your support and help in every way that is appropriate.

Many articles give suggestions of books for further reading. Some of these are the kind of book you would give to the person you are seeking to help. Again, be careful here. Have a look at the book first, to check that it is suitable. And remember that when people are going through difficult situations they may not feel like reading, particularly if the book is on the 'heavy' side. Be willing to accept the fact that the book may remain unread.

Some of the books listed are written for carers and helpers, and are not designed for giving to someone you are trying to help. In that case use the material from such books to enable you to be a better helper, but keep them to yourself.

PART 1

WHO I AM IS MORE IMPORTANT THAN WHAT I SAY

Doubtless there are exceptions, but as a general rule my love, my attitude, my relationship with the Lord and with the individual, my character, and so on, will be more significant in the long run than my words. However wise the advice I give, if it is contradicted by my character or lifestyle, it is not likely to be effective. Equally, genuine sympathy and love will mean a great deal to a person facing a crisis or a problem, however poorly they may be expressed in words. Many times I will not have the answer to the person's need, but will be able to be the answer, or, more accurately, be the means through which Jesus, the answer, is expressed.

For this reason it is important that I ...

- maintain a living personal relationship with God;
- live consistently as a follower of the Lord Jesus;
- accept and, where appropriate, am honest about my own humanness and weaknesses;
- express the love of Christ; and
- demonstrate trustworthiness and dependability.

Mary's husband had just been killed in a road accident. As she drove to Mary's house, Anita struggled to think of what she could possibly say to her. But she needn't have bothered. When she saw Mary, she forgot her carefully prepared speech. Instead, she hugged her and wept with her, and then sat for several minutes with her arm around her. She may have blurted out a few words, but neither she nor Mary remembered them. What meant most to Mary, and what she did remember, was the tremendous comfort Anita herself was, as she shared her grief, and expressed the love of God.

WATCH OUT FOR PLANKS!

There's a worrying passage in James 3 for all those of us who have the privilege of helping others, particularly when that involves helping to change their thinking. 'Not many of you should pre-sume to be teachers,' says James, '… because you know that we who teach will be judged more strictly. We all stumble in many ways. If anyone is never at fault in what he says, he is a perfect man, able to keep his whole body in check' (verses 1–2).

Later in the chapter he adds: 'Who is wise and understanding among you? Let him show it by his good life, by deeds done in the humility that comes from wisdom … The wisdom that comes from heaven is first of all pure; then peace-loving, considerate, submissive, full of mercy and good fruit, impartial and sincere' (verses 13–17).

All the chapter is worth studying, including its warning against 'selfish ambition' (verse 14).

We all have faults; even our motives for helping others may not be wholly pure. So we need to take special steps to make sure that our own faults do not get in the way of our 'correcting' faults in others. Otherwise we shall be subject to Jesus' searching question in Matthew 7:3: 'Why do you look at the speck of sawdust in your brother's eye and pay no attention to the plank in your own eye?'

Perhaps there are three things we need to do. The first is to let the Holy Spirit search our own lives, and show us anything that gets in the way of our helping ministry.

Secondly, we must do all we can to avoid taking up a superior position in our relationship with those we are trying to help. It's not a matter of 'You've got the need and I've got the answer', but rather, 'We're both in this together, and we're both learning. It could well be that you'll minister to me every bit as much as I'll minister to you.'

Thirdly, we need to clothe everything in 'the humility that comes from wisdom'. However much we may be tempted to think how clever we are at analysing and curing other people's problems, our first step must always be to admit that we too are failures and sinners (1 Tim. 1:15), and that without the Spirit of Christ we can do nothing (John 15:5).

NOT US BUT CHRIST

It's amazing how many people want to become counsellors. I'm sure this is a good thing; we need plenty of them. And I'm sure that lots of people who want to become counsellors do so from the best of motives.

But sometimes their motives are less than the best. They may want to study other people's problems as a way of sorting out or even diverting attention from their own. Or they may just love intervening in other people's lives.

None of us has any automatic right to get involved in other people's lives and problems. We shall almost certainly find that from time to time people come to us for help and advice. Additionally we may have a pastoral responsibility for someone who is struggling with a problem and we feel it would be wrong of us simply to stand by and not offer help. But we still don't have an automatic right to intervene.

The foundational factor that gives us the right to intervene in other people's lives is that we can minister Christ to them. We have to be filled with Christ, his love and wisdom and power. They need to be able to see him in us, even if they do not ex-plicitly recognize him. It is not our ideas that will help them, but Christ. If we are filled with Christ, we have what it takes to help them; if we are not filled with Christ, all we can offer is ourselves, and we have no right to force ourselves on anyone.

'Whatever you do, whether in word or in deed, do it all in the name of the Lord Jesus, giving thanks to God the Father through him' (Col. 3:17). To do something in his name is more than just to invoke a formula over our actions. It is to be his agent, the means by which he does it. It means that our name is left out and his name substituted. If someone asks, 'Who helped you?' the reply is 'Jesus.' In this way we don't gain the credit; as the final phrase of the verse reminds us, it goes to God.

So, even if we have a desire to help sort out other people's problems, this must never be our foundational motivation. That must only be Christ.

WE ARE CONCERNED WITH PEOPLE, NOT PROBLEMS

One thing that tends to make me cringe is when people in the caring professions start talking about their 'cases' or 'clients' or 'counsellees'. I accept they have to use these terms, and I guess I'm being oversensitive. But there's something in me that wants to cry out, 'He's not a case – he's a person'; 'She's not a target you direct your counselling at – she's a heartbroken mother.'

Whether my sensitivity is well founded or not, we, as those who have opportunity to care for and help those around us, need constantly to check that we are seeing them as Jesus sees them: people, not problems; individuals personally made and loved by God, not unfortunate sets of circumstances; those who bear the image of God and in whom the Holy Spirit is at work, not clients or cases.

It's all part of valuing and loving them, and of demonstrating that value and love in the way we think of them and relate to them.

After all, Jesus didn't have any clients or cases. Just people, into whom he poured the love of God.

'I SAT WHERE THEY SAT'

Ezekiel's words (Ezek. 3:15, AV) have rightly been used to illustrate a key element of caring, that of feeling and showing empathy before offering help or talking through the issues with those who are in need. We get alongside. We share in their suffering or bewilderment or need. We demonstrate our love by being willing to feel something of their hurt. And in our subsequent talking, we start more or less where *they* are, rather than where *we* are.

As a general rule, avoid saying, 'I know how you feel.' Though we may have a theoretical knowledge, we are certainly not feeling everything they are feeling, and there is the risk that they will feel the comment is superficial and resent it.

But we still need to do all we can to sit where they sit. We can use our imagination to picture how we would feel if our husband or wife had suddenly walked out on us, or what it is like to lose health and independence and dignity. Then we can let our feelings spill over into our attitude and words – our concern, our facial expressions, our body language, our comments, like 'That must have been awful for you', 'You must feel so frustrated at times', 'If that had happened to me I'd be devastated.'

It's all part of following the example of the one who 'took up our infirmities and carried our sorrows' (Is. 53:4).

GO FOR A LIFE, NOT A DAY

'Give a hungry man food and you've fed him for a day; enable him to grow his own food and you've fed him for life.'

In helping others, our attention and energy will be largely focused on the immediate problem and what to do about it. But that must not divert us from our basic aim that each problem situation should become a growth point for the people we are trying to help.

One of the ways we can work towards this is by enabling the people we are trying to help to work creatively at their problem. As a general rule, in analysing their situation and suggesting possible action, we should avoid doing all the work for them. If they work out the answers for themselves, with our help, they are more likely to understand and accept them than if we impose our answers on them. If the decision to follow a possible course of action is theirs rather than ours, they will be more likely to put it into action and stick to it.

Of course, this does not mean that we will not help them in their thinking, and encourage them in their decision-making and action. Our role here may well be a major one; but, even so, it is always better if our input is given subtly, facilitating and encouraging and supporting, rather than in a didactic and controlling way.

This will help avoid a problem that sometimes arises – that of people becoming dependent on their helpers, or even of the helpers, because of their own needs, manipulating the situation so that the people they are helping can't manage without them. We must guard against making ourselves controlling or indispensable; our aim is to bring those we help to the point where they no longer need our help. If they are going to be dependent on anyone, it must be on God.

LISTENING IS A GREAT WAY OF SOLVING PROBLEMS

We toss and turn in the small hours struggling with some issue that seems insoluble. But next morning, when we look at it in the clear light of day, we wonder why we were so worried. Suddenly we can see things as they really are, in proportion; we can even see the beginnings of a way through.

Things don't always work out that way; but quite often one of the most significant ways we can help people who are struggling with problems is to enable them to look at them in the clear light of day. To do this we give them an opportunity to tell us all about them; and all we need to do is listen. In the very formulating of the problem in order to describe it to us, they see it as it really is; they get it in proportion, and they begin to see an answer – all without us having to say a word.

Of course, much depends on the problem and on the person. Some problems are so complex and so deep they can't be formulated clearly. Some people are better than others at putting their feelings and situations into words. But be aware that in some circumstances the describing of a problem can bring its solution simply by your being a good listener.

LISTENING IS LOVING

He sits there, silent. She is telling him something. His eyes wander round the room. He glances at his watch. He leans back in his chair. He yawns. He flicks a speck of dust off his sleeve. He folds his arms. His face shows no reaction to what she is saying. She falls silent. He makes an irrelevant comment.

As those concerned to help others with their problems, we can never allow ourselves the luxury of not listening. We may be tired. We may feel we have heard it all before. There may be distractions. But if they are telling us something, we must listen.

Listening is loving. It is giving ourselves and all our attention to those who are talking to us. We are saying, 'I value you. I'm concerned about what concerns you. I'm giving you all my attention. You matter to me. I want to know where you are at and how you feel.'

Listen with care. Give your full attention. Don't be distracted. Let them see in your face and eyes that you are following what they are saying. Make relevant and perceptive responses. Show by your body language that you are open to what they are saying, that you want to hear more.

Don't just listen. Hear, as well. Hear what they are saying. Absorb it. Digest it. Pick up the subtle nuances of the way they express things. Listen to their body language, the signs, say, that mentioning a certain topic or person causes them anxiety.

Avoid the temptation to be working out how you are going to respond while they are talking to you. There'll be time for that later. For the present, listen.

There's a time to talk, and there's a time to listen. Be a good listener.

OUR WORDS CAN HELP OUR LISTENING

Not everyone is good at communicating. And even those who are usually good at it may find it hard to communicate when they are stressed by some particular difficult situation. So we need to help them.

Putting them at their ease, and talking together in an accepting, relaxed atmosphere, will be a great help. So will our attitude and body language – the signs that we are really interested, the occasional nod or affirming murmur. But we can use words as well.

There are the direct invitations, like 'Tell me about it', or questions: 'How did you feel about what she said?' There's the affirmation that you have taken notice of what they are saying and appreciate how they are feeling: 'That was awful; you must have felt shattered.' There are the comments that show we want to hear more, and lead the person on: 'Discovering like that that you've got cancer must have been incredibly upsetting. I guess it's given rise to all sorts of thoughts and fears in your mind.' Some people make a point of periodically summarizing what they have been hearing and reflecting it back to the person. At times this may sound rather artificial, but, again, it can be a useful way of showing that we have heard what they are saying and want them to go on.

Of course, at times we may not understand what they are saying. They may be confused, or emotionally overwrought, or they may not be able to bring themselves to state something explicitly, or they may assume we know what they are talking about. In these cases we need to be honest: 'I'm sorry, I don't really understand what you are saying. Could you please go through it again?' or even, 'Do you mean you're afraid you've got cancer?'

GOD WANTS US TO LISTEN TO HIM AS WELL

It is essential to listen to those we are trying to help. But God often has something to say about the situation too, and we need to be sure that we listen to him as well.

God speaks in all sorts of ways. Most often he puts his thoughts and ideas into our minds, or the minds of those we are seeking to help. Other times he uses Scripture. Or there are the rather special occasions when he gives a word of knowledge or wisdom, or a prophecy, or a dream or a vision.

It doesn't matter a great deal which way he speaks. The important thing is that we should be listening.

Ask him to speak. This doesn't mean that you've got to be consciously praying, 'Speak, Lord' all the time you are trying to help someone. But pray it when you think of it. Have a general attitude of being open to God's Spirit. Be aware that it's not your wisdom that's needed in this situation, but his. When the person has stopped telling you their problem, don't necessarily plunge straight into giving your response. Stop for a moment. You could say something like, 'That's quite a big problem. It's good of you to share it with me. To be honest, I don't know the answer. But I'm sure God does. I think we ought to spend a few minutes praying now, putting it all into his hands, and asking him to help us. And then perhaps we could spend a few moments in silence, just listening to hear if God is saying something specifically to us.'

Be careful, of course, how you present something you feel God is saying. There are times when we can be very sure and direct, because what we are saying is backed up by the authority of Scripture: 'You need to realize that God is saying that deceiving your wife like that was wrong.' But at other times, we need to be more hesitant, and perhaps to take time to check it out: 'I wonder if God is saying that the best thing is for you to go straight round and apologize. What do you think?' Never force a 'word from the Lord' on others. Wait till they hear it too.

Equally, if they suggest something that God might be saying, don't necessarily take it as gospel, but weigh it up. Take it seriously; never just dismiss it; God has as much right to speak to them as to you. If you feel unhappy with it, take from it the elements you feel are from God, and suggest leaving the other aspects until God shows the way forward more clearly.

See also **prayer ministry**.

MAKE IT EASY FOR PEOPLE TO BE HONEST

The quality of our love and fellowship in our churches and Christian organizations should be such that no-one is ever afraid to be open and honest about themselves and their needs and problems. Sadly, this is not always the case. All too often Christians struggle alone with their problems because they can't bring themselves to share them with someone else.

There could be a number of reasons for this. Maybe they've heard teaching that a Christian should never struggle with doubts or be depressed or whatever. Perhaps they've assumed that keen Christians don't have problems with their singleness or in their marriage – or in any other area. Or they're afraid that if they tell us something personal about themselves it will be round the church in a few days. Or they are so ashamed of their failure or sin that they can't bring themselves to confess it. Or they think that we won't understand.

Whatever the reason, we must do everything we can to make it easy for people to be honest. We must work hard to counter anything that makes it hard for them to be open and ask for help. Acceptance, a high level of confidentiality, a realistic understanding of human nature, a willingness to admit that we all have problems, and a warm relationship of encouragement and love are all vital.

DON'T JUDGE

However we may interpret the words of Jesus in Matthew 7:1, a basic principle of helping others is to accept them as they are. The good Samaritan doubtless felt shock and prejudice and maybe even revulsion at the Jew lying by the side of the road. We may feel the same when we're confronted with someone who is being violent towards his wife, or has got involved in the occult, or was sexually abused when she was a child. But we must not show it. Our model is Jesus with the woman taken in the act of adultery (John 8:3–11).

Learn to listen without being shocked or passing judgment. Accept what people say; remember they may be finding it hard to open up to us; we must avoid doing anything that makes it harder.

If they say something shocking or confess to some sin, make

it perfectly clear by your attitude and body language, and, if necessary, by word, that you still accept them and love them and are committed to helping them with this issue. It may even be appropriate to thank them for being so honest with you.

If you feel there is a danger that such acceptance could be interpreted by them as condoning their sin, find an opportunity later in the conversation to say something like, 'Of course, you'll realize that as a Christian I've got to say that what you've done will have grieved the Lord deeply, and you'll need to get it sorted out.' But even then, make it clear that you are not condemning them, and are committed to standing with them.

ARRANGE YOUR GOLDEN APPLES WITH CARE

One of the quainter sayings of the book of Proverbs (25:11) is

A word aptly spoken
is like apples of gold in settings of silver.

It comes in a passage that emphasizes the importance of saying the right thing at the right time (verses 11–15), a theme that is picked up elsewhere in the Bible and is an essential principle for us as we seek to help others. There are times when it is right to speak, and times when it is right to be silent (Eccles. 3:7). Something we say in all innocence may provoke an entirely unexpected and unhelpful reaction. However valid and true our words may be, there are times when it is inappropriate or unhelpful or unkind to speak them. Additionally, situations are frequently so complex that we could respond in a range of ways – with dismay at the problem, with criticism of the action taken, with compassion for the person, with suggestions as to what to do, and so on; and it takes a lot of wisdom to know what is the right response for the particular occasion.

Ensuring that our words are apt is not easy; we'll have to accept that sometimes we shall say the wrong thing. But we can and should do our best to guard against unwise words, perhaps in the following ways:

- Ask God to direct all our speaking; in particular to prevent us saying inappropriate things (Ps. 141:3).
- Beware of giving instant responses. Think (and pray) before speaking. Follow James's rule: be quick to listen, and slow to speak (Jas. 1:19).
- Develop your ability to read where people are at. One day they may be stressed and unable to take anything we say; the next they are back to normal and we can go ahead. Watch for signs in their attitudes, body language, and so on; learn how to read them, and take notice of them.
- Where appropriate, be tentative in the way you present your words. Prefacing your comment with something like 'I may be wrong, but I tend to feel that …' still allows you to say what needs to be said, but in a way that is less likely to provoke an unhelpful reaction.
- Always be willing to stop what you are saying, and, if necessary, withdraw it.

ARE YOU THINKING WHAT I THINK YOU ARE THINKING?

How can I be sure that what I think you've said is what you think I think you've said? Or that what you think I've said is what I think you think I've said?

Communication can falter in all sorts of ways (see **communication**), especially when the people we are trying to help are upset or nervous or the like. So we need to be especially careful that we check that we are correctly grasping what they are saying, and that they are clearly getting hold of what we may be saying in response, and that we agree on what has come out of the resulting discussion.

One of the ways of doing this is to repeat back to them in your own words what you think they are saying, to check that you've got it right. Avoid doing this too often; and as far as possible try not to let it seem artificial or stop the flow of the conversation. 'I feel that what you've been saying is really important, so I'd like just to check that I've got it right. Are you saying that …?'

Equally, towards the end of our conversations, it will often be valuable to check that we and those we are helping agree over what has come out of them. This can be done by summarizing together, and maybe even writing down, the salient points. We could take the lead in this, but often it will be more helpful if we get them to state in their own words the new insights they've gained. This helps to fix them in their minds, and gives us a good chance to check that they really are thinking what we think they are thinking.

'ALL THINGS WORK TOGETHER FOR GOOD'

Romans 8:28 is decidedly not a verse to quote when seeking to help someone confronted with a disaster or major problem. But it is still a principle that must underlie our own thinking and approach in every situation. God is very wise and very powerful, and he is able to bring ultimate good out of any situation, if we allow him to do so. Any setback, disaster, disappointment, even failure and sin, can be taken and shaped by him into something good. It will take time, and the process may often be a painful one. Gold has to be refined by fire.

Any experience, whether pleasant or unpleasant, can aid or

retard a person's growth as a Christian. Landing a good job can bring joy and thanksgiving, or it can lead to pride or preoccupation. Losing a job can cause anger and bitterness, or it can result in increased dependency on God. Our task is to help the person to respond in as positive and creative a way as possible to each situation, and, where there are negatives, to help turn these into positives.

Many times we will not be able to see what good God is going to bring out of a given situation. Never fall into the trap of trying to predict what it might be. Equally, avoid giving the impression that God is deliberately causing the person to suffer in order to bring about some good end. This could sometimes be the case, but very often the suffering is caused directly or indirectly by sin or evil or the fallenness of the world. We all have a tendency to blame God when things go wrong, but it is generally going to be more helpful to encourage the person to see God as the one who walks with us through our suffering in creative love and wisdom, rather than as the cause of our pain.

See also **suffering**.

PEOPLE IN LONG, DARK VALLEYS NEED EXTRA PATIENCE, LOVE AND SUPPORT

Confronted with people who need help, we soon realize there is wide variety in the extent to which we, or anyone, can do anything that will actually solve the problem they are facing. There are some problems that can and should be solved in the sense of being removed, with the result that the person's situation is transformed. But other problems, in what we might call 'dark valley' situations, do not have any ready solution; we cannot pluck the person out of the dark valley; she or he has to walk through it.

For example, when two people have fallen out with each other, it should be possible to help them to bring their quarrel to an end, to seek and receive forgiveness from each other, to receive forgiveness from God, and to start a new and lovely relationship with each other. Their problem is removed.

By contrast, in a bereavement situation, where, say, a wife has lost her husband, there is no possibility of bringing him back; nor is it desirable to take from her the pain of loss and the long process of grieving. Both of these are a beautiful and necessary expression of her love for her husband and the extent to which she misses him. So, in seeking to help her, our aim is not to take the problem away, but to stand by her and support her as she faces and goes through it. This may be a long process, and it requires patience, understanding and faithfulness. In an age when we like quick results, these qualities are not particularly popular, and the situation is not helped when some well-meaning Christians give the impression that if only our faith is strong enough, we shall find immediate escape from every difficult situation. Undoubtedly, God could give instant solutions to any problem, including raising the dead. But we have to accept that very often he does not do so. Indeed, it would be possible to claim that there are more calls to patience and longsuffering and endurance in the New Testament than there are to bring people back from the dead.

People walking through dark valleys need both sympathy and encouragement. We must give them both a shoulder to cry on, and an arm to strengthen them. Above all, we must be willing to continue to show love and give support however long the valley may turn out to be. True love and support for a bereaved person continues for months and years, not days and weeks. This calls for faithfulness and patience, especially when a person seems to make progress, and then goes through a relapse, and we feel we are back at square one. Remember, patience, gentleness and faithfulness are as much the fruit of the Spirit as love, joy and peace.

BEWARE OF THE SEVEN EVIL SPIRITS

People who seek help are often basically trying to get rid of something from their lives, whether it is a difficult situation, a bad habit, guilt, fear, hurt, anger, or whatever. As we have seen, it may not always be part of God's purpose to take these things away; he may wish to transform them, or use them for some special purpose.

But in many cases it will be our privilege to help the person get rid of the burden. We shall be able to say, 'Your sins are forgiven (or your problem is solved); go in peace.'

It is at this point that we need to remember Jesus' story in Matthew 12:43–45:

When an evil spirit comes out of a man, it goes through arid places seeking rest and does not find it. Then it says, 'I will return to the house I left.' When it arrives, it finds the house unoccupied, swept clean and put in order. Then it goes and takes with it seven other spirits more wicked than itself, and they go in and live there. And the final condition of that man is worse than the first.

Never leave a house empty. Always ensure it is filled, to minimize the risk of the old problem coming back. If you are able to help someone to the point of finding freedom from fear, fill their life up with confidence in the power and trustworthiness of God. If you are involved with a man who renounces fantasizing lust or pornography, give him plenty of Philippians 4:8-type things to fill his mind with and lots of practical advice on what to do when the seven spirits come knocking on his door.

Above all, whenever there is any space in the person we are helping, pray for the infilling of the Holy Spirit. Where that is a living reality, the seven don't stand a chance.

THE PEOPLE OF GOD ARE A FANTASTIC RESOURCE

You may find that, because of your responsibilities or gifts or calling, you have special opportunities to help those who are facing various sorts of problems. But never feel that you have to do this all on your own. It was never God's intention that just one person in a local church should do all the work. In his grace and generosity he has gifted everyone with gifts and abilities, not to mention personal experiences, that are not only helpful but actually essential for the work of caring for and building up the body.

So thank him for his provision, and use the fantastic resource he has given you. Here are a few suggestions:

- When confronted with a person who is in a difficult situation, talk to those in the church who have been through similar situations, or who have special insights into it. For example, a couple who have experienced a stillbirth, or an accountant who can help someone struggling with debt.
- Where appropriate, encourage the person to talk to them as well.
- Back up all your helping ministry with the prayers of others (see 'Prayer is the key', p. 38).
- Mobilize practical help where appropriate – a bed for the night, a cake baked, someone to visit, a letter, and so on. All the gifts of all the people in the church are there to be used sooner or later!
- Get everyone to share in the ministry of encouragement and showing love. People with problems often feel very alone, struggling with the issue on their own. Enable them to know that they have a whole church fellowship standing with them and supporting them.
- Remember that, besides the value of supportive individuals, there is something very special about an understanding and loving group, who together share the burden with the person in need. In our house groups or cell groups or whatever, we can develop strong and trusting relationships where hurting

people find and experience the reality of the love and power of Christ.

One thing to watch in all this is confidentiality. Always check that those you are seeking to help are willing for you to talk to others. As a general rule, never break confidences unless it is clearly in the long-term interests of those concerned to do so. Avoid anything that even borders on gossip.

Martin Luther had a great phrase; writing of the ministry of everyone in the church to everyone else, he said, 'We are Christs to one another.' Now there's a fantastic resource.

WATCH OUT FOR ONE OF THE DEVIL'S NASTIEST TRICKS

We are human. So are the people we are trying to help. Because of their need, they open themselves up to us; they are vulnerable; they look to us for comfort and love.

And we respond. We give ourselves. We get close to them. We give them our love. And before we know where we are we are too close, with the wrong sort of love.

Far too many helping relationships move over into sinful relationships. Far too many helpers get sexually involved with those they are seeking to help. It's one of the devil's favourite tricks, and one of his nastiest.

It is essential to be aware of this danger, and to take every precaution against it. If you think it could never happen to you, remember Paul's words: 'If you think you are standing firm, be careful that you don't fall!' (1 Cor. 10:12). Be especially careful when you are helping someone of the opposite sex. If at all possible avoid situations where the two of you are together with no-one else around, particularly if you are talking about personal issues. Don't take refuge in the thought, 'I could never fall for him (or her).' Remember that even if that is so, he or she may fall for you.

Even in same-sex situations, be careful if you are dealing with sexual issues, lest they provoke an unhealthy interest in your mind or lead you into sexual sin. Remember that the devil isn't just nasty; he's very cunning, as well.

If you feel that there is a risk you might get too close to a specific person, or in tackling a specific issue, do not hesitate to suggest some other person (with their consent!) to do the helping.

Above all, in every situation, seek the protection and power of the living God against every trick of the devil.

GIVE THEM THE WHOLE WILL OF GOD

For simplicity, in the articles in this book it has generally been assumed that those you are seeking to help are Christians, with at least some understanding of basic Christian truths, and a general openness to letting the Holy Spirit work in their lives.

In fact, you will probably find yourself involved with a huge range of people, from those who are not Christians at all and don't wish to be, through those whose Christianity is nominal or vague, to those who are mature and deeply committed followers of the Lord Jesus. Clearly, you will need to adapt your approach according to the individual, selecting and adapting relevant material.

However, I suggest that we should be careful not to water down the Christian content of our helping simply to match the spiritual level of those we are involved with. Of course, we will need to explain it in ways they will understand, and only encourage them to take steps they are ready for. But our task is to minister Christ and the fullness of the gospel, not some watered-down version to suit their taste. We need to follow the example of Paul, who was able to say of his ministry at Ephesus, 'I have not hesitated to proclaim to you the whole will of God' (Acts 20:27), even though all his hearers were new Christians and presumably pretty immature in their faith.

Even when we are dealing with those who are not Christians, we don't need to remove the Christian heart from our helping. Unless we are very good at keeping lamps under bowls (Matt. 5:15–16), they will know that we are Christians, and will expect us to speak as such. We'll not force our Christian beliefs on them, but it is perfectly legitimate for us to say something like, 'I know you're not a committed Christian, but if Jesus was here and you asked him to help with your problem, this is the kind of thing he might say …' I personally have found non-Christians quite ready to listen to the Christian answer, and even to let me pray with them.

Make the most of the Bible

Paul talked about the message of the gospel being 'the power of God' to bring the fullness of salvation into the lives of any who believe (Rom. 1:16). The truths that God has revealed to us are themselves life-changing, because they are the words of the living God. When Jesus said, 'Your sins are forgiven', he wasn't just stating an abstract concept; the person was actually made clean (Mark 2:5).

In the Bible we have the revealed truth of God. But God doesn't want us just to leave it there. He wants us to let it out and set it to work in people's lives. The person who is struggling needs to hear and accept God's promise, 'Never will I leave you; never will I forsake you' (Heb. 13:5); the anxious person needs to know that 'My God will meet all your needs according to his glorious riches in Christ Jesus' (Phil. 4:19).

The old practice of giving people Bible verses or passages to learn by heart and meditate on seems to have fallen out of favour. But it is still worth using where appropriate. After all, the promise of God or the truth of his word in the Bible is likely to carry a lot more weight than any good advice I may offer. Throughout this book Bible passages which may be helpful are listed in the relevant sections. Don't be afraid to encourage the people you are trying to help to learn and digest and be changed by these and other passages as appropriate. Encourage them to write them on a piece of card which they can keep where they can see it often. Get them to learn them by heart. Teach them to meditate on them and apply the truth in various situations.

Of course we must be wise and fair in the passages we choose. Always study the context of the passage to make sure you are using it rightly. And, again, be sensitive to the person to whom you give the Scripture. If they are struggling with intellectual doubts about Christianity, it's not likely to be helpful simply to say, 'The Bible says ...'

PRAYER IS THE KEY

Undeniably there is a lot non-Christians can do to help those with needs and problems. But one thing we have that they lack is the power of prayer. Prayer is the key that lets the supernatural power of God break into the lives of ordinary people. It is an incredible and essential resource. 'Our struggle is not against flesh and blood, but against ... the powers of this dark world ... With this in mind ... always keep on praying' (Eph. 6:12, 18).

Make sure your ministry to others is soaked in prayer; this in turn will make sure it's not your ministry, but the triune God's ministry through you. Get others to pray for you. Pray for yourself. Pray for those you are seeking to help. Pray with those you are seeking to help. Pray when you are confronted with difficulties or problems or needs or setbacks. Pray so that things are put in their right perspective. 'And pray in the Spirit on all occasions' (Eph. 6:18).

Don't just pray that God will solve problems or take away difficulties. Pray that God will reveal himself in the difficulties. Pray for growth as a result of the problems. Pray for the life-changing power of the Holy Spirit. Pray cleansing and forgiveness into the lives of those who turn back to God. Pray wholeness and shalom into those who are broken. Pray faith and hope and the presence of the living God into those who are struggling. In all your prayers, minister Christ, the one who can meet every need.

PART 2

ABORTION

Abortions may legally be performed in the UK up to the twenty-eighth week of pregnancy if the woman's life is at risk from the pregnancy, or if there is a risk to the mental or physical health of the woman or her children, or if there is a substantial risk of serious handicap to the baby. In the first nine weeks of pregnancy the abortion is often achieved through taking drugs. After that, surgery, using a vacuum process to suck out the foetus, is generally required. From about the fifteenth week the foetus is delivered through induced normal labour.

Christians are committed to the principle of the sanctity of life and the protection of the weak and vulnerable. This has generally meant that they have been opposed to abortion on principle, although many Christians would accept that abortion is permissible in special circumstances, such as rape or when the mother's life is seriously threatened by the pregnancy, and some would reluctantly see abortion as a sad but valid option in a fallen world.

Quite apart from the moral issue, any decision whether or not to have an abortion is a very serious one because of its repercussions. Though an abortion rarely has adverse affects on the mother physically, it frequently does so psychologically; some women carry the pain of it for years. Equally, bringing a child into the world is a grave responsibility, especially if that child has particular needs, or the support structures for the child are not likely to be in place. Christians have rightly accepted that if we campaign against abortions we must be prepared to help provide the needed care and support for the mother and for the child.

As with other complex moral issues, we need to be clear on our own basic position, but at the same time to avoid facile dogmatism and quick condemnation of those with whom we disagree. Great wisdom and grace are needed, say, in a situation where we are seeking to care for a bewildered and fearful pregnant schoolgirl who is being pressurized by her parents and advisors to end the pregnancy as soon as possible. In most situations, while continuing to show love and support to those involved, we should encourage them to contact one of the specialist Christian organizations for help and counselling.

What could I say to someone considering having an abortion?

Give yourself time to think through the issues. Since, if you are going to have an abortion, it is best to have it early in the pregnancy, you may feel pressurized to make a quick decision. While you certainly shouldn't put off making a decision unnecessarily, don't rush into it thoughtlessly. Remember that in the early weeks of pregnancy many women are very emotionally volatile; an important decision like this must not be unduly affected by your emotions.

Talk to others. Talk to your doctor, if possible with a gynaecologist, the baby's father, your family, a minister, friends you can trust. Listen to their views, without feeling you have to agree with them. If you talk to someone from a pregnancy clinic or from a pro-life organization, be aware that their advice will be coloured by their views on abortion.

Talk to God. He knows and understands all the issues. You may feel that you have forfeited the right to ask God for help at this time, but that is not so. He longs to help you. If appropriate, pray with a group of close Christian friends. Where necessary, seek God's forgiveness and cleansing. Ask him to enable you to make the right decision.

Weigh up the alternatives to an abortion. If your health or wellbeing is at risk, how big is the risk? If the child is likely to be born with a disability, could you cope with being the parent of a disabled child? If you have and keep the baby, how will you cope with the practical and financial demands? Would adoption be a possibility?

Make up your mind on the moral issues. There is a lot of debate over the rights and wrongs of abortion. None of us are really capable of following through all the arguments. But think it through as far as you can, and ask God to direct you as you make up your mind and do what you are convinced is right for you and your baby, whatever others may say.

Be aware of the possible effects of an abortion. Medical or physical complications are rare, but psychological symptoms, such as depression or feelings of loss and guilt, are fairly common.

Make your choice. In many cases you will do this together with the baby's father. But in the last analysis it is you who have the right and the responsibility to choose to have an abortion or to have your baby. Though they may advise and even pressurize you, no-one else can make this choice for you.

What could I say to those who have had an abortion?

Allow yourself to grieve. Whatever your views on abortion may be, you have suffered a bereavement, and should allow yourself to go through the normal grieving process (see **bereavement**).

Accept the finality of the abortion. Even if you are still uncertain whether it was right or wrong, focusing on 'if onlys' will not do you any good. Accept that you made a decision, and trust that even if it was not the best decision, it is one that you are going to be able to live with, with help, if necessary. Do not allow the abortion to spoil the rest of your life.

Find someone you can talk to. You need someone you can be honest with, like your minister or a close friend, or a counsellor, who will listen and understand. If you have feelings of remorse or guilt, talk about them rather than bottling them up.

Ask God for his healing. If you feel you need to, ask the minister and some of the church 'elders' or other appropriate people to spend a time of prayer with you in which you take to God all the issues that have arisen from the abortion, including, perhaps, things like sorrow, guilt, bad memories, anger, depression or fear. God is able to set you free from these things; you don't have to keep carrying them.

As with any loss, allow yourself time to get over the abortion. However, if you feel you are not making any progress, seek help from a specialist Christian counsellor.

See also **bereavement, depression**.

Two pro-life books

J. Thompson and J. Jeffes, *Someone I Know is Thinking of Having an Abortion* (CARE for Life)
J. Wyatt, *Matters of Life and Death*, chs. 6 and 7 (IVP)

Pro-life organizations

CARE for Life, 1 Winton Street, Basingstoke, RG21 8EN. 01256 477 300. www.care.org.uk. CARE for Life has 130 pregnancy crisis centres throughout the UK, and runs a national telephone helpline: 0800 028 2228
LIFE – Save the unborn child, Life House, 1a Newbold Terrace, Leamington Spa, CV32 4EA. 01926 421 587. National hotline: 01926 311 511. www.lifeuk.org

ADDICTION

People can become addicted to almost anything: gambling, computer games, smoking, chocolate, glue, coffee, drugs, alcohol, a hobby, food, pornography, prostitutes, paedophilia. All addictions have a psychological element, that is, a hold on the person's mind and emotions; many also have a physical element: the body becomes dependent on the substance being used, and failure to supply it causes illness.

Some addictions involve the use of illegal substances or activities. In others the substance or activity is perfectly legal, but it tends to lead the user into illegal or antisocial activity. Other addictions have no illegal or antisocial aspects, but exercise an inappropriate control over the addicts' lives, causing damage to them or those around them.

For Christians any form of addiction is unacceptable in that we have given ourselves, including our minds and bodies, to God; we are his 'slaves' and must not become enslaved to anything else.

It is always a matter of debate where the line is crossed between controlled use of the substance or activity and addiction to it. Addicts will almost invariably insist they still have the habit under control, even when others are sure it is controlling them.

Sources of addiction can be very varied. Some hard drugs are so powerfully addictive that using them only once or twice, even unintentionally, can form a habit. Other habits are built up over a long period. Some addictions arise from or are intensified by factors already existing in the person, such as low self-esteem, depression or loneliness. In these cases any attempt to set the person free from the addiction will need to analyse and tackle the underlying issue as well.

An essential for helping people conquer addictions is their own co-operation and commitment to getting free. Without this no progress will be made. Even where addicts are so committed, they are likely to go through phases where the commitment appears very weak, and may disappear altogether. Patience and tenacity are therefore vital in those seeking to help them.

In all cases of serious addiction, trained and specialist help is essential. There are a number of Christian specialist organizations, most of which operate long-term help programmes.

Bible teaching relevant to addiction

Offer the parts of your body to [God] as instruments of righteousness ... offer them in slavery to righteousness leading to holiness (Rom. 6:13, 19. See the whole chapter).

I will not be mastered by anything ... Do you not know that

your bodies are members of Christ himself? … Do you not know that your body is a temple of the Holy Spirit, who is in you, whom you have received from God? You are not your own; you were bought at a price. Therefore honour God with your body (1 Cor. 6:12, 15, 19–20. See the whole passage, verses 12–20).

My grace is sufficient for you (2 Cor. 12:9).

I can do everything through him who gives me strength (Phil. 4:13).

Since, then, you have been raised with Christ, set your hearts on things above, where Christ is seated at the right hand of God. Set your minds on things above, not on earthly things. For you died, and your life is now hidden with Christ in God (Col. 3:1–3).

Helping those with addictions

Clearly, the type of help needed will vary according to the substance or activity the addicts are using, the extent of their addiction, whether or not it involves illegal activity, and so on. Here, however, are some general principles that may be applicable in most situations. In many cases much of the work will be done by the counsellor, though it is always important that other Christian friends stand with the addict and support and further the work of the counsellor by their attitude and love.

Where appropriate, encourage them to see their doctor, both for help during the period of breaking the addiction, and for a general medical check-up.

Build a strong relationship of acceptance and trust with those you are trying to help. Remember addicts are often people who find strong relationships difficult to form or to cope with, so work especially hard in this area. If the relationship is not strong, it risks foundering as soon as a setback occurs. Acceptance is essential. You may feel and even show distaste at the habit, but you must always show the grace and love of Jesus Christ for the individuals, even when they let you down. Equally, it is vital they trust you and are willing to commit themselves to be completely honest with you.

Help them to understand and agree with the reasons why they should stop what they are doing. Give them high motivation to quit. Addicts tend to minimize the seriousness of what they are doing; you need to stress it and give them the whole picture. Point out and talk through the damaging effects of their habit on themselves, their minds, their bodies, their spiritual lives, and on others. Get others to back you up. Talk through relevant Bible passages. Pray with them and ask God to make his mind clear to them.

Help them reach the point where they clearly commit themselves to getting free of the habit. Since it is likely there will be tremendous pressure on them to go back on this commitment, we must help them make it as significant and real a decision as possible. For example, it could take the form of a solemn covenant before witnesses and before God; it could be written down and signed; it could be made widely known.

Help them see and admit that they can't solve the problem on their own, but that God has the resources to solve it if they are willing to let him work in them. Get them to give the problem over to God, to open up their lives to him and the power of the Holy Spirit. Where appropriate, keep repeating this.

Talk things through with the family or friends of the addict. Enlist their help. Make it a real team effort.

If there is a physical dependency which results in a difficult period of withdrawal, ensure there is someone available to talk and pray with the addict at any time.

Keep encouraging them to stick to any programme the counsellor or helping organization is offering.

If issues like low self-image or loneliness underlie their problem, do what is appropriate to tackle these.

Where appropriate, facilitate and encourage alternative activities to fill the gap left by the addictive activity.

If there is a relapse, be gracious and forgiving. Allow a relapse to throw them more heavily back on God and cause them to renew their original solemn covenant.

Keep praying. Keep others praying. This is a spiritual battle.

As time goes on, encourage them with the progress that has been made. But warn them against complacency; the battle will probably have to be fought for the rest of their lives. Be specially aware of the risk of a relapse during a period of depression or the like.

See also **alcohol abuse, drug abuse, lust, masturbation, pornography, solvent abuse.**

A useful book about drugs

O. Batchelor, *Use and Misuse: A Christian Perspective on Drugs* (IVP)

Useful resources

ECOD (Evangelical Coalition on Drugs), Whitefield House, 186 Kennington Park Road, London, SE11 4BT.
020 7207 2100. www.eauk.org
Hope UK, 25(f) Copperfield Street, London SE1 0EN.
020 7928 0848. www.hopeuk.org

AIDS

To face death by Aids is an awful experience. Sadly, our culture continues to make the experience even worse by surrounding it with exaggerated fears and prejudice. Christians, more than any others, need to set aside such fears and prejudice in order to minister the love and grace of Jesus to Aids sufferers. There can be little doubt that if the disease had existed in his day, Jesus would have been known as 'friend of Aids sufferers' as well as a friend of prostitutes and lepers and the like.

The HIV virus is spread through blood-to-blood contact and sexual intercourse (heterosexual or homosexual). Apart from mother/baby infection, it is not spread any other way. Even the re-use of infected needles stands only a very small chance of spreading the virus.

A person who has been infected with HIV may live for many years with no adverse symptoms, and even be unaware of the disease. Indeed, it would seem there is no inevitability that it will develop, though, medically, there is still no way of making sure that it doesn't.

Where it does develop, the sufferer will show various physical symptoms, such as fevers, weight loss and skin rashes. Then, as the disease invades the nervous system and the brain, there will be confusion and loss of memory and co-ordination. In the final stages, when the person's immune system has broken down completely, there is a wide range of terminal illnesses that may develop and from which the patient will die.

Those who are diagnosed as HIV positive are likely to experience a reaction similar to that of anyone faced with a terminal illness. But it is likely to be compounded by additional factors such as the prejudice against Aids, the knowledge that there is no cure, fear of the particularly nasty aspects of the disease, and the uncertainty over when and if Aids as such will develop. There may also be worry over having infected others, and guilt over how the disease was contracted.

Helping those who are suffering from HIV/Aids

Most of the suggestions in the section on **terminal illness** will be applicable.

The greatest need of sufferers is love. Many sufferers are innocent victims of the disease, but where this is not so, we must be able to set aside any prejudice we may feel against them. Demonstrating the love of Jesus in no way condones any sinful acts in which they may have been engaged, but our gospel has at its heart the love of God poured out on sinners. Love is shown in acceptance, friendship, willingness to spend time with them (especially if other friends begin to boycott them), willingness to talk about the disease and its effects, faithful ongoing loyal commitment and support, and walking with them through the various stages of the disease.

We shall also need to ensure that the family and close friends of the sufferer are cared for and supported. Help them to talk through their own reaction and fears, including fear of infection.

Christian organizations have been at the forefront of caring for Aids sufferers. Encourage them to get in touch with one of these organizations and benefit from their wide experience and practical help.

Be ready to minister the grace and healing of Christ where issues of fear and guilt arise.

Make a special point of valuing and affirming the person. All illnesses dehumanize us, turning us into 'patients' or 'victims'; we lose control over our lives, our decision-making and our bodies. Aids sufferers have the added problems of being particularly rejected by many in our culture. We need to do all we can to counter these tendencies and to show by our attitude that in the eyes of God they are still whole persons who are accepted and loved.

If necessary, give appropriate help to any in the church community who find it difficult to cope with the situation.

Help the sufferers to set right any wrong relationships or the like, and to draw very close to God.

As far as is possible, encourage a positive attitude to the life they have left. The period between contracting the HIV virus and developing Aids is often a long one, and can be indefinite. This time is God's gift to them; many sufferers have found it a beautiful and enriching time, or a time in which they have been able to achieve much for the glory of God.

Be aware of the range of feelings and reactions they will go through. Walk with them as they struggle with anger, shame, depression, weakness, frustration or despair.

See also **anger, carers, depression, fear, guilt, illness, suffering, terminal illness**.

Useful books

P. Dixon, *The Truth about Aids* (Kingsway)
D. Jarvis, *HIV Positive* (Lion)
A. Marcetti and S. Lunn, *A Place of Growth* (Darton, Longman and Todd)

National Aids helpline

0800 567 123

Two Christian organizations

ACET (AIDS Care, Education and Training), PO Box 3693, Putney, London SW15 2BQ. 020 8780 0400. www.acetuk.org
Grandma's, PO Box 1392, London SW6 4EJ. 020 7610 3904

ALCOHOL ABUSE

Alcohol is the most dangerous addictive substance in widespread use in our society. Besides the direct damage it does to the body, its harmful indirect effects are horrific, ranging from carnage on our roads to serious crime; over 90% of crimes of violence, for instance, are committed by those who have been drinking. However, alcoholism is to be distinguished from the other harmful effects of the use of alcohol; a person described as an alcoholic is psychologically, or psychologically and physically, addicted to alcohol and unable to stop drinking.

The nature of alcoholism is such that most alcoholics will insist they are not addicted and may keep their problem secret even from those closest to them. So statistics are difficult to assess. It may be that up to 5% of the population are alcoholics to a greater or lesser degree, with a high growth rate among teenagers.

Some alcoholics are able to cover up their habit, and control it so that it is not detrimental in any serious way to their lives or those around them. Others will hide their drinking, but its bad effects become apparent; these may include financial issues, mood swings, violence, deteriorating work performance, and increasing time off work. Others will make no secret of their drinking.

Danger signals are increasing alcohol intake; drinking at several points during the day; an increased tolerance for alcohol, necessitating even more intake to get the same effect; and behaviour changes, such as defensiveness, secrecy, irrationality and aggression. More serious danger signs are physical reactions such as blackouts and pronounced inability to control drinking.

However clear it may become to friends and family, the alcoholic is likely to continue to insist that she or he has no problem. Getting to the point of admitting a problem is frequently the hardest and most significant stage of moving to a solution. Some would say nothing can be done to help until the addict hits bottom.

Though some argue that a programme of 'controlled limited social drinking' can be successful, many still believe that the only real solution to alcoholism is total abstinence. For the ex-alcoholic, the risk involved even in very limited drinking is unacceptable. It may be that one of the most significant steps we could take in seeking to help alcoholics is to give up drinking ourselves as a sign of our commitment to their cure.

As in any form of addiction, the underlying causes of alcoholism are complex. Though not always so, it is likely that people become dependent on alcohol in the first place because of some other need in their personality or situation, ranging from loneliness to stress in marriage or at work. Clearly, those who are going to be helped to get free from their alcoholism will need help with the underlying problem as well.

An alcoholic will normally need the help of a specialist organization or trained counsellor. Besides Alcoholics Anonymous, which many Christians have found helpful, there are several Christian programmes, often based on the insights of the AA programme, which itself was influenced by Christian concepts when it was compiled in the 1930s. One of the strengths of AA and similar programmes is group meetings and the opportunity to hear testimonies from those who have come off alcohol.

The Alcoholics Anonymous Twelve Steps

It is emphasized that these are not to be imposed rigidly; they can be interpreted and adapted as appropriate.

1. We admitted that we were powerless over alcohol – that our lives had become unmanageable.
2. Came to believe that a Power greater than ourselves could restore us to sanity.
3. Made a decision to turn our will and our lives over to the care of God as we understood him.
4. Made a searching and fearless moral inventory of ourselves.
5. Admitted to God, to ourselves, and to another human being, the exact nature of our wrongs.
6. Were entirely ready to have God remove all these defects of character.
7. Humbly asked him to remove our shortcomings.
8. Made a list of all persons we had harmed, and became willing to make amends to them all.
9. Made direct amends to such people wherever possible, except when to do so would injure them or others.
10. Continued to take personal inventory and when we were wrong promptly admitted it.
11. Sought through prayer and meditation to improve our conscious contact with God as we understood him, praying only for knowledge of his will for us and the power to carry that out.
12. Having had a spiritual awakening as the result of these steps, we tried to carry this message to alcoholics, and to practise these principles in all our affairs.

Helping alcoholics

See the suggestions on helping those with **addictions**.

Get alongside them. Build a good relationship of caring and trust. They need to be at the point where they can accept what you say, be honest and open with you, however costly that may be, and trust you to stand with them whatever happens.

Help them accept that they have a problem and that it is a major one that needs drastic action. Get others to back up what you are saying.

Encourage them to get help from a specialist organization, counsellor or group.

Talk with them about the AA Twelve Steps. Explore ways they could be applied to their situation.

Give them hope. Lots of alcoholics have been set free. Encourage them. Build up their motivation.

Encourage them to start the journey with a solemn commitment before God and other witnesses to come off alcohol altogether.

Commit yourself to pray. Get others to pray regularly and consistently. Specific times of prayer ministry may be appropriate, though it is important to stress that there is no short-cut to the long process of recovery.

In situations where alcohol was used to counter things like boredom, loneliness and inadequacy, help them fill the gap left by their drinking with something positive, such as tasks to do or biblical truths to focus on.

Ensure that you or some other Christian friend is available for the person to contact at need.

Support the family of the alcoholic. Help them as they seek to help her or him. Encourage them to get help and guidance from a suitable support group.

Encourage the alcoholics to stick to whatever programme the counsellor or helping group proposes. Support them in it.

Encourage continuing openness and honesty.

Where appropriate, help them to get involved in helping others, turning away from their self-preoccupation and helping to boost their self-confidence.

Be especially aware of times when they are vulnerable, for example when they are depressed or stressed.

If there are factors that have contributed to the development of their alcoholism, such as personality needs or external stresses, help them as they face them and seek to sort them out. Pray these things through with them.

Be patient. Recovery is a long process, and there will be setbacks. Be accepting, gracious and understanding, but at the same time firmly hold them to their basic aim of keeping clear of alcohol altogether. When there are relapses, help them to come back to God for grace and renewal.

Some of the Bible's teaching on the abuse of alcohol

Wine is a mocker and beer a brawler;
  whoever is led astray by them is not wise (Prov. 20:1).

Let us put aside the deeds of darkness and put on the armour of light. Let us behave decently, as in the daytime, not in orgies and drunkenness ... rather, clothe yourselves with the Lord Jesus Christ, and do not think about how to gratify the desires of the sinful nature (Rom: 13:12–14).

I will not be mastered by anything ... Do you not know that your bodies are members of Christ himself? ... Do you not know that your body is a temple of the Holy Spirit, who is in you, whom you have received from God? You are not your own; you were bought at a price. Therefore honour God with your body (1 Cor. 6:12, 15, 19–20. See the whole passage, verses 12–20).

My grace is sufficient for you (2 Cor. 12:9).

Live by the Spirit, and you will not gratify the desires of the sinful nature ... The acts of the sinful natures are ... drunkenness, orgies, and the like... But the fruit of the Spirit is ... self-control ... Since we live by the Spirit, let us keep in step with the Spirit (Gal. 5:16, 19, 21, 22, 25).

Be very careful ... how you live ... Do not get drunk on wine, which leads to debauchery. Instead, be filled with the Spirit (Eph. 5:15, 18).

See also **addiction**, **drug abuse**.

A helpful book

A. DeJong and M. Doot, *Dying for a Drink* (Eerdmans)

Alcoholics Anonymous

PO Box 1, Stonebow House, Stonebow, York YO1 7NJ.
01904 644 026. Helpline 020 7352 3001

Christian organizations that offer help to alcohol abusers

ECOD (Evangelical Coalition on Drugs), Whitefield House, 186
Kennington Park Road, London SE11 4BT. 020 7207 2100.
www.eauk.org
Hope UK, 25(f) Copperfield Street, London SE1 0EN.
020 7928 0848. www.hopeuk.org
Life for the World Trust, Wakefield Building, Gomm Road, High
Wycombe HP13 7DJ. 01494 462 008. www.doveuk.com/lfw
Yeldall Christian Centre, Yeldall Manor, Hare Hatch, Reading
RG10 9XR. 0118 940 1093. www.yeldall.org.uk
Details of local help organizations and rehabilitation centres can
be obtained from ECOD.

ALIENATION

We live in a culture that has increasingly become detached from
reality. We watch pictures on a screen instead of experiencing real
things. Our food comes from tins or supermarket shelves with no
seeming link with real crops growing in real fields. We communicate by machine instead of face to face with real people. We purge
our emotions with 'soaps' instead of real-life situations. When it
gets dark we switch on lights; when it gets cold the central heat-
ing comes on. Our lives are cocooned in artificiality. As a result we
suffer from alienation.

Other cultures have lived much closer to the world as it
really is. They lived in communities, face to face with real people,
working with their hands to grow and prepare their own food, fit-
ting their lives to the rhythm of day and night, summer and winter,

and so on. As a result they were secure, they belonged, they fitted.

Allied to feelings of alienation is a sense of meaninglessness and of the emptiness of life, often expressed in an attitude of boredom.

Christianity calls us to be real people in a real world. It gives the ultimate and total answer to alienation: reconciliation, restoring the wholeness of our relationship with God, with others, with the world around us, and with ourselves. But even so, because of their circumstances, many Christians still have to struggle with feelings of alienation, meaninglessness and boredom. Such feelings can be caused or aggravated by a living environment such as a city high-rise flat, or a work situation such as a monotonous task with no creative or satisfying element.

What could I say?

Look at the big picture. Real meaning and purpose come from your place in the universe, not from your job or circumstances. You are a child of God, specifically and personally created and loved by him, individually chosen and redeemed by Jesus Christ, and indwelt by the Holy Spirit.

Think through the implications of reconciliation. Use the Bible teaching on reconciliation to counter your feelings of alienation.

Do what you can to counter the alienating influences of your environment or job or other situation. Find ways of using even a boring, repetitive job creatively. Counter the effects of your environment by growing flowers in a window box, or having a pet, or finding ways of getting back in touch with nature.

Develop friendships and relationships that are as real and personal as possible. Avoid treating people as things or machines. Be honest, be open, be yourself.

Take up a creative hobby. Instead of watching other people doing things, do something worthwhile and satisfying yourself.

Some of the Bible's teaching on reconciliation

The whole creation has been groaning as in the pains of childbirth right up to the present time ... We know that in all things God works for the good of those who love him, who have been called according to his purpose ... If God is for us, who can be against us? ... Who shall separate us from the love of Christ? Shall trouble or hardship or persecution or famine or nakedness or danger or sword? ... No, in all these things we are more than conquerors through him who loved us (Rom. 8:22, 28, 31, 35, 37).

If anyone is in Christ, he is a new creation; the old has gone, the new has come! All this is from God, who reconciled us to himself through Christ and gave us the ministry of reconciliation: that God was reconciling the world to himself in Christ (2 Cor. 5:17–19).

[Christ] himself is our peace ... You are no longer foreigners and aliens, but ... members of God's household (Eph. 2:14, 19).

God was pleased to have all his fulness in [Christ], and through him to reconcile to himself all things, whether things on earth or things in heaven, by making peace through his blood, shed on the cross.

Once you were alienated from God ... but now he has reconciled you by Christ's physical body through death to present you holy in his sight, without blemish and free from accusation (Col. 1:19–22).

See also **communication, loneliness, rejection.**

ALZHEIMER'S DISEASE

Some people maintain excellent health right through into old age. But most suffer a certain amount of physical and mental decline, particularly in their seventies and eighties. The mental decline generally shows itself in forgetting names or losing familiar objects. Though annoying, this is not a problem in itself, and is to be accepted as part of growing older.

However, the deterioration of mental capacity can reach a more serious stage, when it is to be classified as Alzheimer's disease or dementia. Proneness to the disease is increased if there has already been an incidence in the family.

Symptoms include loss of memory, loss of concentration, loss of the ability to perform more complex mental activities, and deterioration of verbal and mathematical ability. The disease is progressive, though its progress is gradual and may be very slow. In later stages the loss of mental abilities is greatly increased; sufferers retreat into a world of their own and become physically inactive, regressing to childish and even foetal conditions.

These symptoms, especially in the earlier stages, are not necessarily a sign of Alzheimer's. Parallel symptoms can be caused by other conditions, such as hormone deficiencies, infection, vitamin deficiency, minor strokes or depression, or they can be the by-products of medication or of the use of alcohol. The symptoms can also be produced by stress; ironically, the fear of developing Alzheimer's can itself aggravate the normal decline of mental facilities and produce worrying symptoms. All older people should talk with their doctor about any such symptoms that might concern them.

Helping those who have to live with Alzheimer's

Where symptoms do occur, it is important to obtain medical analysis and help, particularly to clarify whether this is truly a case of Alzheimer's, or something else. As far as is possible, this should be done without causing extra anxiety to the person.

Offer reassurance. Almost all older people suffer a decline in mental capacity. Many are able to cope with the early stages of Alzheimer's without any loss of their quality of life.

Some sufferers may deny that they have a problem. This may be a way of deliberately rejecting the condition, or because, as part of the outworking of the illness, they are genuinely unaware of it. In either case we do not have to disillusion them, as long as safeguards are in place to minimize the risk that they will harm themselves in any way.

Do all you can to maintain their privacy, dignity, and right to make their own decisions and live their own lives. The time may come when these things will have to be curtailed, but seek to postpone it as long as possible.

Support spouses, family and carers. Watching a loved one decline in mental capacity can be very stressful. If possible, ensure they have periodic breaks; it is usually possible to arrange for a week or two of respite care for the sufferer so that the carer can have a holiday.

Continue to converse as normally as possible with those who have Alzheimer's. Keep praying with them; the act of praying will often be accompanied by clarity of mind. Remember that Bible verses and hymns learnt in childhood may well be particularly significant for them.

Assure them of the unchanging nature of God and his continuing faithfulness and love to them.

Helpful books

S. Fish, *Alzheimer's* (Lion)
R. Taylor, *Love in the Shadows* (Scripture Union)

ANGER

Anger is an emotional response to something that hurts or upsets us. We feel angry when we think we are being attacked in some way; our blood pressure mounts, our adrenalin flows, our emotion tunes our body up to react. Anger can arise from frustration, fear, or perceived injustice (to ourselves or someone we care about), or be a recurring experience with its roots way back in past experiences of hurt and pain.

Though some are less prone to anger than others, even the most placid of people may well react with anger to a trauma such as bereavement. In this case they are subconsciously feeling anger at death and what it does; but, since it is not easy to express anger at an abstract thing like death, they may find themselves off-loading the anger on to, say, the medical staff or God or even a loved one. This can be disturbing and upsetting for all concerned, and such people need special understanding and compassion.

Anger can have constructive or destructive results. We may feel angry at the ease with which a man can gun down young children in a school gym, and fight to ban hand guns. Or we may give vent to our anger at a cutting remark from the boss by shouting at the secretary. We can express anger in open aggression or hostility, or in more subtle ways such as sarcasm or withdrawal. We can bottle it up, consciously or unconsciously, until it explodes in a bout of temper, or festers into bitterness or depression. We can turn it in on ourselves, giving rise to self-rejection or guilt.

Anger is dangerous when we ignore it or express it in action without stopping to think out the consequences. For anger to have positive results it is essential that, with God's help, we control and channel it constructively, for the good of others and ourselves.

Helping those who have a problem with anger

There may be times when someone specifically seeks our help over a problem with anger. Quite often, however, the person concerned may not be aware of the problem; we all seem to have a tendency to deny or minimize our own anger. In this case we need to be very careful about broaching the subject, choosing the occasion carefully, and raising the issue in a gracious, non-threatening way. Whatever we may feel, we must avoid being judgmental, and make it clear that our concern is to help the person channel his or her feelings in a positive way that glorifies God, rather than in damaging anger.

If we feel that anger is a major issue, or if it is complicated by, for instance, having deep roots in some experience in the past, or if it is giving rise to effects such as depression or violence, we should urge the person to consult a trained counsellor.

Some Bible teaching on anger

A gentle answer turns away wrath (Prov. 15:1).

A fool gives full vent to his anger,

but a wise man keeps himself under control (Prov. 29:11).

Live by the Spirit, and you will not gratify the desires of the sinful nature ... The acts of the sinful nature are ... fits of rage ... But the fruit of the Spirit is ... peace, patience ... gentleness and self-control ... Since we live by the Spirit, let us keep in step with the Spirit (Gal. 5:16, 19, 20, 22, 23, 25).

In your anger do not sin. Do not let the sun go down while you are still angry, and do not give the devil a foothold ... Do not grieve the Holy Spirit of God ... Get rid of all bitterness, rage and anger, brawling and slander, along with every form of malice (Eph. 4:26, 27, 30, 31).

I want men everywhere to lift up holy hands in prayer, without anger or disputing (1 Tim. 2:8).

Everyone should be quick to listen, slow to speak and slow to become angry, for man's anger does not bring about the righteous life that God desires (Jas. 1:19–20).

See also John 2:13–17.

What could I say?

When people have a problem with anger, it is probably not wise to talk to them about it when they are angry. Find a time when you can talk and pray with them and help them to face the issue reasonably objectively. Here are some issues and suggestions you may find useful.

Anger can and must be controlled. It is a natural human emotion which can be directed creatively or destructively. Sadly, it is far easier to let it be destructive than creative, so it is essential to submit all our reactions to the directing of the Holy Spirit.

Try and understand why you get angry. The reason may be very obvious, such as being continually taunted or provoked; or it may lie a lot deeper, and need the help of a trained counsellor to sort it out.

When you feel anger, stop! Don't react in an uncontrolled way. It is almost certain to harm you and others. You are not a slave to your passions.

Pray! Ask for God's help, and the guidance of the Holy Spirit.

Think! Your reaction is going to be a Spirit-controlled, thought-out one, positive, creative, not destructive. Think of a reason for not getting angry, even if it takes some ingenuity. Make allowances. That bad driver may be rushing to see a dying parent. The person who upset you may not have done it deliberately. The boss may have a headache. Use your brains to think out that 'gentle answer'. There's got to be some way you can find, with God's help, to keep calm.

Avoid escalation. Your angry response will almost certainly threaten or hurt the other person and lead to further anger. Break the chain. Saying, 'I'm sorry, but that upset me', may give the same message as shouting or swearing, and it stands a better chance of getting a 'Sorry, I didn't mean to do that.'

Find ways of expressing your anger constructively. This may take some working out, but you ought to be able to do it. Instead of screaming at the child, channel the emotional energy your anger produces into changing his or her behaviour pattern. When you are passed over for promotion, channel it into improving your performance, or looking for another job. You can even try responding to someone's bad driving with a good laugh.

Be wise in your approach to those whose actions trigger your anger. It may not be possible or helpful to talk things through with them. But if you do decide to do it, choose a time and an approach that will give you the highest chance of a constructive outcome. Avoid blaming the person. Avoid saying, 'You make me angry.' If you can bring yourself to say it, try, 'I know I've got a problem with my temper, and I need your help in cracking it.' Do everything you can to make it easy for them to respond positively.

Avoid nursing your anger. Stop yourself reliving the situation in your mind again and again, or practising the cutting retort you wish you'd made. Pray for the renewing of your mind. If you can't dismiss the issue from your mind, concentrate on your constructive, Christlike response, not on the hurt.

Watch out for long-term, negative results of anger. These could be reactions such as resentment, bitterness, self-pity or depression. If necessary seek help from a trained counsellor.

Be very honest with God about your anger. Talk it through with him, maybe with the help of a minister or close friend. Daily ask him to be Lord of your emotions and reactions. Ask for his special grace any time you know you are going into a situation that is likely to provoke your anger.

See also **changing thought patterns, conflict, depression, stress, trauma, violence.**

A helpful book

T. Ward, *Taming Your Emotional Tigers* (IVP)

ANOREXIA

Anorexia nervosa is characterized by under-eating and its consequent weight loss. The large majority of sufferers are teenage girls, though boys and adult women are also affected. The loss of weight can be severe and, if continued, fatal. Early indications of the disorder are fastidiousness over food, overactivity and obsessive dieting or exercise. Later effects include lethargy, muscle deterioration, poor sleep, the ceasing of the menstrual cycle, and heart and kidney damage. Additional indications can include vomiting and the growth of fine body hair. Anorexia often occurs in girls belonging to apparently successful middle-class families, where about 1% are affected. Athletes, dancers and models are particularly at risk.

There is a wide range of possible explanations for anorexia. Possible contributory factors range from the unrealistically thin body image promoted by advertisers to deep psychological needs. One pattern, though by no means the only one, is where the sufferer has a hidden emotional need which, stimulated by a trigger event, gives rise to the beginnings of the disorder. This then develops, sometimes rapidly, to the point of serious danger, where one third of the normal body weight has been lost.

The trigger event could be a bereavement, a trauma, the onset of menstruation, boyfriend or girlfriend issues, school exams, or simply following the fashion of dieting. The underlying factor generally includes an element of self-rejection or low self-esteem, and could be childhood abuse, inability to achieve or to satisfy parental or other standards, the suppression of legitimate emotions ('I was never allowed to be angry or upset'), rejection, or overbearing parents or other authority figures.

One way of understanding the condition is to see it as a means to an end. The sufferer feels unable to cope with life, and finds that the condition supplies an escape from its pressures. This is not just the ultimate escape of death, but intermediate escapes such as escape from the responsibilities of adulthood or adult sexuality, escape from the controlling pressures of school and parents and society into a world where she has control, or escape from the adolescent crisis of identity, uncertainty and insecurity into the tangible realities of body and food.

The sufferer will frequently refuse to accept that she is anorexic; where others see an emaciated body, she will remain convinced she is overweight, or that eating will cause overweight. She is likely to claim that she is eating normally, and resort to considerable subterfuge (conscious or unconscious) to persuade others that she is doing so. While terrified of eating, sufferers are frequently obsessed the whole time with food and calories.

When the sufferer does accept that she is anorexic, the illness itself, exacerbated by other people's reactions and its terrifying hold on her mind, can become another intolerable pressure, a power that dominates her. The physical, mental and emotional weakness that arises from starvation leaves her without any resources to fight it.

Anorexia is a very serious condition. While there is a great deal Christian friends can do to support the sufferer and her family, it is essential to ensure she gets professional medical and counselling or psychiatric help as soon as possible. Since it is obviously beneficial to catch the illness in its early days, it is important to keep an eye on vulnerable people in case early signs arise, such as fastidiousness or deceit over food, or obsessive dieting or exercise.

Helping an anorexia sufferer

Get immediate professional help. Get her to a doctor. Quite apart from the possibility that the weight loss is being caused by some illness other than anorexia, it is essential to have an informed opinion on the extent to which the anorexia is health- or life-threatening. If the situation is serious the doctor may take immediate action, ranging from professional counselling, attendance at a hospital out-patients' department, or hospitalization.

Show acceptance and understanding. The last thing an anorexia sufferer needs is rejection on account of her behaviour. We don't condemn or blame someone for having an illness such as glandular fever or leukemia; rather, we show special concern and love and support. The same must apply to anorexia.

Help them to get to the point where they accept they have anorexia. Sufferers typically refuse to accept that they are seriously underweight. They need to realize that they are ill and need treatment.

Be careful how you encourage them to eat. Get professional advice. You may need to use ingenuity, but be very wary of using tricks to get them to eat. The sufferer needs to be able to trust you; avoid any approach that might destroy this relationship of trust. Avoid bullying or exercising overbearing authority.

Accept ambivalence and mood swings and setbacks. These occur with any illness, but are especially present in anorexia, where the sufferer is caught in a trap between the desire to get better and the pressure to destroy herself.

Encourage the sufferer to trust the professionals who are seeking to help her. Where appropriate, liaise with them.

Where root causes of low self-esteem or the like are identified, work hard, in co-operation with the counsellor, at dealing with them: for example, by helping her to correct false ingrained beliefs, and giving consistent and genuine affirmation and love.

Don't minimize the trigger events. If you can remove the pressure of a trigger event, for example by together taking the decision to postpone exams indefinitely, do so.

Support the family. Parents in particular feel bewildered and helpless. Avoid blaming them for their daughter's anorexia. But encourage them to talk with her counsellor and doctor to explore ways they may be able to help.

Accept that recovery will take time. It is generally a long process, and support and care will continue to be needed for a considerable period after the person has returned to normal body weight. Be especially on the watch for any traumatic experience that could trigger another bout.

What could I say?

Be encouraged. Most sufferers recover.

Face the issue. Accept that there is a problem. It is a big one, and you will need help in solving it. It is a complex one, more than just the trigger event. But it can be solved.

Make a choice. Choose life rather than death, health rather than years of sickness.

Give yourself back to God. Give every part of your life to him – your thoughts, your relationships, your feelings, your past, your future, and your body. Remember Paul's words: 'Do you not know that your body is a temple of the Holy Spirit, who is in you, whom you have received from God? You are not your own; you were bought at a price. Therefore honour God with your body' (1 Cor. 6:19–20).

Get help. Find someone you can trust, and talk to them about how you feel. Be real with them. Listen to what they say. See a doctor. Be prepared to see a counsellor. Trust these people; they are experts; they understand why you feel as you do; they are able to set you free. If you get the opportunity, join a self-help or support group.

Be honest. Stop telling yourself lies, and stop trying to deceive others.

Be positive. You are a real person, unique, of great value, individually shaped and loved by God, who sets a great life before you. Refuse to listen to the voices that keep telling you the negatives; the positives are more real than the negatives.

Be patient. As with any major illness, it takes time to recover.

National helpline

Eating Disorders Association: 01603 621 414

A Christian resource

Anorexia and Bulimia Care, 15 Fernhurst Gate, Aughton, Ormskirk L39 5ED. 01695 422 479

Five helpful books

D. Lovell, *Hungry for Love* (IVP)
E. Round, *Dying to be Thin* (Lion)
H. Wilkinson, *Beyond Chaotic Eating* (Marshall Pickering). A book to help understanding of anorexia.
H. Wilkinson, *Doorway to Hope* (CWR)
H. Wilkinson, *Puppet on a String* (Hodder and Stoughton). A book for anorexia sufferers to read.

ANXIETY

Like fear or stress, anxiety or worry can be helpful or unhelpful, creative or destructive. It is quite natural for the parents of a lost child to feel anxious; their anxiety prompts them to do something to find the child. A measure of anxiety over an approaching job interview can gear us up to present ourselves in the best possible light.

Anxiety becomes a problem when it is excessive, when instead of improving our performance it makes us less effective or paralyses us, or when it has no clear source and becomes a continuing and damaging attitude of mind.

There have been many different analyses of the causes of the widespread anxiety in our culture. Among contributory factors are:

• The breakdown of many of the traditional structures that gave people security, value and stability, such as the family, a clear set of moral standards and belief in God.

- The pace of life, the dominance of technological and urban living, and the loss of contact with nature with its clear cycles and rhythms.
- Continual change.
- The pressure to succeed.
- The example of others; our parents or those around us are anxious, so we learn to be that way too.
- The build-up of anxiety-producing factors, each of which may be small in itself, but which have a cumulative effect. For example, we may know there is only a remote chance of being mugged; but to the fear of being mugged we add fear of getting Aids, worry about our job and anxiety arising from today's news.

The Bible's teaching on anxiety is very clear. It recognizes it as a natural human emotion (Jesus sweating drops of blood in the Garden of Gethsemane) which should lead us to positive action such as prayer (Phil. 4:6) or action (Phil. 2:19–23; Paul specifically uses an 'anxiety' word – rather weakly translated 'takes [an] interest in' – to describe Timothy's attitude in verse 20). It recognizes, however, the danger of getting stuck in anxiety, but stresses that Christians always have a way of escape, since all the resources of the love and power of God are there to rescue us.

Some of the Bible's teaching on anxiety

Do not worry about your life, what you will eat or drink; or about your body, what you will wear. Is not life more important than food, and the body more important than clothes? Look at the birds of the air; they do not sow or reap or store away in barns, and yet your heavenly Father feeds them. Are you not much more valuable than they? Who of you by worrying can add a single hour to his life? …

Do not worry, saying, 'What shall we eat?' or' What shall we drink?' or 'What shall we wear?' For the pagans run after all these things, and your heavenly Father knows that you need them. But seek first his kingdom and his righteousness, and all these things will be given to you as well (Matt. 6:25–27, 31–33).

Peace I leave with you; my peace I give you. I do not give to you as the world gives. Do not let your hearts be troubled and do not be afraid (John 14:27).

My grace is sufficient for you, for my power is made perfect in weakness (2 Cor. 12.9).

Rejoice in the Lord always ... The Lord is near. Do not be anxious about anything, but in everything, by prayer and petition, with thanksgiving, present your requests to God. And the peace of God, which transcends all understanding, will guard your hearts and your minds in Christ Jesus.

Finally, brothers, whatever is true, whatever is noble, whatever is right, whatever is pure, whatever is lovely, whatever is admirable – if anything is excellent or praiseworthy – think about such things. Whatever you have learned or received or heard from me – put it into practice. And the God of peace will be with you (Phil. 4:4–9).

Cast all your anxiety on him because he cares for you (1 Pet. 5:7).

See also the passages quoted in the article on **fear**.

Helping those who struggle with anxiety

Be understanding and sympathetic. Don't dismiss their anxieties as unimportant. They may seem petty to you, but they are big to those who suffer from them.

Avoid adding to the pressure they are under by making them feel guilty for being anxious. Assure them that anxiety is a normal human reaction to difficulties and stress, which can be positive and helpful. It's not having anxious thoughts that is the problem; it's what we do with them when we have them.

Encourage them to use their feelings of anxiety as reminders to turn to God, prompting them to pray or to hand the issue over to him, each time they arise.

Recognize that anxiety can have all sorts of sources, some of which may not be at all obvious. But where there are obvious sources, help the person to deal with them as far as is possible.

Where the roots of the anxiety are hard to trace, suggest the help of a trained counsellor.

In all cases, whether or not the source of the anxiety can be removed or lessened, stress the grace and power and love of God.

Besides bringing the specific worries to God in prayer, it may be appropriate to arrange a time of special prayer ministry, in which they commit themselves to trusting their heavenly Father in all circumstances, and pray for special strength and grace to do so.

Do what you can to encourage those who suffer with anxiety to live a wholesome and well-balanced life, thus, hopefully, enabling them to get a more healthy perspective on the things that worry them. Possible suggestions you could make might include: watch less TV, get more exercise, have a holiday, get out into the country, keep fish, take up gardening.

See also **alienation, changing thought patterns, depression, fear, guilt, insomnia, low self-image, phobia, rejection, stress.**

A useful book

N. T. Anderson, *Freedom from Fear* (Monarch)

BEREAVEMENT

Losing someone we love through death is perhaps the most shattering of all our experiences. Even where we have faith that there is life after death, we still have to go through the pain of parting, the sense of loss, and the grieving process.

Occasionally death is something we welcome, a merciful release, or the timely closing of a long and good life. In those circumstances the pain of loss and grieving will be less. At other times the pain will be greatly increased by, say, the suddenness or the circumstances of the death, or because the person is young or dies tragically.

The death of a loved one is not the only form of bereavement. Divorce, retirement, or the loss of anything we hold dear, such as a limb, a special pet, or our home, is a form of bereavement, and can lead to sorrow and a grieving process.

The grieving process

There is a broad general pattern to the way people react to bereavement, often known as the 'stages of grief'. It isn't a fixed pattern; not everyone goes though every stage, and though there is a general development from one stage to another, some people may move backwards as well as forwards in the process.

People suffering bereavement often find it hard to cope with their feelings and experiences. Perhaps everything feels unreal, or a gracious Christian shows signs of uncharacteristic anger. We and they need to know that these symptoms are part of everyone's reaction to bereavement. It's not that there's anything wrong with them; they are not going mad. It's just that they are working through the shock and the awfulness of the bereavement experience.

Shock. For the first few days our bodies and minds cushion the awfulness of the loss by denying it. There is a numbness, an unreality: 'This can't be happening to me.' This cushioning is helpful, saving us from having to face reality all at once.

Emotional release. Our culture tends to inhibit the expression of grief: 'Stiff upper lip', 'Men don't cry', 'Christians don't grieve', 'I'm silly to cry', and so on. This is quite contrary to biblical teaching, and can be very harmful. Of course something as big as death affects us emotionally; we need to express that emotion, generally through the God-given means of tears. Bottling up our emotion can lead to serious problems later in the grieving process.

Anger and guilt. We feel a natural hostility towards the awfulness of death and loss. But it is hard to express anger at something so abstract as death, so often our anger is directed on to something or someone else, such as the medical staff, the person responsible for the road accident, God, or even ourselves (in the form of guilt). Christians in particular will be bewildered and even frightened at the strength of these feelings. We need to help them to understand that such feelings are a common part of the reaction to death, and to do what we can to help them to off-load them positively rather than destructively.

Yearning. For maybe two years and more, bereaved people experience disorientation, apathy, listlessness, loneliness, restlessness, irritability, sadness, depression and despair. These are all normal reactions to loss, and an expression of how much the person who has died meant to them.

Illness. Quite often a bereaved person will go through a bout of illness which, though genuine enough, is actually part of the body's reaction to the shock of loss. Such an illness can in some ways be helpful; it gives others the chance to express the special love and caring the bereaved person so much needs.

Acceptance and reorientation. The grieving process can last for a few months or five years or more. But, gradually, with many ups and downs, the bereaved person grows in acceptance of the loss, and in adjusting to life without the loved one.

Christians and bereavement

Some Christians feel that since death has been conquered and that our loved ones are now 'with Christ, which is better by far' (Phil. 1:23), they should not grieve at all, but rather give expression to Christ's triumph over death. This is a mistake. It is not a question of either rejoicing in Christ's victory or feeling sad at our loss; we should do both. Jesus both wept at Lazarus' grave, and raised him from the dead.

Grieving is an expression of love. Of course we are glad our loved one is in the presence of God, but we are also sad, because something beautiful has gone from our lives, something that has meant so much to us, in a sense a part of ourselves. Where there has been no love we won't feel the loss; but where the love has been deep the loss will be deep and painful, and we need to express that pain through grieving.

1 Thessalonians 4:13 strikes the right balance. It does not say Christians shouldn't grieve. But it does say our grief is different from that of non-Christians, because we have hope.

Some Bible passages on bereavement and grief

> Even though I walk
>> through the valley of the shadow of death,
> I will fear no evil,
>> for you are with me;
> your rod and your staff,
>> they comfort me (Ps. 23:4).

> The Spirit of the Sovereign LORD is on me,
> He has sent me to bind up the broken-hearted,
>> to … provide for those who grieve in Zion –
> to bestow on them a crown of beauty
>> instead of ashes,
> the oil of gladness
>> instead of mourning,
> and a garment of praise
>> instead of a spirit of despair (Is. 61:1–3).

> Blessed are those who mourn,
>> for they will be comforted (Matt. 5:4).

They went and told Jesus [of the death of John the Baptist].
    When Jesus heard what had happened, he withdrew by boat privately to a solitary place (Matt. 14:12–13).

… the God of all comfort, who comforts us in all our troubles, so that we can comfort those in any trouble with the comfort we ourselves have received from God. For just as the sufferings of Christ flow over into our lives, so also through Christ our comfort overflows (2 Cor. 1:3–7).

We do not want you to be ignorant about those who fall asleep, or to grieve like the rest of men, who have no hope. We believe that Jesus died and rose again and so we believe that God will bring with Jesus those who have fallen asleep in him … So we will be with the Lord for ever. Therefore encourage each other with these words (1 Thess. 4:13–14, 17–18).

The book of Psalms contains many passages written by those passing though darkness and grief; sometimes the writers are very honest about their feelings, but always they come back to the faithfulness of God who will in the end bring them through. See for example Psalms 6; 22; 31; 57; 69; 71; 90; 130.

Helping those who have been bereaved

If possible, as soon as you hear of the death, call to see the bereaved person. Don't worry about what you will say; a hug and shared tears are worth a thousand carefully thought-out words.

Offer help. Look for small, practical ways of expressing your support and love.

Be understanding. Help them to cope with the numbness, or denial, or expressions of grief and anger and so on.

Be patient. The process is slow and long. Keep up the support and caring.

Watch out for mood swings and steps 'backwards' in the grieving process. The fact that the bereaved person says, 'I'm fine now', does not prevent him or her going through a bad patch next week.

Encourage talking about the person who has died. Where a wife has lost her husband after years of marriage, for example, it is cruel to expect her suddenly to cut him out of her thoughts and conversation.

Where anger or guilt surfaces, be sympathetic and gentle, and help the bereaved person deal with it positively.

If you believe the process of grieving is not going forward satisfactorily, encourage the person to seek help from a suitable counsellor.

Watch out for anniversaries. Send a card or flowers and give special support.

What could I say?

As we have seen, love and support are far more significant in the shock and darkness of bereavement than well-thought-out comments and attempted explanations. But, when the time is right, some of these suggestions may well be helpful.

Allow yourself to grieve. Don't underestimate the shock and sadness the death of a loved one brings. Go easy on yourself. Don't keep a stiff upper lip.

Accept help. Don't try and manage on your own. You need love and support from others; and they need to be able to express their love and support for you.

Be patient. Grieving takes time. Wounds don't heal overnight. Where you have loved much you will need to grieve much. Expect good days and bad days, progress and setbacks.

Don't worry if you have vivid dreams or strange experiences of the person being near you. When we've been used to having someone around for years, the mind takes time to adjust to his or her absence. But resist the temptation to fantasize or to try and get in touch with your loved one. However hard it is, you need to adjust to the reality of your loss.

Talk about the person to others. Treasure memories. Relive the good experiences of the past. But don't get stuck in the past; use it as a foundation to build a good future.

If possible, avoid major changes in the early days of bereavement. It might be unwise, for example, to move to a new area and thus lose a supportive circle of friends.

Use resources that are available. You may find it helpful to join a local group, such as a Cruse group, of those who, like you, are going through bereavement. Even if you don't feel the need for it, it may be an opportunity to help someone else.

Be prepared to get specific help. If you are finding the grieving process difficult in any way, don't hesitate to seek help from a minister or a counsellor.

Have someone who is willing to let you contact them at any time if you are feeling particularly low. It doesn't need to be a professional counsellor: just someone who will listen, provide a shoulder to cry on, make you a cup of tea, and generally stand by you in your need.

Have someone you can be honest with. We can't pour out our innermost feelings to everyone, but there are times when we need to talk through our anger, fears, loneliness and so on.

As time goes by, work at developing new interests and friendships.

Don't forget to pray, both with and for the bereaved person, from the first day right through the grieving process.

Four questions bereaved people might ask

1. 'Why has God allowed this?'
Particularly in the early stages of bereavement this question is more an expression of bewilderment or protest than a request for a reasoned answer, and the best response is, 'We don't know', perhaps with, 'We don't understand now, but one day we will.' But if the question persists, we might in due course try sensitively pointing out that in a fallen world death is the inevitable lot of all men and women; that God has entered into and overcome the darkness of death in the cross of Christ; that he promises us that he will be with us even in 'the valley of the shadow of death'; and that though we cannot understand it, he knows the purposes he is working out through the years and they are all beautiful.

2. 'Will I see my loved one again?'
The Bible doesn't give much teaching on this. But while it says that exclusive relationships do not exist in heaven (Matt. 22:30), it does suggest we will see and recognize each other there (Matt. 17:3).

3. 'Can my loved one see what is happening to me now?'
The probable answer to this is 'No', at least not in the way we would tend to think. The Bible clearly warns against the danger of trying to get in touch with a loved one who has died. A helpful response to the question might be: 'What we do know is that God can see everything that is happening to you; he is caring for you, and for your loved one as well, and will certainly pass on anything she or he needs to know.'

4. 'How can I cope with the knowledge that my loved one, who was not a Christian, is now in hell?'
Very sensitively we could point out: (1) It is not for us to say for sure that any specific person is in hell. There is always the possibility that at some time (even at the very last moment) he or she called on the name of the Lord (Acts 2:21). (2) God alone is 'the Judge of all the earth' (Gen. 18:25). All who die are in his hands,

and their fate is his responsibility, not ours, a responsibility he fulfils with justice and with love. (3) However heavy such knowledge, or fear, may be to bear, he will give us the strength to bear it (2 Cor. 12:9; Jas. 4:6a).

Some things *not* to say

'Don't cry.'
'You'll soon get over it.'
'I know how you feel.'
'Make new friends and you'll soon forget the one who's died.'

See also **anger, fear, loneliness, loss, suffering**.

For further help

The DSS publishes a helpful booklet, *What To Do After a Death* (D49)
Cruse – Bereavement Care, Cruse House, 126 Sheen Road, Richmond, TW9 1UR. 020 8940 4818. Helpline 020 8332 7227 Cot-death helpline: 020 7235 1721

Helpful books

H. Alexander, *Experiences of Bereavement* (Lion)
H. Bauman, *Living through Grief* (Lion)
V. Ironside, *Finding God in Bereavement* (Lion Pocketguide)
I. Knox, *Bereaved* (Kingsway)
A. Pearson, *Growing Through Loss and Grief* (HarperCollins)

BULIMIA

Bulimia is an eating disorder in which the sufferer (most are female) periodically binges, eating large amounts of food, and then disposes of it through vomiting, starvation, laxatives or the like. Like anorexia, bulimia is an expression of a deeper problem than one of eating. But, unlike anorexia, most sufferers are able to continue to hide their bulimia; indeed, it is generally very important to them that they do so.

The problems that underlie and give rise to bulimia are generally complex and deep-rooted. Sufferers will need the help of a trained counsellor, preferably one who specializes in eating disorders, both to find what the problem is, and to face and overcome it. Seeking to deal with bulimia just on the level of controlled eating is rarely sufficient.

Helping those who suffer with bulimia

Bulimics are generally very ashamed of their 'secret'. They are likely to deny that they have any problem, and so we need to make a point of showing them extra love and acceptance so as to make it as easy as possible for them to be honest with us.

Help them to get to the point where they acknowledge that they have a problem, and that their eating problem is the expression of an inner need which they have to face and meet.

Give them hope. There is a very high recovery rate among bulimics who face up to their problem.

Carefully but strongly encourage them to get help from a counsellor, or possibly from a support group for bulimia sufferers.

Keep their secret. There is no need for lots of people to know.

Pray with them. Pray for self-control over eating, and, more importantly, for the power and love of God to heal whatever it is that is driving them to it.

Do what you can to help them turn the focus of their attention away from themselves and their feelings and their eating problem. Encourage an upward and outward focus – on God and their relationship with him, and on others.

National helpline

Eating Disorders Association: 01603 621 414

A Christian resource

Anorexia and Bulimia Care, 15 Fernhurst Gate, Aughton, Ormskirk L39 5ED. 01695 422 479

BULLYING

In essence, bullying is the causing of distress and damage to a vulnerable individual by someone or a group of people in a dominant position. It doesn't necessarily involve physical violence; it can take the form of emotional abuse, deliberate acts that provoke or cause problems, like hiding possessions, spreading rumours, or any abuse of power to the detriment of the victim. It happens throughout life in every sort of situation, though it is most frequently associated with school, home and workplace.

Schools have become increasingly aware of the problem of bullying and its effect on both the victims and the perpetrators, and will generally have procedures in place to deal with cases when they are reported. Procedures may also be laid down in workplace situations, though where the bully is the boss victims may well feel that more damage than good will be done by following them. In the home and other situations there are no established procedures, except in cases of clear physical violence, and many victims feel hopelessly trapped.

Bullying is an expression of power. Many bullies feel they need to express their power in this way because of their own insecurity or low self-image; but bullying can also be a learned behaviour pattern (many victims of bullying go on to bully others), or even an expected role (such as the traditional sergeant-major or the sarcastic schoolteacher). At root it is a blatant rejection of the Christian principle of loving and valuing the other person.

Victims are often picked on because they are vulnerable in

some way. Additionally, the process of being bullied tends to destroy any self-confidence they may have had. As a result they will be all the more reluctant to take any decisive action to deal with the situation.

In seeking to help perpetrators of bullying the hardest task is usually to get them to admit they are doing anything wrong and need help in changing their behaviour. Typically they will seek to excuse themselves, to say it is all meant in fun, or that the victim is exaggerating.

What could I say to victims of bullying?

See the suggestions under **violence**.

Bullying is wrong. It damages both the victim and the perpetrator. It is directly contrary to God's foundational principle of love. Even if you feel that some of your suffering is your own fault or deserved in some way, God wants it to stop.

God knows what you are going through. His love and grace reach out in a very special way to those who are weak, vulnerable and persecuted. Take refuge in him and allow him to give you the special strength and wisdom you need to face and come through this situation.

Take some steps to stop the bullying. This may not be easy; you will need to be careful not to make things worse. But in every situation there must be some way of tackling the problem. Check out the procedures laid down in your workplace or school; talk to personnel officers or others in authority; talk with a social worker.

While the bullying is continuing, try using these Bible truths and passages where appropriate:

- They bullied Jesus; you are sharing in his sufferings (Phil. 3:10).
- 'Love your enemies and pray for those who persecute you, that you may be sons of your Father in heaven' (Matt. 5:44–45).
- Our God can bring good out of any evil situation or suffering – and he promises that he will, if we let him. Hold firmly on to the hope that he will do that here.
- The people of God have always been bullied. Many of the Psalms, for example, show this. Where appropriate, use the

experiences and thoughts of others to help you through your time of suffering. Study and pray through Bible passages such as Lamentations 3; Psalms 22; 31; 37; 57; etc.

Do all you can to fight the temptation to respond to the bullying with anger, fear, self-pity and so on. These things only destroy, multiplying and spreading the damage done by the bullying. When they do arise, take them to the Lord and let him deal with them. If necessary, talk them through with a Christian friend or counsellor.

Get others to pray for you and with you. Pray for yourself, that you will have strength to cope with the situation, wisdom to know what to do about it, and God's protection against any form of harm. Pray also for the bully.

What could I say to bullies?

However you may view it, what you are doing is wrong. It does not measure up to the standards of love that God calls us to follow. It's not the kind of thing we can picture Jesus doing.

Since it is wrong, it must stop. It needs to be replaced with a truly loving, Christlike relationship and behaviour.

Accept that the grace and power of God can change you, and that you want him to do so.

Admit your sin to God. You could choose to do this during a time of prayer ministry in the presence of Christian friends you can trust. Ask and receive his forgiveness and cleansing.

Again, if appropriate, in the presence of others, recommit your life solemnly to God. Promise him that by his grace you will avoid anything that even begins to look like bullying. Ask for the anointing of the Holy Spirit, to give you both discernment and strength.

Admit to your victim that you have sinned against him or her. Ask for forgiveness. Together, commit yourselves to a new and wholesome relationship of Christlike love and trust.

Use the question 'What would Jesus do?' to help shape your reaction in every situation.

Where you do begin to slip back into the old pattern, immediately admit your mistake and ask for forgiveness.

Be prepared to seek the help of a counsellor. You may well need to sort out and deal with the underlying cause of your tendency to bully.

See also **anger**, **child abuse**, **conflict**, **manipulation**, **prejudice**, **rejection**, **suffering**, **violence**.

National helpline

Childline, 0800 1111

BURNOUT

Most human beings have remarkable reserves of physical, mental, emotional and spiritual energy which are needed from time to time to cope with crises, pressures, stress and the like. However, if we are confronted with a series of crises, or the pressures or stresses continue at a high level over a long period, we can reach the point where we have used up all our reserves, and there is nothing left to keep us going. This is burnout. The term is most frequently used for conditions arising from excessive pressures at work, but it can be the result of a whole range of pressures.

Burnout is characterized by a range of features:

- *Physical:* fatigue, exhaustion, headaches, gastrointestinal upsets.
- *Mental:* loss of drive, loss of interest, demoralization, inefficiency.
- *Emotional:* dullness, blunting of the emotions; but also loss of control over emotions, leading to irritability, outbursts of anger, etc.
- *Spiritual:* helplessness, depersonalization, detachment, hopelessness.

It is not easy to tell when a person moves from a state of excessive stress to a state of burnout; the two tend to merge. But whether it is burnout or not, a person showing these characteristics is in urgent need of help.

Burnout is a serious condition. There is a high risk that without decisive action it will remain permanently. Be quick to spot the symptoms and take action. People with burnout do not necessarily recognize there is anything seriously wrong. You will need to help them see the seriousness of their condition by talking either with them or with their family or friends.

In most cases it will be essential that they seek professional help, both from their doctor and from a trained counsellor.

Clearly, burnout is best avoided. Keep a careful eye on those who have heavy work or home pressures and additionally take on church or ministry responsibilities. Watch especially those who are driven by a need to find their self-worth in work or achievement. Encourage people to practise the principle of the Sabbath, both by having adequate holidays, and by having periods free from church responsibilities. Do what you can to ensure your church provides good teaching on the Sabbath principle, the place of work, priorities, the source of self-worth, and so on.

What could I say?

Realize that this is a serious condition that needs drastic steps to deal with it.

Try and find ways of removing the source of the pressure. If, for example, the problem is a high-powered job, consider giving it up, or at the very least get your doctor to sign you off for a lengthy period to give you a break. If it is impossible to escape from the pressure, find ways of lessening it. If, say, you are caring for a terminally ill relative, find others who can share some of the responsibility, or get help from a supportive counsellor, the medical team, or the social services. If you have responsibilities in the church that are adding to the pressure, obey the command of the Bible and take a sabbatical.

Give yourself another major interest. Maybe, as in many cases of burnout, work or the specific situation causing the stress has taken over the whole of your life. Reverse this by finding something that interests you, a new hobby or a new friendship. Because burnout produces lethargy, this will take some doing. But work at it; don't let the disengagement and hopelessness of burnout have the last word.

Check your priorities in life. Is work or status or money worth the price of health, peace of mind, your family, and so on? What is life really for? Does God really intend your secular or even Christian work to destroy you? Do you have to have a high-powered job or a certain salary level even if it kills you or wrecks your marriage or family life? Are you indispensable? Take the opportunity to sort out your priorities, and the things that really matter. Remember the words of Jesus: 'What good is it for a man to gain the whole world, yet forfeit his soul?' (Mark 8:36).

Get help. Have a medical check-up; it could be that some physical condition has contributed to or arisen from the burnout. If you are able, see a works counsellor or someone specializing in stress and burnout. If you can't find a professional counsellor, find someone you can talk to honestly and openly, and who will speak honestly and openly with you, and whom you feel you can trust.

Give yourself time. Be prepared to work through a slow process of returning to normal. Pace yourself; don't take on too much too early.

See also **depression, stress**.

CARERS

Carers carry a double burden. They share the suffering or problems of the person they are caring for. In addition, they have to cope with their own needs and suffering. In many situations, for example when caring for an ill or elderly family member, they find themselves constantly giving to meet the needs of the other person, but never receiving to meet their own needs.

The Christian community can be an invaluable source of help and strength to those in a caring role, expressing love and support in a range of ways, from prayer and empathy, through to practical help such as providing respite care.

What could I say?

You are not alone. We want to help carry the load; it's our way of showing Christian love. Please ask us to help you as appropriate; don't struggle on your own. Where we can help, we will. Where we can't, we will be honest and say so.

Make sure you are getting all the help and support you can. All sorts of help can be got from other helpers, statutory bodies, medical staff, support groups and the like.

Be willing to be honest about your feelings. Carers often have feelings of frustration, injustice, bewilderment, anger, guilt, fear and so on. When these things arise, talk them through with a minister or other suitable person.

Don't feel that you must always put on a brave face in front of the person you are caring for. There may well be some times when the best thing is for you both to be honest about your feelings and even to have a good cry together.

Make sure you give yourself space. From time to time have a break from your caring responsibilities. However vital your role, resist the pressure to feel you are indispensable. You will be able to care all the better if you give yourself regular times off.

Get people to pray for you and for the person you are caring for. You both need the support and grace of God. Make prayer a central feature of all your caring; if appropriate, pray regularly with the person you are caring for.

Be especially careful that minor things don't get out of proportion. Physical weakness or emotional stress can cause irritability and frustration in the person you are caring for, and these feelings may at times be off-loaded on to you. This can be very upsetting, but do your best not to let it hurt you or to spoil your relationship with him or her.

Be encouraged. Caring is a very Christlike ministry. You are able to show love and encouragement and the graciousness of God. See it as an opportunity to exercise the caring and helping ministry of Jesus. Ask specifically for his presence in you in all that you do.

See also **disability, illness, terminal illness, stress, suffering**.

Support organizations

Carers National Association, 1st Floor, 20 Glasshouse Yard, London EC1A 4JS. 020 7490 8898. www.carersuk.demon.co.uk
Carers Christian Fellowship, 14 Yealand Drive, Ulverston LA12 9JB.

Useful books

C. Ledger, *Caring for Carers* (Kingsway)
N. Leach and S. Smith, *Practise Hospitality with CARE* (CARE Guide)
H. Vogel, *Strength to Care* (CWR)

CHANGE

Change is such a common feature of our culture that most of us tend to feel we are experts at coping with it. But the very fact that it is so common can mean that we are all the more obstinate when some situation arises where we feel we ought to resist change. A man who has just gone through, say, the takeover of the company he works for, the restructuring of his job, moving to a new office, and getting used to a new computer system, may feel that that is as much as he can possibly cope with, and will adamantly oppose the introduction of a new hymnbook at church.

People frequently resist change because they are in some way threatened by it. It may threaten their comfort or security or position; or it may threaten them as a person: they feel fearful, or hurt, or not in control of things.

Not all change is for the better, and there may be times when we feel it right to encourage someone to stand firm in resistance to it. But on many occasions change, for better or worse, is inevitable, and continuing resistance will serve only to damage all concerned. Our task in that case will be to help people to accept the change, and to find ways of making it creative and productive.

What could I say to those facing unavoidable change?

God can handle it. The Bible accepts that some change is good and some is not so good. But it also teaches very clearly that God is big enough to cope with and bring good out of any situation, and that if we keep him at the centre, he promises to fit everything else into place.

Be open to giving way. None of us has time or energy to fight every battle, however worthwhile we may think the cause. There are some things we need simply to accept. A good rule of thumb is to ask, 'Is this an issue worth dying for?' If the answer is 'No', then it's probably not worth fighting for. Remember that 'submitting' is a Christian virtue (Eph. 5:21).

Resist the tendency to focus in on all the negative aspects of the changing situation. Instead, work hard at thinking of potential positives. Write out a list of these; talk about them positively to others.

Pray. Ask for grace and acceptance, the ability to cope with change, and that you will grow as a person and as a Christian as a result of the changes. Pray that the promises in Matthew 6:33 and Romans 8:28 will be fulfilled in your situation.

Trust God. Be sure that the basis for your security is firmly in God, and not in things around you. Accept that God may even be allowing the things on which you have been basing your security to be taken away so that you will be thrown more on to him.

Bible passages relevant to facing change

I tell you, do not worry about your life, what you will eat or drink; or about your body, what you will wear ... But seek first his kingdom and his righteousness, and all these things will be given to you as well (Matt. 6:25, 33).

In all things God works for the good of those who love him, who have been called according to his purpose (Rom. 8:28).

We fix our eyes not on what is seen, but on what is unseen. For what is seen is temporary, but what is unseen is eternal (2 Cor. 4:18).

I have learnt to be content whatever the circumstances ... I can do everything through him who gives me strength (Phil. 4:11, 13).

Here we do not have an enduring city, but we are looking for the city that is to come (Heb. 13:14).

Do not love the world or anything in the world ... The world and its desires pass away, but the man who does the will of God lives for ever (1 John 2:15, 17).

CHANGING THOUGHT PATTERNS

The kind of people we are is profoundly affected by the beliefs and attitudes within us, which are expressed in our basic thought patterns. These thought patterns may be conscious or unconscious. Ideas and attitudes that have been planted in our mind and constantly reinforced become a powerful and sometimes controlling influence on our thoughts and actions. A woman who throughout her childhood has been told that she is useless and stupid is very likely to believe that evaluation for the rest of her life, and all her actions will be affected by that belief.

Similarly, even though a man becomes a Christian, he will still carry with him beliefs and attitudes that have become firmly lodged in his mind, and they will take a fair bit of shifting. One of the major causes of problems in people's Christian lives is that though they have become Christians, they still think and react as they did when they were non-Christians. As a result, their behaviour is hardly different from of that of people who are not Christians. We need to take action on Paul's words: 'Do not conform any longer to the pattern of this world, but be transformed by the renewing of your mind' (Rom. 12:2).

Often we are not consciously aware of the attitudes and beliefs that we have, just as we are not aware of our eyes when we are looking at something. Nevertheless, our thinking and so our living are channelled through them, and can be profoundly affected by them.

When we want to change some external aspect of our living, such as our outward attitude or actions, very often the key is to change our inner thought patterns. This is rarely an easy thing to do. We tend to be creatures of habit, and our minds slip automatically into the ways of thinking we have been following for years.

So changing a thought pattern takes conscious effort and time. A belief that was indoctrinated into us throughout our childhood, a period when we were particularly susceptible to the forming of thought patterns, will need to be dug out thoroughly, and continually and consciously rejected when, due to our habits of thought, it keeps popping up again. More positively, the new pattern of thought needs to be deliberately adopted and continually reinforced.

Typical thought patterns we may encounter that need to be changed include:

- prejudices, such as prejudice against certain ethnic groups;
- some phobias, such as fear of bearded men;
- false beliefs, like 'Everything I do is wrong';
- anti-Christian beliefs, like 'I can live a good life on my own';
- indoctrinated beliefs, such as 'I have to get everything right.'

Helping people to change their thought patterns

The best place to start, as far as Christians are concerned, is with Romans 12:2, which in its context calls on us to give our minds as well as our bodies to God for him to change in any way he chooses. But we don't leave all the work to him. He shows us what things we should be believing and thinking, and promises his power to believe and think them. But we then have to get on with the task of implementing these new beliefs and thoughts, and that can take some doing. To help, here are ten suggestions, which I've called 'Ten steps to changing thought patterns'. The suggestions may well need to be adapted to fit specific individuals. As you suggest these steps to people, particularly encourage them to implement them in conscious and prayerful dependence upon the Holy Spirit.

Ten steps to changing thought patterns

1. Accept that you are not going to stay as you are. You are determined to change. Even more importantly, God wants you to change and has promised he will give you what you need to change. Changes in feelings and actions start with change in the thought patterns that express our basic attitudes and beliefs. See the words of Jesus in Mark 7:21–23 and Matthew 12:35. Commit yourself before God to change at every level.

2. Write down, preferably with the help of a friend or a counsellor, the attitudes and beliefs that underlie the thought patterns that influence the area of your life you are concerned about. For example, if you cannot take criticism, you might write down: 'Criticism is rejection', 'People criticize me because they don't like me', or 'I need to be accepted fully by everyone.'

3. Look as objectively as possible at what you have written, or, better still, ask a friend to comment on it. Are your statements true? Are they partially true? Can they be rewritten or rephrased to make them nearer the truth? Most importantly, what would God say about them? How do they tally with the teaching of Jesus and the rest of the Scriptures? Can you find any Scripture passages which comment on them or correct them?

4. Write down alternative or revised statements. In our example,

you might write: 'Criticism is not necessarily rejection', 'Sometimes people criticize me in order to help me', 'I don't have to believe everything everyone says', 'Jesus lived a great life without being accepted by everyone.' Try to make this second list as positive as possible, but don't put on to it anything that is impossible for you to believe. For example, you might feel it impossible to write, 'I don't care what anyone says about me'; but you could write, 'I need to take more notice of the positive things people say about me than of the critical things.' Add to the list any relevant Bible teaching.

5. Now the real work begins! Your task is to reprogramme your thinking by continually feeding in the second list of attitudes and beliefs, such that your old beliefs get pushed out. Remember this will take time, since your old beliefs and attitudes are so well entrenched in your mind. Start by clearly and decisively rejecting the first list. Ask the Holy Spirit to purge those beliefs from your mind and life. Then equally decisively commit yourself to the second list. 'From now on, with the help of the Holy Spirit, these are going to be the things that form my thought patterns.' Aim for nothing less than that great statement at the end of 1 Corinthians 2: 'We have the mind of Christ.'

6. Enlist the help of a friend who will pick you up when you revert to the old pattern, and will encourage you to keep going when you feel like giving up.

7. Find ways of continually reminding yourself of the points on the second list. Write them on cards and put them where you can see them often. Learn the relevant Bible passages by heart and keep reciting them to yourself.

8. Keep a journal, and record progress or otherwise in it each day. This will be a stimulus to you to keep the process going. Pray over the ups and downs of the process. Don't be too discouraged if the progress is slow. Any progress at all towards the renewing of our mind is worth it.

9. The hardest time to apply the second list is when you have to respond or act in the heat of the moment. Someone criticizes you, and, without thinking, you respond as you always have, completely forgetting your new set of beliefs. So train yourself not to make instant responses. Stop. Wait. Think before you respond. Respond on the basis of your new beliefs.

10. Keep reinforcing your new beliefs and thought patterns. Remind yourself of their importance. Watch out for additional ways of confirming their truth. After a time, you may even be able to build further on them and reshape them into even better forms. Above all, keep praying for the ongoing renewing of your mind.

CHILD ABUSE

Child abuse can be defined as any action by a responsible person that damages a child in any way.

Physical abuse is tragically still very common. The NSPCC has estimated that in the UK three or more children die every week as a result of physical abuse from their parents.

Statistics concerning *sexual* abuse vary widely, often according to the varying definitions of what constitutes sexual abuse. Here, as with physical abuse, children are most at risk in their own homes. (See **child sexual abuse**.)

A third form of abuse, which frequently accompanies the other two, but also often occurs alone, is *emotional*. This can take all sorts of forms, such as rejection, threats, lack of love, taunting, shouting, or verbal attacks like 'You're stupid', 'Drop dead!'

There is still considerable controversy over *ritual* abuse. This does not necessarily have to be linked with satanic groups; as a technical definition it can be any bizarre form of organized group abuse. In practice it appears that sexual elements are often involved.

Much of the material under **child sexual abuse** will be applicable in other cases of abuse. The two key principles are:

- Take reports of abuse seriously, particularly if it is the victim who is telling you. You may feel they are imagining it or trying to manipulate you; but it is vital to give them a fair hearing in case what they are saying is true.
- Take immediate action. If you are sure ongoing abuse is taking place, you must report it. If you are not sure, or if you feel that

the abuse is a minor isolated incident, you should still talk it over with someone who has some knowledge in this field. Many churches are appointing children's advocates, who would normally be the person you would turn to. Most denominational groupings have someone who has special responsibility to give advice in this area.

See also **bullying, child sexual abuse, prejudice, rejection, violence**.

National resources

Childline, Royal Mail Building, Studd Street, London N1 0QW. 020 7239 1000. Helpline: 0800 1111. www.childline.org.uk
National Society for the Prevention of Cruelty to Children (NSPCC), 42 Curtain Road, London EC2A 3NH. 020 7825 2500. Child protection helpline: 0800 800 500. www.nspcc.org.uk

A Christian resource

PCCA Christian Child Care, PO Box 133, Swanley BR8 7UQ. 01322 667 207. www.doveuk.com/pcca

CHILD SEXUAL ABUSE

Statistics on child sexual abuse vary greatly, often as a result of differing definitions of what abuse is. Technically, it is a very wide term, including sexually motivated exposure or touching of primary or secondary sexual parts of the body. The number of children subjected to such abuse, perhaps just once or twice, is likely to be high. Estimates of those suffering abuse in its more narrow sense of involving some form of intercourse, generally over a period of time, range from 3% to 10% of all children. Girls are considerably more at risk than boys. The great majority of abuse is by people the child knows well: other children, relatives, babysitters, and especially fathers and stepfathers. Almost all adult abusers are male.

Abuse can start at any age, often beginning in a small way and developing to regular intercourse over a long period and continuing well into teenage. Pressure is put on the child not to tell, perhaps through threats of violence, or promises of rewards. Most children hate the experience, but there may be an element of enjoying the attention it gives them and the rewards it brings. In father/daughter situations, the mother will often know what is happening but will be afraid to do anything about it for fear of the consequences.

An increasing number of churches are setting in place procedures and structures, both to safeguard against abuse, and to clarify what should be done if abuse is suspected. This may include the appointment of a person with knowledge and specific responsibility in this area, who can act as a children's advocate. Where such a person has not been appointed there will usually be someone with this responsibility in a wider ecclesiastical structure, such as a diocese or denominational office.

Possible indications of abuse

Should there be a risk that a child is being abused, it may be appropriate to watch out for some of these indications, though, of course, the existence of these things in themselves is no proof of abuse.

- Changes in mood or behaviour, particularly where a child withdraws, regresses, starts underachieving, or becomes clingy, for no apparent reason.
- Inappropriate relationships with peers or adults.
- Injuries which are not readily explainable, or have not received medical attention.
- Inappropriate sexual knowledge in the child, or preoccupation with sexual matters.
- Persistent tiredness; bad dreams, possibly with sexual connotations.

When a child tells you he or she has been abused

Listen seriously. You may find it hard to believe; you may even suspect the child is lying or fantasizing. But still listen; take the child seriously. If the allegations are true, the child may have been threatened with dire consequences if they tell anyone; we must not make it harder for them to tell by showing unbelief.

Don't probe; don't ask leading questions; don't put ideas into the child's mind.

Don't promise that you won't tell anyone. You may well be legally required to do so.

After the conversation, write down what the child has said.

If the child is linked to your church, consult and follow agreed procedures; in particular, talk things through with the children's advocate.

If the allegations are of serious abuse and there are grounds for believing they are true, you must inform the authorities, say through an NSPCC officer or the local Social Services department.

If there is serious doubt about the truth of the allegations, every effort must be made to decide one way or the other. Things must not just be left unresolved.

Helping a child who has been abused

In cases of serious abuse, it is the responsibility of the Social Services and other authorities to arrange counselling and care for the child. But even where that is fully provided, children will still need a great deal of help and support from all those around them.

Sadly, the immediate result of abuse becoming known can be more terrifying for the child than the abuse itself. It involves the intrusion of all sorts of authority figures, and possibly the break-up of the family. In such circumstances, do everything you can to reassure and comfort the child.

A child who has been abused by an adult in a position of trust may find it hard to trust other adults. Take special care over a period of time to build wholesome, trusting relationships with the child.

Specific problems arising from the abuse should be dealt with by the counsellor. They may include guilt, fear of adults, bad dreams, low self-worth, fear of sex, overemphasis on sex, and insecurity. Even where such counselling is being given, sensitive support will still be needed to assist the child to deal with them.

Helping adults who have been abused as children

It is only comparatively recently that the issue of child sexual abuse has been recognized as a widespread problem. Many adults who were abused as children were given no help at the time. Though some have learnt to cope with the experience and have few problems as a result, others are still struggling with the hurt and damage that were done.

While it is very important not to minimize the seriousness of such abuse and its possible effects, we need also to bear in mind that damage can be sometimes be done by digging out long-past and even forgotten experiences (real or imagined) which are not in fact having serious, adverse effects on life in the present. In some cases the wisest course will be to take the person through a time of 'just in case' prayer ministry in which we seek God's grace and healing for anything of this sort that may be in the person's past, without having to focus specifically on it, and then accept that the issue has been handed over to him, and so can be forgotten.

However, where the abuse suffered was real and is clearly having adverse effects in the present, it will almost certainly be necessary to encourage the person to see a specialist Christian counsellor for help in dealing with it. While leaving most of the helping to the counsellor, here are some things you may feel able to say in your talking with the person.

What could I say to adults who have been abused as children?

Don't carry it alone. Find someone you can talk to about the abuse, your feelings about it, and how it has affected your subsequent life. This person could be a professional counsellor, or a minister, or a trusted friend.

Check out areas of your life that could be linked to the abuse. It can (though doesn't have to) lead to guilt, anger, feelings of powerlessness and betrayal, bad memories, the inability to trust men or those in authority, difficulty in showing or receiving affection or love, low self-image, self-rejection, rejection or abuse of the body, eating disorders, feelings of uncleanness, obsessive cleanliness, and sexual problems (including frigidity, promiscuity and abusing children). Where any of these have arisen as a result of child sexual abuse, understanding their source can be a big step on the way to dealing with them.

Hold on to hope. Though it is very understandable that abuse in childhood can have a deeply damaging effect on the whole of life, it does not have to be that way. Make up your mind that the result of the abuse in your life will not be allowed to be destructive. Fight the temptation to let anger dominate you, or to pass the abuse on to the next generation. Talk through with your friend or counsellor each of the damaged areas and find healing for them.

Use all the resources available to find healing. For some issues, such as forgiveness, cleansing, inner healing, and the severance of the psychological or spiritual hold the abuser may have over you, you may need specific help from a minister or trained Christian counsellor. Make use of the great resources available through prayer, the love of God and the power of the Holy Spirit. Consider the possibility, at an appropriate time, of specific prayer ministry for issues that may arise in counselling.

Work towards forgiveness. If you can bring yourself to forgive the abuser, do so. If you cannot, pray that eventually you will be able to; you don't want to be eaten up with bitterness and anger all your life.

Consider carefully any other steps you may need to take. It may be that no useful purpose will be served by confronting the abuser; if you have left it all these years, go on leaving it. But if there is any likelihood that any children should still be at risk from the abuser, action must be taken.

Helping abusers

Since abuse is a serious criminal offence, we must resist the pressures to hush things up. In particular, if there is any risk at all that abuse will continue, immediate action must be taken. In borderline cases, where, for example, the abuse is a 'minor', one-off occurrence, such as inappropriate cuddling of a child, advice and guidance should be sought from the children's advocate or similar person.

What could I say to abusers?

Face up to the seriousness of what you have done. Quite apart from being a very serious criminal offence, it has the potential to ruin another person's life, all for your sexual gratification. Be willing to accept the responsibility for your actions; there may have been factors which influenced you, but they didn't make you do it. You did it.

If the police do not already know, go voluntarily to them and tell them what you have been doing. You may wish to consult a solicitor first, and you would be wise to take a trusted friend with you. Willingness to take the initiative in going to the police, co-operation with subsequent enquiries, and willingness to receive counselling can all count as mitigating factors should the police choose to prosecute.

Set up structures to make sure there will never be any repetition. In the most solemn way in which you can conceive, before witnesses who will hold you to them, take upon yourself four vows. First, never again to abuse any child in any way. Secondly, to avoid any situation (e.g. being a babysitter or being involved in youth work) when the possibility of abusing might arise. Thirdly, to work through a programme of counselling until you reach the point where the counsellor is satisfied that all the issues have been adequately dealt with. Fourthly, to remain accountable to your counsellor or some other suitable person with whom you will be totally honest should temptations continue to arise.

Co-operate fully with your counsellor. The process of counselling may be painful, digging out things from your past that you do not wish to face. Accept that they need to be faced, and co-operate with your counsellor in every way.

Ask others to help you. Because of the seriousness of the offence, you will have to face rejection and worse from those who know about it. To help you through the pain of this, you will need two or three loyal friends or family members who will stick with you and give you the love and support you need. Don't be too proud to admit your needs. Be honest with them; let them be honest with you.

Pray for your victim. You may choose, if it is appropriate and others advise it, to write briefly to the victim and their family saying how sorry you are for what you have done. Don't make excuses; don't go into detail; don't ask for their forgiveness. (If they give it, great! But it is too big a thing for you to ask for.)

When you feel you are ready, go and talk to your minister or church elders about receiving forgiveness from God.

See also **changing thought patterns, forgiveness, guilt, rape, sexual issues, suffering**.

National resources

Childline, Royal Mail Building, Studd Street, London N1 0QW. 020 7239 1000. Helpline: 0800 1111. www.childline.org.uk
National Society for the Prevention of Cruelty to Children (NSPCC), 42 Curtain Road, London EC2A 3NH. 020 7825 2500. Child protection helpline: 0800 800 500. www.nspcc.org.uk

A Christian resource

PCCA Christian Child Care, PO Box 133, Swanley BR8 7UQ. 01322 667 207. www.doveuk.com/pcca

CHILDLESSNESS

Many couples have difficulty conceiving, and a surprisingly large number never do so, despite the lack of any obvious cause of infertility. Most of these couples desperately want a child, and go through a continuing painful cycle of hope and disappointment. Additionally, their problem tends to isolate them from their friends and peers, most of whom are having few difficulties pro-

ducing children, and some of whom show considerable insens-
itivity ('You're lucky you haven't got any children; I'd gladly give
you one of mine').

A childless couple will suffer many of the feelings of those
coping with bereavement and loss, particularly, of course, where
the longed-for pregnancy does occur, only to end in a miscarriage
or stillbirth.

For Christians the problem of childlessness can be to some
extent accentuated by the Old Testament passages which speak of
children as a sign of God's blessing, with their implication that
lack of children is a sign of God's displeasure. Additionally,
though there are a number of childless women mentioned in the
Bible, they all end up bearing children. This was doubtless a sign
of God's miraculous grace to them, but it may not always seem
helpful to present-day couples who remain childless despite ardent
prayers for God's intervention.

Whatever the teaching of the Old Testament, where at times
God's blessing did tend to be demonstrated to his people in material terms, the New Testament makes it clear that, for Christians,
suffering, so far from being a sign of God's displeasure, can even
be a means of God's grace and blessing (see **suffering**).
Additionally, however important the natural family, God has
given us, as his sons and daughters, an even more significant
family – that of the people of God. Though it is not for us to
understand why one couple is fertile and another is not, to the
childless couple who are able to accept childlessness as his calling
to them, Jesus promises: 'I tell you the truth … no-one who has
left home or brothers or sisters or mother or father or children or
fields for me and the gospel will fail to receive a hundred times as
much in this present age (homes, brothers, sisters, mothers, children and fields – and with them, persecutions) and in the age to
come, eternal life' (Mark 10:29–30).

Care needs to be taken in raising the issue of adoption. Avoid
suggesting adoption as though it is the simple answer to the childless couple's problems. If they are willing to consider it, before they
make up their minds, encourage them to talk the possibilities
through with someone from an adoption agency or local Social
Services department. Be aware that the assessment process can be

a lengthy one, and that, though there is no shortage of older children, many couples who set their hearts on adopting a newborn baby have ended up finding that no suitable baby is available.

One of our biggest contributions to a childless couple is to ensure the acceptance and love of a caring church fellowship. Do all you can to minimize thoughtless remarks and uncaring attitudes. Encourage fertile couples to share something of the pain of childlessness, while at the same time helping the childless couple to get to the point where they can in some ways share the joy of those who have children.

What could I say?

God knows your pain and your longing. He hears all your prayers. None of us can understand why his answer at present is 'No', but we can be sure that the answer is given in love and wisdom, with the promise of his presence and grace. (See **suffering, unanswered prayer**.)

Hold on to hope. But don't let the hope of a child be your only hope. God has lots of good things in store for you. A child may be one of them, but there will be plenty of others – some of them, in God's wisdom, even better than a child.

Stay close to God. You need his comfort and strength through this difficult time. If you find yourself feeling resentful and even angry towards him, talk to him about it – he'll understand. If necessary, talk these feelings through with a minister or wise Christian friend.

Be sure to get all the help you can from medical specialists and the like. If they offer some special course of action such as drugs or IVF, we will pray for you and stand by you as you think through all the issues and make a decision.

Be prepared to talk about how you feel with other childless couples. No two situations are exactly the same, but they may be able to help you and you may be able to help them. Consider joining or forming a mutual support group.

Use the God-given resource of prayer to the full. Remember, it is given primarily to bring us into the presence of our gracious God and to help us to stay there, walking with him day by day, experiencing his grace and strength for each situation. But it is also right to bring our requests to him, knowing that he has the right to answer 'Yes' or 'No' to our prayer. You may feel a time of special prayer ministry is appropriate, where you ask very specifically for a child. You may choose to follow Paul's example, where he seems to have prayed very specifically on three occasions, and then left the outcome with God (2 Cor. 12:8–9; see **suffering**).

Work at preventing your childlessness from dominating your lives. It is, of course, a major issue; but make sure there are other major interests and concerns in your lives.

Receive God's special grace when others fail to understand. At times you will be hurt by the thoughtless comments of other people, including those close to you, and by the way some Christians apply Old Testament teaching to suggest that your childlessness is a sign that God is displeased with you in some way. Seek God's special grace at these times; hold on to verses such as Psalm 27:10 and John 9:2–3.

Guard your relationship with each other with great care. It is well known that childlessness can put a major strain on a marriage. But equally, a shared burden like this can draw you closer together. Love and support each other through the disappointments and hurt.

Helpful books

H. and S. Anson, *Some Mothers Do 'Ave 'Em, Others Don't* (Eagle)
B. McCarthy, *Fertility and Faith* (IVP)
P. Moore, *Trying for a Baby* (Lion)
B. Spring, *Childless* (Lion)
J. Wyatt, *Matters of Life and Death* (IVP), ch. 3

COMMUNICATION

Human communication is much more than the conveying of facts, like an old-fashioned history lesson or an e-mail message. It is a form of relating to another person, expressing our feelings and our inner selves as well as pieces of information. It covers not just what we say, but who we are, how we communicate, our tone of voice, our emphasis, our body language, and so on.

Communication is a two-way process made up of a number of elements and stages.

1. Mary has a thought or a feeling, or the like.
2. She expresses that thought or feeling. She could do this in words, or with an action, or with a look, or with all three.
3. John hears Mary's words, sees her look, or whatever.
4. John adds at least two things to what he hears or sees: (a) what he already knows about Mary, and (b) his own expectation of what she is trying to communicate.
5. In the light of these, John interprets what he hears and sees.

All sorts of problems can arise. At stage 2, instead of expressing the thought or feeling clearly, Mary may express it badly, or send out a double signal, saying one thing with her words, and another with her tone of voice or body language. At stage 3, John may hear the words, but not really listen to them, or only partially take them on board. He may have rushed impatiently on to stage 4, and be so sure he knows all about her and what she wants to say, she may as well not have spoken. At stage 4 he may add in the wrong information, perhaps so that he hears only what he wants to hear. At stage 5, even if he has listened carefully, and added in no false information, he still may misunderstand her and not get the interpretation right. If Mary's communication to John goes wrong at any of these stages, the whole process has failed.

We all need to learn to communicate better, and in our attempts to help people with things like marriage problems or conflict in a church, better communication can sometimes be the first stage to solving the problem. So here are some suggestions we might find useful.

Ten keys to good communication

1. Learn to listen. Listening is a skill we all need to develop. To listen well:

- Listen with an open mind. Don't assume you know what the person is trying to say. Don't prejudge or jump to conclusions.
- Show by your attention and body language that you respect the person and are genuinely interested in what is being communicated. Make it easy for the other person to communicate.
- Concentrate. Don't be thinking ahead to your response while the other person is speaking.
- Listen to everything that is being communicated: facts, feelings, looks, tone of voice, and so on.
- Take time over listening. If you are unsure you are getting the message right, encourage the person to go through it again.

2. Make what you say clear and straightforward. Avoid ambiguities and vagueness and double meanings. Don't hint at things or use innuendo. Avoid exaggerating and generalizing. Be truthful.

3. Avoid giving a double message by contradicting your words by some other aspect of your communication, such as tone of voice. Don't use sarcasm.

4 Be calm. Too many conversations turn into battles. Don't attack the other person in what you are saying. Avoid feeling threatened and under attack by what he or she says, and rushing to defend yourself. Keep things peaceful, positive, polite and pleasant.

5. Include plenty of encouragement, gratitude, praise and the like. When you have to say negatives, make it easier for the person to take them by surrounding them with positives. As a general rule use 'You' for positive statements ('You've been very helpful'), and 'I' for negatives ('I don't feel much further forward' rather than 'You've been unhelpful').

6. Be loving. Have a genuine concern for the well-being of the other person. Encourage and enrich him or her by your attitude and by who you are, as well as what you say. Have the aim that everyone you talk to goes away blessed.

7. Be tactful and wise. Some things may be true but best left unsaid, or kept for a more suitable occasion. Know when to be silent and when to speak (Eccles. 3:7). Know how much the other person can take. Don't push too far or expect too much.

8. Be fair. Don't manipulate. Don't take advantage of your superior knowledge or better communication skills, or of weak-

nesses in the other person. Never bully or nag or ridicule or 'put down'. All of these things belittle the other person and fail to show respect and love.

9. Where communication is difficult, or it is specially important to get things right, repeat back in your own words to the person what you think she or he has been saying, so you can both be sure you've got it right.

10. Remember, God is a God who communicates; Jesus is the Word. Model your communicating on Jesus. Carry on every conversation as though he was involved in it. Indeed, make sure that he *is* involved in all your communication.

Some Bible teaching on communication

> He who answers before listening –
>   that is his folly and his shame (Prov. 18:13).

Let your 'Yes' be 'Yes' and your 'No', 'No' (Matt. 5:37).

In Christ we speak before God with sincerity, like men sent from God (2 Cor. 2:17).

Do everything without complaining or arguing (Phil. 2:14).

Speaking the truth in love ... each of you must put off falsehood and speak truthfully to his neighbour (Eph. 4:15, 25).

You must rid yourselves of all such things as these: anger, rage, malice, slander and filthy language from your lips. Do not lie to each other, since you have taken off your old self with its practices and have put on the new self, which is being renewed in knowledge in the image of its Creator ...

Let the peace of Christ rule in your hearts, since as members of one body you were called to peace. And be thankful. Let the word of Christ dwell in you richly as you teach and admonish one another ... And whatever you do, whether in word or deed, do it all in the name of the Lord Jesus (Col. 3:8–10, 15–17).

Everyone should be quick to listen, slow to speak (Jas. 1:19).

CONFLICT

Conflict arises because every one of us is a unique individual, with our own set of values, experiences, backgrounds, goals, personality traits, and so on. We never see things exactly as other people do, nor will we want exactly what they want, or make decisions precisely as they do.

Conflict does not have to be destructive or even divisive. Ideally, its outcome will be the enriching of each side with new understanding and the pooling of resources for future action.

Conflict takes many forms and arises in all sorts of relationships. We may, for instance, disagree with a fellow church leader on what to do about the youth group, or we may be unhappy with our boss over the way she runs the section. Different reactions will be called for in different situations. According to the circumstances, some of the suggestions below may be applicable and helpful to those in conflict situations.

Conflicts develop in all sorts of ways. Here is a fairly typical pattern of what can, sadly, happen in a local church:

1. The church, like all churches, contains within it the potential for conflict. Members come from all sorts of social and cultural and theological backgrounds. Some are mature Christians, some immature, some old, some young, and so on. There are lots of potential areas of conflict, but, by the grace of God and in the power of the Holy Spirit, none of them has yet become an issue.

2. Something happens, a 'trigger event' that highlights an issue over which people disagree. Instead of resolving it positively, it's allowed to fester and become divisive.

3. Individuals take up positions. They state their view clearly and strongly. They don't bother to listen to the view of the other side, and may well have a distorted understanding of it.

4. As the conflict continues, each side will use a number of devices to bolster its position:

- Caricaturing the position of the other side.
- Using exaggeration or half-truths.
- Quoting Bible verses. The fact that the verses were not written

with the particular conflict situation in mind is ignored. Anything that can be used to support the position taken is good grist for the mill. After all, the Bible sounds so much more authoritative than my opinion.

- Using 'theological' arguments. It sounds so much better to say, 'It can be shown that hard rock music accompanies devil worship in some parts of the world', than to say, 'I don't like the loud noise.'
- Using 'the thin end of the wedge' argument. 'If we allow the church hall to be used for a christening party we'll soon be having discos there.'
- Insisting on principles. 'I know I'm being awkward, but it's a matter of principle. These pews have been sat on by generations of worshippers; to remove them would be to dishonour their memory.'
- Drawing in allies. Being a voice in the wilderness is a lonely business. Persuading other people to join you, generally by giving a distorted view of the issues, helps boost your position.

As things hot up, even nastier steps may be taken:

- Making personal attacks on the people on the other side. The focus switches from issues to personalities. These attacks can take many forms; one of the nastiest is 'I don't see how anybody who is a true Christian can hold that position.'
- Making manipulative threats. 'The Lord won't bless us' (or 'I'll resign') 'unless we do X.'
- Abusing one's position as a spiritual leader. 'God has told me we must do it this way,' implying that the other side is opposing God.

5. Positions become more and more entrenched. It can even happen that the original trigger issue is forgotten, as a wider and wider range of ammunition is brought in. It gets progressively harder for either side to climb down.

6. A 'death or glory' point is reached. No holds are barred (Jas. 4:2).

7. The only possible resolution is victory for one side, and mass resignation by the other.

Small-scale conflicts between two individuals, such as in a marriage or work situation, will follow a different pattern, though several of the above steps will be included.

Helping those in conflict situations

It may be that you find yourself in a position where you can act as mediator. Be warned that this is no easy task, though it is always worth trying. It will be essential, of course, that both sides accept you and trust you and are willing to let you be involved.

The key to mediation is Jesus, the greatest mediator of all. This is no arbitration situation in which the task of the mediator is to find a compromise solution that does as much face-saving as possible for each side. Rather, the task is to enable the two sides to hear what God is saying in this situation. Though talking together will be important in finding this out, the best thing of all is for both sides, together, to wait on God in prayer.

As mediator, you may choose to listen to each side separately at first. But, sooner or later, bring the two sides together. It will probably be wise to draw up clear guidelines for such a session, to avoid it getting out of hand. For example:

- The mediator has the right to control proceedings.
- Individuals will speak only when invited to do so by the mediator; there are to be no interruptions.
- Whenever one side has stated an aspect of its case, the other side will be asked to re-state it in their own words. Discussions will not go forward until it is clear that each side is truly hearing and understanding the other.
- When a point has been clearly understood (and not before) the mediator will invite a response.
- At the end of the session the mediator will normally summarize what has been said, what progress has been made, and what action has been decided on.
- Every session will open and close in prayer. At relevant places in the session (or if things begin to hot up) the discussion will stop to allow issues to be taken to God in prayer.

In other situations you will not need to be involved as mediator, or it would not be possible for you to do so, since you are particularly involved with one side and the other would not accept you. You can still, however, make a significant contribution to help avoid the conflict escalating and becoming destructive. Here are some suggestions.

What could I say?

Commit yourself to resolving the conflict constructively. Your goal is not to get your own way, or to win, but to enable all those involved to find the best way of going forward at this time, given all the complexities of the situation and of the people involved.

Pray. Pray for yourself and those who agree with you. Pray for the other side. Pray for the wisdom and grace of the Holy Spirit. Pray for the mind of Christ. Pray that both sides will be protected from anything that would grieve the Spirit in this conflict situation.

Study the Bible's teaching on conflict, and its principles for resolving it.

Be determined that dealing with the issues will not be divisive. 'This thing is not going to drive us apart, but bring us closer together.'

Watch out for things like anger, resentment, or feelings of hurt or rejection. If they are in you, take great care not to let them affect your attitudes and relationships. If they appear on the other side, be especially gracious and understanding.

Accept that the insights of the other side mixed with yours will be richer than your insights alone.

Be willing to accept that you may have to give way entirely on the issue. However sure you may be that you are in the right, be willing to climb down. Remember Jesus in Philippians 2:5–8.

Be very careful of refusing to give way because 'a principle is at stake'. Many 'principles' are not worth sticking up for at the cost of a major conflict. After all, people matter more than principles, and love must be the overriding principle at all times (Col. 3:14). Give the 'principle' over to God and let him take care of it.

Be very careful how you use the Bible. In a conflict with fellow-Christians there is a great temptation to use it to bolster your particular position. All through church history people have greatly misused the Scriptures in times of conflict, forcing them to back up their views in a huge range of situations. The fact is, the Bible does not provide clear answers to many of the specific issues we face. If it is a matter of quoting verses here and there, a case can usually be made for either side. Use the Bible rather to provide broad principles on how you should behave in a conflict situation – with love, grace, humility, etc.

Beware of 'spiritualizing' the issues in a way that bolsters your case. 'God will never bless our church while we allow heavy rock music in our services' (or, 'until we make our services more contemporary') may sound very spiritual, but it is actually a bit of cunning manipulation.

Beware of using your 'spirituality' to take up an intransigent position. 'The Holy Spirit has told me in a dream that we must do it this way, and I cannot disobey the Holy Spirit.'

Go out of your way to respect and love the person or people on the other side. Speak well of them. Demonstrate to everyone that though you may disagree with them, you love them with the love of Christ. Never fall into the trap of seeking to bolster your case by attacking them personally (for example, by insinuating that the members of the heavy rock band have loose sexual morals).

Confine the conflict. Don't let it spread. Resist the temptation to bolster your case by drawing in allies.

Listen. You may think you know what the other side is saying, but work very hard at making sure you have got it right. Don't believe rumours. Create a situation in which you can listen to their point of view in a calm, non-confrontational atmosphere. 'I'm not here to argue the case; I just want to hear clearly what it is you are saying.'

Don't take seriously things said in the heat of the moment. When people are worked up they exaggerate their case or say things they are sorry for afterwards. Make allowances. Don't store up such things to use as ammunition later.

Avoid being pushed to extremes, and ignore extreme statements from the other side. Emphasize the points you agree on; build on the elements you have in common.

Check all your assumptions. Everyone makes assumptions.

Accept that the future is more important than the past. Never rake up the past (Love 'keeps no records of wrongs', 1 Cor. 13:4); concentrate on building a good foundation for the future. Work hard at forgiving and forgetting.

Where necessary, call in someone acceptable to both sides to help resolve the conflict. It is vital to trust and follow this person's advice, even if it seems biased towards the other side.

Do everything you can to improve communication. Poor communication often lies at the heart of continuing conflict situations.

Check to see if there are external factors that exacerbate the conflict. These may be things like as tensions and stresses from other sources, or poor living or working conditions. Do what you can to address them.

Where there is a complex range of issues, try selecting one to deal with at a time. Pick one of the less difficult ones. Talk it through; plan specific practical steps. When that one has been sorted out, go on to another.

Be willing to deal with any conflict-related issues in yourself. If you have a particular difficulty in coping with conflict (for example, if you feel fear in a conflict situation and have to withdraw, or you find yourself overcome with anger) you will need to address these issues, possibly with the help of a counsellor. Similarly, if you frequently find yourself in conflict situations, be willing to accept that there may be some source of conflict in you that needs dealing with. You may, for example, be insecure, or have problems relating to certain types of people. Be prepared to get help in dealing with these issues.

Get in early. Remember, conflicts tend to escalate. Deal with them while they are still relatively small.

Some of the Bible's teaching on conflict

If you are offering your gift at the altar and there remember that your brother has something against you, leave your gift there in front of the altar. First go and be reconciled to your brother; then come and offer your gift.

Settle matters quickly with your adversary (Matt. 5:23–25).

If your brother sins against you, go and show him his fault, just between the two of you. If he listens to you, you have won your brother over. But if he will not listen, take one or two others along, so that 'every matter may be established by the testimony of two or three witnesses.' If he refuses to listen to them, tell it to the church; and if he refuses to listen even to the church, treat him as you would a pagan or a tax collector (Matt. 18:15–17).

I appeal to you, brothers, in the name of our Lord Jesus Christ, that all of you agree with one another so that there may be no divisions among you and that you may be perfectly united in mind and thought (1 Cor.1:10. It is worth reading through Paul's response to the divisions at Corinth in the first four chapters of 1 Corinthians).

Submit to one another out of reverence for Christ (Eph. 5:21).

If you have any encouragement from being united with Christ, if any comfort from his love, if any fellowship with the Spirit, if any tenderness and compassion, then make my joy complete by being like-minded, having the same love, being one in spirit and purpose. Do nothing out of selfish ambition or vain conceit, but in humility consider others better than yourselves. Each of you should look not only to your own interests, but also to the interests of others.
    Your attitude should be the same as that of Christ Jesus:

Who, being in very nature God,
    did not consider equality with God something to be grasped,
but made himself nothing,
    taking the very nature of a servant,
    being made in human likeness.
And being found in appearance as a man,
    he humbled himself
    and became obedient to death – even death on a cross!
                                                    (Phil. 2:1–8)

Therefore, as God's chosen people, holy and dearly loved, clothe yourselves with compassion, kindness, humility, gentleness and patience. Bear with each other and forgive whatever grievances you may have against one another. Forgive as the Lord forgave you. And over all these virtues put on love, which binds them all together in perfect unity.

Let the peace of Christ rule in your hearts, since as members of one body you were called to peace (Col. 3:12–15).

What causes fights and quarrels among you? Don't they come from your desires that battle within you? You want something but don't get it. You kill and covet, but you cannot have what you want. You quarrel and fight ...

Submit yourselves, then, to God. Resist the devil, and he will flee from you. Come near to God and he will come near to you. Wash your hands, you sinners, and purify your hearts, you double-minded ... Humble yourselves before the Lord, and he will lift you up.

Brothers, do not slander one another ... who are you to judge your neighbour? (Jas. 4:1–2, 7–8, 11–12).

See also **bullying, communication, forgiveness, prejudice, violence**.

A useful book

J. Huggett, *Conflict: Friend or Foe?* (Kingsway)

DEBT AND FINANCIAL PROBLEMS

Four million people in Britain have problems arising from debt. In many cases these are the result of financial mismanagement, though often the cause is something for which the person cannot be held responsible, such as redundancy, the death of a spouse, or divorce.

The huge growth in debt has been fuelled by the materialistic mindset and persuasive advertisers of our culture, together with the ready availability of credit. But perhaps the most significant factor in many cases is simple greed; people are not content with what they have; they assume they have a right to have what others have and to live as they do, and they seek to exercise that right, without a great deal of thought for the consequences.

The Bible's basic principle is clear: greed and unnecessary debt are to be avoided. Poverty and a simple lifestyle are not a disgrace or to be shunned; they often go hand in hand with true godliness.

Some New Testament teaching on money and debt

Do not store up for yourselves treasures on earth ... Store up for yourselves treasures in heaven ... For where your treasure is, there your heart will be also ...

You cannot serve both God and Money.

Therefore I tell you, do not worry about your life, what you will eat or drink; or about your body, what you will wear ... The pagans run after all these things, and your heavenly Father knows that you need them. But seek first his kingdom and his righteousness, and all these things will be given to you as well (Matt. 6:19, 20, 21, 24, 25, 32–33. See the whole passage, verses 19–34).

The worries of this life, the deceitfulness of wealth and the desire for other things come in and choke the word (Mark 4:19).

Be on your guard against all kinds of greed; a man's life does not consist in the abundance of his possessions (Luke 12:15).

All the believers were one in heart and mind. No-one claimed that any of his possessions was his own, but they shared everything they had ... There were no needy persons among them (Acts 4:32, 34).

Let no debt remain outstanding, except the continuing debt to love one another (Rom. 13:8).

Out of the most severe trial, their overflowing joy and their extreme poverty welled up in rich generosity ... they gave as much as they were able, and even beyond their ability ... They gave themselves first to the Lord and then to us in keeping with God's will (2 Cor. 8:2, 3, 5).

I know what it is to be in need, and I know what it is to have plenty. I have learned the secret of being content in any and every situation, whether well fed or hungry, whether living in plenty or in want. I can do everything through him who gives me strength ...

And my God will meet all your needs according to his glorious riches in Christ Jesus (Phil. 4:12–13, 19).

Godliness with contentment is great gain. For we brought nothing into the world, and we can take nothing out of it. But if we have food and clothing, we will be content with that ... the love of money is a root of all kinds of evil (1 Tim. 6:6–8, 10).

Keep your lives free from the love of money and be content with what you have, because God has said,

> 'Never will I leave you;
>   never will I forsake you,'

So we say with confidence,

'The Lord is my helper; I will not be afraid' (Heb. 13:5–6).

If anyone has material possessions and sees his brother in need but has no pity on him, how can the love of God be in him? (1 John 3:17).

Basic theological principles for Christians

- Our trust is in God and not in possessions of any sort. He must have first place in our set of values; anything else is idolatry. But if we put him first, he can and will supply what we need.

- The money we have is his and not ours; it is lent to us for us to use wisely as good stewards. We are answerable to him for how we use it. See the parable of the talents in Matthew 25:14–30.
- It is the privilege of each Christian community to care for those in its midst who are poor, both by giving and lending – in neither case expecting anything back (Luke 6:34–36).
- Unnecessary debt is to be avoided. Unavoidable debts are to be paid or forgiven (Matt. 6:12).

The incredible complexity of contemporary society and its finances makes the application of these principles and the general New Testament teaching difficult. Even so, we need to keep them at the centre of our thinking, and not allow ourselves to be swept along by the culture around us.

Helping those who are struggling financially

The primary source of help for Christians who are poor or trapped in debt should be their local Christian community. Some churches, many of them serving Christians from oppressed or ethnic minority groups, have been able to develop workable schemes to this end. Wisdom needs to be shown in setting them up and ensuring they are rightly used and protected from abuse, but such schemes can be an impressive practical expression of Christian love.

In talking their situation through with them, careful analysis needs to be done of the causes of their financial problems. These are likely to be complex, but it should be possible to separate out contributory factors such as:

- a basic unwillingness or inability to take responsibility for their finances;
- naïvety and bad management: they were unaware of the mess they were getting themselves into;
- an unavoidable disaster or situation, such as death of the main breadwinner, or a single parent in a poverty trap;
- the insidiousness of 'credit';
- a specific weakness such as gambling or heavy smoking.

Where you feel there is an unwillingness to recognize that there is an avoidable problem such as mismanagement, or an unwillingness to face it and take responsibility for doing something about it, do everything you can to stress the seriousness of the situation and to bring the person to the point of taking action. But if he or she is not willing to do this, you may have to accept that no progress can be made until the person hits rock bottom. In that case it would probably be wisest to withdraw financial help, although making it clear that this is being done for the person's long-term good.

Where the problems have arisen from bad financial management or the pressures of those who offer credit, help the person develop sound principles and procedures, such as prioritizing spending, budgeting, refusing credit, resisting impulse buying, keeping careful records, and so on. It should be possible to find someone in the local church whose experience or expertise will be of value here.

Where a personal weakness such as gambling lies at the root of their financial problems, help them to get to the point where they acknowledge they need help over that problem, and enable them to get appropriate counselling.

Encourage them to seek help from organizations like Credit Action and any local mutual help group.

In some cases practical help will need to be given in areas such as writing letters to creditors, sorting out a workable programme of debt repayment, and so on. Someone with experience in finance and especially in dealing with debt could be called in to help here.

Help them to model their thinking about money and possessions on the New Testament teaching rather than on our 'spend, spend, spend' society. Ideally they should be able to see the application of the New Testament principles in the church at large.

Watch for dangerous results of the financial pressures, such as tension in a marriage, depression, or neglect (especially of children), and call in appropriate help or counsellors.

A Christian resource

Credit Action, 6 Regent Terrace, Cambridge CB2 1AA.
01223 324 034. www.creditaction.com

Helpful books

B. Rosner, *How to Get Really Rich* (IVP)
K. Tondeur, *What Jesus said about Money and Possessions* (Monarch)
K. Tondeur, *Finding the Balance* (CWR)

DECISION-MAKING

Every day we make hundreds of decisions. To get up, what clothes to wear, what to have for breakfast, whether or not to have another cup of coffee – and all that before we've really woken up!

Most decisions are easy, and we spend no time over them. But some we find hard, and we struggle over them. These are usually the ones that we know will have a significant effect on our future, or that of our family, or the like. How do we know what is for the best? How do we find what is the 'right' decision? How do we avoid making a dreadful mistake? Above all, how do we find out what God wants us to do?

People have tried all sorts of ways to make decisions, from tossing coins to reading their stars. Even the Scriptures themselves seem to offer a bewildering variety of ways people decided things in biblical days, ranging from dreams to casting lots, from waiting on God in prayer to following circumstances. Often this only adds to our confusion; at a time when we want a clear decision, the way to make that decision seems anything but clear.

The very fact that the Bible does not give us a straightforward method for making decisions is significant in two ways. In the first place, it tells us there is no one right way of making a decision. There are lots of ways. God can speak to us through an ass (Num. 22:28) or through a word of prophecy. He can show us his will through the Scriptures, or through the inner conviction of the Holy Spirit.

Secondly, it gives us a hint that overemphasis on the issue of how we make decisions is a mistake. That isn't what interests God most. For him the thing that really matters is our relationship to him, not what we are deciding to do. If we can get the first right, the second will fall into place. If we don't get the first right, then we won't get the second right either.

So helping people to make decisions, such as which job to go for, how to invest their money, whether or not to take on a position of Christian leadership, and the like, becomes a much deeper issue than simply weighing up the pros and cons of a specific course of action. Each point of decision becomes a challenge to the person to reassess his or her relationship with God. In a sense, once we have got them to the point where that relationship is all that it should be, we can more or less tell them to forget the decision-making. God has promised that he will open up his way; he guarantees he will not let them down. We could almost say that it no longer matters what they decide; whatever decision they make, God promises that in his wisdom and power he will work it out for good (Rom. 8:28).

Even so, people still find it difficult to make major decisions, and are likely to seek our help. Here is a suggested process we could use or adapt in trying to help them.

Ten steps to making a major decision

1. Accept that there is no fixed pattern of Christian decision-making. God guides in all sorts of ways; in the Bible he uses a pillar of fire, a talking ass, a choir of angels, a storm, a still small voice, the drawing of lots, individuals, a church meeting, and many other things. Accept, further, that very often he gives *us* the privilege of doing the actual decision-making. He superintends the process, but he treats us as mature and wise adults, not as robots. In effect, he tells us: 'You're a child of God; you have the mind of Christ; I've given you my Holy Spirit. Now I'm going to trust you to make the decision; and you, in your turn, must trust me that I'll not let you make a mess of it.'

2. Recognize that, as a Christian, your life does not belong to you. What you want is God's way forward, not yours. Though God undoubtedly takes account of your preferences, your attitude

must be that of Jesus in Gethsemane: 'Not my will, but yours be done' (Luke 22:42).

3. Tell God very clearly that you are willing to do whatever he wants you to do, both with regard to the specific issue and in any other area. Write this down so that you are very clear what you are saying to God and what implications could follow. It is no good saying to God, 'Please guide me over whether I should go for job A or job B, but, whatever you do, don't start talking about me becoming a missionary.' There is only one thing you can truly ask God: 'Lord, I'm puzzling over job A or job B. I'd like you to show me if one of them is right; but if you want to show me something completely different, please do so. I'm ready for anything.'

4. Check your motives. Since we are very good at deceiving ourselves, specifically ask the Holy Spirit to help you see things clearly. 'Why do I want a different job? Am I really motivated by the higher salary or the status?' It may be that God wants you to have more money or increased status, but if these are your major motives you need to admit that to God and ask him to sort you out. The issue for God may well be not whether or not you have more money, but whether or not your relationship with him is strong enough to avoid the spiritual damage the 'love of money' could do to you (1 Tim. 6:10).

5. Get close to God. It's always easier to hear someone speaking if we are near them. Spend a day with him. Fast and pray. Don't spend the day repeating, 'Guide me, guide me, guide me'; you need to say that only once (Matt. 6:7–8), so you'll have lots of time for more important things. Spend the time in worship; in letting the Spirit search and renew your heart; in loving Jesus; in realizing afresh the power and glory of who God is, what Christ has done and what the Bible teaches, and so on. Whether or not God says anything on the specific issue (and there's a fair chance he won't), he'll be thrilled to spend that time with you; for him you are much more important than the decision.

6. Check that there is no area of your life where you are acting contrary to what you know is the will of God. Recall the things he has said to you in the past, the great commands of Jesus, the major principles of Christian living. It's not a question of 'Unless I've got everything perfectly right he won't show me the right way now' –

if we had to get every detail right every time, we'd never get anywhere. Rather, this is giving God the opportunity to point out something to us that is important to him, something he wants us to get right for our sakes, something that in his purposes needs to be in place before he can lead us forward on the next step.

7. Take the opportunity to make a general inventory of your life, who you are, the way you've come and where you are going. You are a unique creation of God; you only have one life to live; you want to enter heaven with the words 'Well done, good and faithful servant' (Matt. 25:21) ringing in your ears. How are you shaping? How do you want to shape? How does this time of decision tie in with it all?

8. Do all the investigation you can on the specific issue. Gather information. Make lists of pros and cons. Read through relevant Bible passages. Consult wise and discerning friends – several of them, not just the ones you know will push you in the direction you secretly want to go. Depending on your theology, collect prophecies (again, beware of putting too much weight on just one) and words of knowledge, write out Bible verses that 'jump out at you', even draw lots. Put the results of all this investigation together. If everything points in the same direction, or nearly so, take very careful note. It doesn't necessarily settle the issue, but it looks like being a strong pointer.

9. When you are getting near to making the decision, put the onus on God to stop you if, despite all the above points, you are getting it wrong and are deciding to do something he really doesn't want you to do. Ask him to intervene in such a way that you will get the message clearly. Then relax. He'll have no problem intervening if he needs to.

10. Decide. Do what you think is right. It's as easy as that. If you get hit by a thunderbolt, think again. But if not, go ahead. If you still have doubts, give them over to God. As a last resort, remember that our God is so clever and so loving that if, even after all these steps, we still make the 'wrong' decision, he can sort it out; it is just one more of those 'all things' that he will work together for good (Rom. 8:28). So stop worrying. Accept his peace. Praise him and love him for his grace and guidance.

Some Bible teaching on decision-making

> I will instruct you and teach you in the way you should go;
>   I will counsel you and watch over you (Ps. 32:8).

> Trust in the LORD with all your heart
>   and lean not on your own understanding;
> in all your ways acknowledge him,
>   and he will make your paths straight (Prov. 3:5–6).

When you pray, do not keep on babbling like pagans, for they think they will be heard because of their many words. Do not be like them, for your Father knows what you need before you ask him. This, then, is how you should pray:

> 'Our Father in heaven,
> hallowed be your name,
> your kingdom come,
> your will be done
>   on earth as it is in heaven.
> Give us today our daily bread.
> Forgive us our debts,
>   as we also have forgiven our debtors.
> And lead us not into temptation,
> but deliver us from the evil one (Matt. 6:7–13).

When he, the Spirit of truth comes, he will guide you into all truth … He will bring glory to me by taking from what is mine and making it known to you (John 16:13–14).

We have an obligation – but it is not to the sinful nature, to live according to it … The Spirit helps us in our weakness. We do not know what we ought to pray for, but the Spirit himself intercedes for us with groans that words cannot express. And he who searches our hearts knows the mind of the Spirit, because the Spirit intercedes for the saints in accordance with God's will.

And we know that in all things God works for the good of those who love him, who have been called according to his purpose ... What, then, shall we say in response to this? If God is for us, who can be against us? He who did not spare his own Son, but gave him up for us all – how will he not also, along with him, graciously give us all things? (Rom. 8:12, 26–28, 31–32. The whole chapter is well worth studying).

> 'Who has known the mind of the Lord
> that he may instruct him?'

But we have the mind of Christ (1 Cor. 2:16).

[We ask] God to fill you with the knowledge of his will through all spiritual wisdom and understanding. And we pray this in order that you may live a life worthy of the Lord and may please him in every way (Col. 1:9–10).

May the God of peace, who through the blood of the eternal covenant brought back from the dead our Lord Jesus, that great Shepherd of the sheep, equip you with everything good for doing his will, and may he work in us what is pleasing to him, through Jesus Christ, to whom be glory for ever and ever. Amen (Heb. 13:20–21).

A helpful book

L. and D. Osborn, *Decisions, Decisions ...* (IVP)

DEPRESSION

Almost everyone gets depressed at some time or other. For some it is just a matter of feeling down for a few days. For others it is an experience of darkness and hopelessness that lasts months or years. Still others develop a lethargic and weary lifestyle without realizing they are depressed. Others experience swings between deepest darkness and periods of unnatural elation and energy.

Just as there are many types of depression, there are many causes or contributory factors. Some of these are wholly physiological, such as exhaustion, or imbalance of body chemistry, or an inadequate supply of oxygen to nerves and brain. Others are linked with external circumstances or experiences. Traumatic events such as bereavement, illness, a road accident, redundancy or divorce can all trigger a bout of depression, sometimes months after the event. Additionally, emotional, psychological or spiritual factors, such as suppressed anger, low self-image, or a broken relationship with God, may lie behind depression.

Depressions vary widely in intensity and duration. In many cases a bout appears to need to run its course. Perhaps we have been overdoing things, or have gone through a traumatic experience, and we have used up our physical and emotional reserves. Our body and our emotions need time to recuperate, to take things slowly and gently for a while. Or perhaps our body chemistry or hormones have got out of order, and need time to get back to normal, something that is often the case after a pregnancy. (Fifty per cent of women experience postnatal depression during the first six weeks after having a baby.) In these cases a person who is suffering depression may have to accept that there is little that can be done to shorten the period of depression. In other cases, and particularly where the depression is severe, both medical and psychological help will be able to lessen its severity and shorten its course. Anyone who experiences a depression that lasts for more than two or three weeks should have a medical check-up and be encouraged to see a trained counsellor. If the depression is severe, especially if the person appears suicidal or if, in the case of postnatal depression, the baby is in any way at risk, professional help must be obtained urgently.

Helping those who are depressed

There are still some Christians who seem to believe that any form of depression is sinful. Sufferers are already struggling with feelings of worthlessness and guilt, and adopting such an attitude is pretty sure to push them deeper into depression. Instead, we must demonstrate that we accept and love them as they are; we no more condemn them for feeling depressed than we would for having a broken leg. Our acceptance and love should both reflect and express the acceptance and love of God, countering the feeling, so often experienced by depressed Christians, that God has forsaken them.

Those who are depressed tend to withdraw. While it may be right to release such people from some of their responsibilities, try to discourage excessive withdrawal. Help them to avoid spending long periods on their own, and try to keep their interest going in things and people outside of them.

Be patient. Depression, like a broken leg, takes time to heal. Signs of improvement are often slight or non-existent, and there are frequent setbacks. Never get frustrated; never give up.

Watch yourself. It is easy for those helping depressed people to become depressed themselves. Give yourself space. Make sure you have ways of switching off. Keep things in perspective. Get others to share the load. Beware of letting a depressed person become too dependent on you.

Prayer is a lifeline when all else seems to have failed. Promise to pray. Those who are depressed often feel unable to pray for themselves. Get a small group together to pray regularly, not just for a cure, but for strength to live one day at a time until the cure comes. Where those suffering depression are willing, pray with them regularly, giving their feelings and fears over to God, and assuring them of his grace. In particular, help them to off-load any feelings of guilt.

Seek to strike a balance between excessive cheerfulness (which will be counterproductive) and allowing yourself to be dragged down to their depressed level. Counter negative thinking and comments graciously but firmly: 'Your illness may make you feel there is no light at the end of the tunnel, but I know that there is.'

Show love and provide help in practical ways, but remember that in many cases it will be more helpful to encourage them to do things with you rather than you doing everything for them.

Try to introduce topics and suggest activities that interest the depressed individuals and help lift their depression for a while. Activities together involving exercise can be particularly helpful.

Keep offering hope and encouraging patience. Cures come, but they take time.

Gently radiate faith, in God, in them, and in their future. Be a rock when everything else around them is giving way.

Demonstrate to them the faithfulness of God.

The greatest need of those suffering depression is a faithful friend who will love and support them as they walk with them through the dark valley. This will count for far more than multitudes of words. Below, however, are some points to bear in mind and to raise at the appropriate time.

What could I say to someone who is depressed?

Depression is an illness. Almost all people who are ill with depression get better. There is no need to feel guilty for being depressed, any more than you would for getting pneumonia.

You need time and space to recover. You need to fight the tendency to think, 'In my case there is no cure.'

If you can, talk about the possible source of your depression. Explore the possibility that it might be a reaction to a traumatic experience or the outcome of stress or exhaustion. Understanding the cause of depression helps dispel some of its mystery and hopelessness.

Seek and accept all the help you can find, from friends, family, minister, doctor and counsellor.

Try not to focus solely on negatives. Find a positive – something you have enjoyed, or the love of a friend, or some small achievement – and try to focus on that.

Some Bible passages relevant to depression

See the experience of Elijah, recorded in 1 Kings 19.

Many of the Psalms express feelings experienced by those suffering depression: for example Psalms 42; 77; 107; 116; 130.

We do not lose heart. Though outwardly we are wasting away, yet inwardly we are being renewed day by day. For our light and momentary troubles are achieving for us an eternal glory that far outweighs them all. So we fix our eyes not on what is seen, but on what is unseen. For what is seen is temporary, but what is unseen is eternal (2 Cor. 4:16–18).

There was given me a thorn in my flesh, a messenger of Satan, to torment me. Three times I pleaded with the Lord to take it away from me. But he said to me, 'My grace is sufficient for you, for my power is made perfect in weakness.' Therefore I will boast all the more gladly about my weaknesses, so that Christ's power may rest on me. That is why, for Christ's sake, I delight in weaknesses, in insults, in hardships, in persecutions, in difficulties. For when I am weak, then I am strong (2 Cor. 12:7–10).

Dear friends, do not be surprised at the painful trial you are suffering, as though something strange were happening to you, But rejoice that you participate in the sufferings of Christ, so that you may be overjoyed when his glory is revealed ...

Humble yourselves, therefore, under God's mighty hand, that he may lift you up in due time. Cast all your anxiety on him because he cares for you ... And the God of all grace, who called you to his eternal glory in Christ, after you have suffered a little while, will himself restore you and make you strong, firm and steadfast. To him be the power for ever and ever. Amen (1 Pet. 4:12–13; 5:6–7, 10–11).

See also **alienation**, **anxiety**, **burnout**, **changing thought patterns**, **low self-image**, **stress**, **suffering**.

Some useful books

S. Atkinson, *Climbing out of Depression* (Lion)
R. Fowke, *Towards the Light* (CWR)
T. Ward, *Taming Your Emotional Tigers* (IVP)

DISABILITY

We live in a society that is constantly promoting health, good looks, and physical and mental achievement. Though not explicitly stated, the message is clear: anyone lacking these things is a failure, not a real person, a reject.

The Christian teaching is totally opposed to this. In God's eyes our worth is in no way dependent on our physical appearance, our mental ability or the condition of our body. Indeed, it is arguable that, perhaps to counter the view of the world, God has a special concern for the poor and the broken and the hurting. Certainly those with disabilities were a special focus of the love and ministry of the incarnate Lord Jesus.

Paul's 'thorn in the flesh' (2 Cor. 12:7–10) may well have been some form of disability, possibly sight impairment. The principles underlying his approach to it may be applicable in a range of situations involving a disability:

1. He recognized that the disability came both from Satan and from God. In an ideal world such things would not exist; they are the result of living in a fallen and broken world. Yet they are not outside of the control of God (see a parallel concept in Job 1:6–12). God is committed to using even the damage that Satan has inflicted upon the world for his glory.

2. He asked God to take away the disability. He had seen God do many miracles of healing, and he knew that God could heal him if he chose. His asking was fervent, pleading with the Lord, and in faith. He prayed on three specific occasions.

3. He accepted God's answer, 'No.'

4. He trusted God for the additional grace that he would need to cope with his disability.

5. He accepted his disability as something that God was allowing for a purpose. In his case he understood the purpose as twofold: to stop him becoming conceited because of the great revelations he had had of God, and to enable him to experience more of God's power.

6. He was able to move from acceptance of his disability to 'boasting' and 'delighting' in it.

Helping in situations that involve people with disabilities

Many able-bodied people still find people with disabilities difficult to cope with. But the church must be a place where such people can feel a real welcome and experience the fullness of the love of Christ in his people. We need to educate and assist the local congregation in this, perhaps in the following ways:

- Help them to put aside the element of embarrassment and self-consciousness they may feel. Encourage them to think wholly of the need of the other person, not of their reaction to something that is unfamiliar or upsetting.
- Enable them to train themselves to look beyond the disability to the person. This is not a paraplegic, it's Andrew.
- Try to avoid all terminology that people with disabilities find unhelpful or upsetting.
- Help them to learn to communicate as normally as possible, or, where communication is especially difficult, to develop suitable skills.
- Enable them to cope with any disturbance the disability may cause in services and church activities. It is in fact remarkable how quickly a congregation can learn to accept, say, the sounds made by someone with severe learning difficulties in a service, and how the welcoming and loving of such a person by the church congregation can enrich worship together.

Inevitably the question 'Why has God allowed this?' will be asked, both by those with disabilities and by those close to them. This may not necessarily be a request for a carefully argued response, though that may be appropriate at times. Sometimes it is more of a protest, or a cry of anger or frustration, and is best answered by admitting that we don't understand, but at the same time demonstrating the reality and strength of God's love through the way we ourselves treat them (see **suffering**).

Give them hope. Hope was a tremendous source of motivation and strength for the early Christians who struggled with all sorts of problems and suffering. Most of us today have such an easy life we no longer need hope. But those who struggle with a disability need, like Paul, to look with hope to the day when they will be released from the limitations and frustrations of their earthly body and given a new and perfect body in heaven (2 Cor. 5:1–9).

Where necessary, help them move towards a biblical understanding of suffering so that they can begin to view their disability in a positive way.

Those who were born able-bodied but become disabled can be expected to go through a process of loss or bereavement, in which they need to grieve for what they have lost. Be understanding of this, and help them to work through the process. If you feel they are not working through the process satisfactorily, encourage them to get counselling help.

Parents of a child born with a disability will need a great deal of love, support and help. Counselling as such should be arranged by the medical staff, but they will still need help from the Christian community in dealing with their feelings of bewilderment, anger and guilt.

If the issue of faith and regeneration arises in connection with those with serious learning difficulties, err on the side of grace in accepting them as fellow-Christians. It is true that their understanding of the gospel and of doctrine may be very limited; but none of us have got it entirely right, and God accepts us. Remember that Jesus used a little child as the pattern for entering the kingdom of heaven (Matt. 18:2–5).

Liaise where possible with medical staff, social workers, therapists and the like. They will generally be delighted to show you ways the church community can support and help.

Accept that many people with disabilities have psychological problems which may make them harder to love or help. Be aware of the possibility of anger, frustration, self-centredness, manipulation, low self-image, oversensitivity, resentment and depression. Be understanding and, where possible, help them to cope with these feelings and attitudes. Where necessary, encourage them to get help from a counsellor.

Be particularly sensitive about the issue of prayer for healing (see **prayer ministry**). Talk with them about Paul's thorn in the flesh. Do what you can to prevent well meaning Christians causing extra pain by thoughtlessly imposing their view of healing on them. But still pray with them and for them, that God's strength will be made perfect in their disability.

Be aware that people with disabilities generally wish to be as independent as possible. But where practical help is needed and welcomed, do what you can to arrange it, preferably involving a team of people rather than just one or two.

Encourage them to be involved in church and other activities as far as is possible, and to develop skills and hobbies. Many people with disabilities have time on their hands. Where possible, encourage them to develop gifts and use opportunities to help others.

Be particularly conscious of the needs of the carers. Support and pray for them. Make it possible for them to have breaks; use the facilities of respite care. Encourage them to get help from specialist bodies or mutual help groups. Watch for any signs of stress or failure to cope, and if necessary get the help of a doctor or counsellor.

Many church buildings are unfriendly to those with disabilities. Do what you can to make sure suitable facilities are provided.

See also **carers**, **illness**, **suffering**.

Support organizations

MENCAP, 123 Golden Lane, London EC1Y 0RX.
020 7454 0454. www.mencap@org.uk
RADAR (Royal Association for Disability and Rehabilitation),
Unit 12, City Forum, 250 City Road, London EC1V 8AF.
020 7250 3222. www.radar.org.uk
There is a wide range of support organizations for people with specific disabilities. Details can be obtained from your doctor or the local Citizens Advice Bureau.

Christian support organizations

Disability Network, Whitefield House, 186 Kennington Park Road, London SE11 4BT. 020 7207 2100. www.eauk.org
PROSPECTS for People with Learning Disabilities, PO Box 351, Reading RG1 7AL. 0118 950 8781. www.prospects.org.uk
The Agape Trust, 118 Hastings Road, Battle TN33 0TQ.
01424 775 042.
There are many local Christian centres, residential homes, and support organizations for people with disabilities throughout the

country. Contact the Disability Network if you are unable to locate these locally.

Useful books

T. Harrison, *Disability: Rights and Wrongs* (Lion)
G. Lay, *Seeking Signs and Missing Wonders* (Monarch)
M. Sinclair and R. Bravo, *Living with Limits* (Lion)

DIVORCE

Divorce in itself is tragic because it is an expression of the breakdown of what should be the most beautiful of all human relationships. Something God intended to be good and pure and creative and enriching ends up in hurt and disaster. But additionally, divorce is tragic because of its repercussions. Literally millions of people in our society bear life-long scars of hurt arising from divorce situations, which express themselves in things like insecurity, depression, violence, low self-image, anger, inability to trust or form lasting relationships, and so on.

Though united in their commitment to marriage as a permanent, God-given relationship, Christians continue to disagree over the details of the application of the Bible's teaching on divorce. Some would stress the unacceptablity of divorce in all but the most extreme circumstances. Others would interpret the teaching of Jesus (Matt. 5:32; 19:9) and Paul (1 Cor. 7:10–16) as reluctantly allowing divorce in just two circumstances, where there has been adultery or where a Christian is married to a non-Christian. Others would feel that these categories might be extended to include things like violence or total breakdown of relationships. But even those who would interpret the biblical teaching very strictly for themselves need to show grace towards others who find themselves in a divorce situation, and be willing to leave the judging of the rightness or otherwise of their actions to God alone.

Helping people avoid a divorce

Whatever our view on divorce, our first task, when becoming aware of a situation in which divorce is being considered, is to do anything and everything we can to save the marriage. The most obvious thing is to persuade the couple to get help. Far too many couples drift towards divorce without seriously seeking help to save their marriage; and by the time they are willing to consider it, it is often too late. A statistic from the United States claims that once divorce proceedings have been started, only one in eight couples are willing to go for counselling; but of those who do, half save the marriage permanently.

Clearly, the chances of saving a marriage will be considerably increased if both partners are willing to make an effort to do so. Where only one of the partners is willing, the chances become very much slimmer.

Counselling at this stage should be done by a skilled and experienced counsellor, though some more general suggestions about helping those who are having problems in their marriage can be found in **marriage issues**.

Helping people who are going through a divorce

For Christians, the pain of a divorce can often be made worse by the attitude of our fellow-Christians, some of whom tend to express their disapproval of divorce as disapproval of those who are going through divorce. But those who are going through divorce desperately need love and support. We must work hard not to let our feelings or our theology prevent us showing them these things, even if, to salve our conscience, we have to say, 'I don't agree with what you are doing, but I'm still going to love you with the love of Jesus while you do it.'

Be aware that divorce is a kind of bereavement and that a person going through it will share some of the experiences that a person going through bereavement will have. These may include shock, numbness, unbelief ('This can't be happening to me'), the expression of a complex range of emotions (especially anger, grief, panic, and depression), and the slow acceptance of and coming to terms with the divorce after what can be a long period of grieving. (See **bereavement**.) We will need to show acceptance, patience and grace, and faithful friendship and love.

The divorce process often involves making difficult decisions. Our role here must not be to make the decisions for the individuals concerned or to pressurize them in any way. Rather, we need to help them work through the issues and come to their own decision, all the time standing by them and supporting them with love and prayer. Remember that the crisis of deciding to start proceedings can often be more painful than the issuing of the actual divorce itself.

All sorts of reactions can occur during a process of divorce and in the time immediately afterwards. Watch for them and help the person through them, encouraging them to get counselling help where appropriate. Reactions can include:

- guilt: 'I could have done more to save the marriage';
- a sense of failure;
- relief, which in itself could lead to guilt;
- hope that the marriage may yet be saved or restored;
- anger at what they are experiencing, or at the tragic breakdown of their marriage.

Special help will be needed over the feelings and issues arising from continuing contact with the partner and with children and other family members.

Keep praying that in all the complexities and pain God will continue to work and in the end bring about his own gracious purposes for good. Encourage those involved to keep praying and seeking God, whatever their feelings may be.

If some people in the church find the concept of divorce difficult to cope with, make a special point of helping them to show grace and love to those involved.

Where children are involved in the divorce, ensure that their needs are being met, especially for security at a very insecure time. Don't forget the needs of other family members, particularly the parents of those being divorced.

Be aware of possible practical issues, such as finance, accommodation, and the need to build a new circle of friends. Encourage others to help in these areas where appropriate.

It may sometimes be appropriate for a person who has gone through a divorce to be involved in a time of prayer ministry, perhaps with the elders of the church, in which all the many issues are finally brought before God for his mercy, grace, forgiveness, healing and so on. Then there could be a time of rededication, of starting this new phase of life with a wholesale recommitment to the Lord.

See also **bereavement, failure, loss, marriage issues, single parents**.

Some useful books

A. Cornes, *Divorce and Remarriage* (Monarch)
M. Kirk, *Divorce* (Lion)
F. Retief, *Divorce: Hope for the Hurting* (Nelson Word)
S. Ridley, *Finding God in Marriage Breakdown* (Lion Pocketguide)

DRUG ABUSE

The abuse of drugs has been practised for centuries. The special feature today is the number of people who do it. Factors behind the huge increase in drug abuse include:

- The ready availability of drugs. Some drugs can be bought over the counter or got on prescription. Others have to be obtained illicitly, but that is rarely a problem. However hard customs and police try to prevent it, drugs are almost always obtainable by those who want them.
- Commercial pressures. The illicit drug scene is big business. People are making fortunes out of spreading the use of drugs.
- The wide variety of drugs available. If one doesn't suit you there are always plenty of others to try.

- The concept of 'recreational drugs', with its message that we have a right to enjoyment however obtained.
- The attitude of society. Whatever the official stance may be, most people tend to adopt an attitude that says, 'If you want to do it and it doesn't affect me, get on with it.'
- The emptiness in many people's lives. Too many people have no purpose in life or principles to guide them. Yet they hunger for spiritual reality and feel drugs may lead them to it.
- The high incidence of loneliness, boredom, hurts, feelings of inadequacy, stress and the like. The very risks inherent in drug-taking can increase its attractiveness to some.
- Peer pressure, especially among young people.

Drugs differ widely in potency, addictiveness and effect. The same drug may have different effects on different people. Because there is no control over illegal drugs, they may be contaminated or too pure; in either case they can kill.

Possession of illegal drugs is an offence punishable by a fine or imprisonment. It is also an offence to have illegal drugs on premises for which you are responsible and to fail to report this to the police. The law does not require you, however, to tell the police if you know or suspect that someone is taking illegal drugs.

Since drugs vary so much, the effects they produce differ considerably. Possible indicators of drug abuse include sudden changes of mood, drowsiness, aggression, decline in performance, apathy, loss of appetite and furtiveness. Serious effects include a range of damage to the body, including liver disease, leukaemia, infertility and heart failure.

There is no strict stereotype for an addict. He or she could be a highly skilled and very successful professional person, or an unemployed youngster living rough on the street. However, as a result of the hold the drug has on their minds, and because a large proportion of those who become addicts do so at least partly as a result of personality problems already existing or latent in them, a high proportion of addicts will show some of the following characteristics:

- instability, emotional immaturity and antisocial behaviour;
- self-centredness and manipulation;

- inability to form real relationships, except within the drug culture;
- lack of concern for others, including their immediate family;
- willingness to go to almost any lengths to support their habit;
- lack of will-power or sense of responsibility.

Helping the drug abuser

Many of the points suggested under **addiction** and **alcohol abuse** will be relevant here.

Clearly, our main task in seeking to help an abuser or addict is to persuade them to seek help from one of the specialist agencies. These normally operate long-term programmes, including getting the person off the drug and helping him or her to develop a drug-free lifestyle.

Getting those on drugs to the point where they are willing to seek help may not be easy. They may be quite satisfied with their lifestyle as it is. In that case, our task, with the help of prayer, will be to work on them to give them motivation for change, pointing out such facts as the damage they are doing or could do to their health; the effect of their habit on their family or close friends; and the incompatibility of their drug dependency with basic Christian principles.

Your role as a faithful and consistent friend can be a very significant one. You may feel your contribution is limited and that progress is slow. But stand by them; they need someone like you who will show them the love of Christ and the faithfulness of God in action.

All sorts of issues may arise during counselling, perhaps pinpointing underlying needs and traumas that have helped to contribute to the drug dependency. Be aware of these, and support the counsellor or team in their efforts to deal with them.

Be prepared for disappointments. But be encouraged by the fact many users who manage to get completely clear of drugs had relapses along the way but still made it.

Use the power of prayer. Mobilize prayer support for the battle that is being fought. Encourage the drug user to bring the whole issue to God, maybe in a time of specific prayer ministry. This may include confession and cleansing, an acknowledgment of the goodness and grace of God and his willingness to bring healing and wholeness, a dedication of body and mind to God, and prayer for the infilling of the Holy Spirit. This kind of ministry should be repeated from time to time, in recognition of a developing process of recovery and healing.

Ensure that there is always someone the person can contact for help if in need or under particular pressure.

Give appropriate support to the family of the drug user. Encourage them to get guidance and help from specialist organizations.

Help those with drug problems to understand the Bible's teaching about our bodies and God's right to them. See the passages quoted under **addiction** and **alcohol abuse**.

If you feel it would be a significant step of support and solidarity with the person, give up your own use of alcohol.

Help them develop new interests and a healthier lifestyle. Give them things to do that will help their self-confidence. Encourage them; help give them hope and purpose.

See also **addiction**, **alcohol abuse**, **solvent abuse**.

A helpful book

O. Batchelor, *Use and Misuse: A Christian Perspective on Drugs* (IVP)

National drugs helpline

0800 776 600

Christian organizations that offer help to drug abusers

ECOD (Evangelical Coalition on Drugs), Whitefield House, 186 Kennington Park Road, London SE11 4BT. 020 7207 2100. www.eauk.org
Hope UK, 25(f) Copperfield Street, London SE1 0EN. 020 7928 0848. www.hopeuk.org

Life for the World Trust, Wakefield Building, Gomm Road,
High Wycombe HP13 7DJ. 01494 462 008.
www.doveuk.com/lfw
The Matthew Project, 24 Pottergate, Norwich NR2 1DX. 01603
764 754. www.gurney.co.uk/watton/social/matthew
Yeldall Christian Centre, Yeldall Manor, Hare Hatch, Reading
RG10 9XR. 0118 940 1093. www.yeldall.org.uk
Details of local help organizations and rehabilitation centres can
be obtained from ECOD.

FAILURE

All Christians fail from time to time. Sometimes the failure is a
blatant falling into sin by a Christian leader, which hits the head-
lines in the press. More often it is something on a smaller scale by
an ordinary believer; but it can still be a humbling and even shattering experience.

Mercifully, Christianity is specifically designed for failures.
Indeed, an awareness of our failure appears to be essential. Paul,
perhaps as much as thirty years into his Christian life, still called
himself the worst of sinners (1 Tim. 1:15). It is the man who is
aware of his failure that gets the approval of Jesus (Luke 18:9–14).
Peter failed disastrously, but even before he had done so Jesus was
talking about his future ministry, perhaps even arising in part
from his failure (Luke 22:31–32).

There are perhaps three possible reactions by Christians who
have failed in some aspect of their Christian lives.

- They may look on it as a one-off lapse, for which they are truly
  repentant. They are determined that by God's grace it will never
  happen again.
- Though they are repentant and would be delighted if it never happened again, they know only too well that this is an area of weakness in their lives where they are likely to fail again and again.

- They have no desire to repent of their action, and continue to repeat it.

Clearly, in the third case our responsibility is to help them to come to a position of repentance. Our approach to those in the second category will depend to some extent on the issue in question, our own theological convictions, and perhaps on how we interpret Paul's words in Romans 7:15–25. My own feeling is that though we are all seeking to reach the point where we can be confident that we will not fail again in a specific area, most of us have not reached that point yet, and God in his grace is aware of this. So, apart from true repentance, he asks not so much for a firm commitment that we will never fail in that area again, but rather for a true dependence upon him as we struggle with our failures. There is a parallel, perhaps, with the father in Mark 9:24, who cried to Jesus, 'I do believe; help me overcome my unbelief!'

What could I say?

God can cope with failure. Failure hurts us, has the potential to harm others, and saddens God. But it doesn't take him by surprise; he knows we all fail, and has given us a gospel of hope and restoration for those who fail.

Be sure you are truly repentant over your failure. Confess all that is sinful to God, and ask for and receive his forgiveness. If there are aspects where you are not too sure whether they are sinful or not, still bring them to God and ask him to cover them with his grace. If you find it helpful, ask someone else or a small group to share with you in this act of confession and receiving forgiveness.

Where necessary, confess your failure to others whom it directly affects. Seek their forgiveness, and make appropriate restitution.

Accept the forgiveness of others. If they refuse to forgive, accept that you have done what is required of you in asking for their forgiveness, and that in God's eyes you are in the clear.

Forgive yourself. This is essential. Repentance means viewing the issue as God views it; God now views it as forgiven and finished. You must not let your sense of shame or a false sense of humility stop you seeing yourself as God sees you. Indeed, failure to forgive ourselves can be a form of pride: 'I know the truth of the situation better than God does.'

Make an opportunity, ideally together with a wise Christian friend or counsellor, to analyse what went wrong, why you failed. Think through and set in motion any steps you can to prevent a recurrence. Commit yourself solemnly to following these, and pray for God's strength and help as you do so.

If the situation is one where you continually fail again and again, consider whether or not you should seek special help. This could be from a counsellor, or though specific prayer ministry. Clearly, there are some areas (for example, failing to love God fully or our neighbour as ourselves) where most Christians fail very often, and we may have to accept we'll never reach perfection this side of heaven. But there are other issues, such as failure to control anger or lust, where specific help could enable you, in God's strength, to conquer your weakness.

Remember God can use every situation, even one of disastrous failure, for his ultimate glory. It is not for us to tell him how to do this, but we can pray that somehow he will bring good out of this failure. Be determined that, at the very least, you will grow in your understanding of God's ways and in your relation to him as a result of this experience.

See also **forgiveness, guilt, low self-image.**

FAITH

At the start of his letter Peter writes:

> For a little while you may have had to suffer grief in all kinds of trials. These have come so that your faith – of greater worth than gold, which perishes even though refined by fire – may be proved genuine and may result in praise, glory and honour when Jesus Christ is revealed. Though you have not

seen him, you love him; and even though you do not see him now, you believe in him and are filled with an inexpressible and glorious joy, for you are receiving the goal of your faith, the salvation of your souls (1 Pet. 1:6–9).

Peter seems to be saying that one of the outcomes of living through difficult situations and facing problems is the confirming and strengthening of our faith, and, in its turn, the experience of the joy of salvation, the outcome of our faith.

Times of testing, of course, do not always strengthen faith; they can sometimes destroy it (see **loss of faith**). Nevertheless, the New Testament teaching is clear: faith is something that grows stronger with use; and one of the best places to grow our faith is in those situations where things seems to count against it, just as the best time to grow our love is when we are confronted with those who hate us (Jas. 1:2–3; Matt. 5:43–48).

So, in seeking to help people, we need to remember that part of God's purpose in the situations in which they find themselves is that their faith may be tested, refined and strengthened. Though it will often be wisest not to mention this particular aspect specifically to them, we need to keep it in mind in all our dealings with them and in our praying for them.

There will be times when an individual's faith will sink very low. Here we need to follow the example of Jesus, whose ministry could be summed up in Isaiah's words 'A bruised reed he will not break, and a smouldering wick he will not snuff out' (Matt. 12:20). Never condemn someone whose faith is being tested; rather, stand with them and help them through the time of testing. There may be times when it is right to say, 'I know your faith is pretty low at the moment, and that you find it hard to trust God or pray. But we are (or I am) going to carry you on the shoulders of our faith; we will trust God to bring you through; we will keep praying. And God will bring you through to the point where your faith is strong again.'

The practice of sharing testimony to what God has been doing can be a very valuable one for strengthening faith. But be wise how you use it; encourage people to be truthful, and to accept that, as with the psalmists, there will be times when our 'testimony' will be pretty negative, as well as times when it will be gloriously positive (see, for example, Pss. 42 and 77).

The articles in this book have generally assumed that the people we are trying to help already have faith in Jesus Christ. But that, of course, will not always be the case, and it may be that, as we talk to some who are not Christians, they will reach the point where we can help them to put their faith in him for the first time.

Helping those who are ready to put their faith in Jesus Christ as their Saviour

As a reading of the New Testament will show, there is no one way of entering the kingdom of God. Just as we are all different in personalities and experience, so the way God works in us will vary greatly. For some it will be a deeply emotional experience; for others a simple decision and commitment. Some may need to study profound theological truths before they are ready to take the step; others will come with a naïve and childlike trust. We need to accept each person as she or he is, and be very sensitive to what God is saying. Nevertheless, there are some steps we probably need to take.

Check that they know what they are doing. Do they have enough understanding of God and what he has done in Jesus, and of the Christian message and its implications, to make an informed response? In a former generation it was fairly safe to assume that most people had at least some idea of Christian truth, but that is not so today. If you are not sure that they do understand enough, encourage them and pray with them that God will come into their lives, but persuade them to do some Bible study with you, or attend an 'Introducing the Christian faith' course, so that they can in due time make a more informed commitment.

Talk with them about the implications. Explain that Jesus called people to a radically new lifestyle when he asked them to follow him. Talk with them about aspects of their life they will have to leave behind in order to follow Jesus. Explain that they don't have to sort everything out and make themselves perfect before they can follow him, but that they must be willing to let him change anything that he doesn't like. Discuss any possible implications for the future, in their relationships or attitudes or lifestyle.

Explain that we can't make ourselves Christians. Only God through the Holy Spirit can do that. We can open our lives to him; but only he can come in and change them and make us children of God.

Encourage them. Though it is right to check that they know what they are doing and help them 'count the cost', we shouldn't do it in such a way as to put them off! Encourage them with the love and goodness of God; speak to them of the grace of Jesus, the miracle of forgiveness and a new life, and the wonder of having God in our lives through the Holy Spirit. Use verses like John 3:16; 1 John 1:9 and Revelation 3:20 to express the love and grace of God.

As appropriate, choose an image that expresses clearly the decisive step of putting their faith in Jesus Christ. It can be in terms of opening the door of our lives and asking Jesus to come in and take control. Or of our moving over and letting him take the driving-seat. Or of crossing over (the cross as 'the bridge to life') from building our lives on the foundation of ourselves and what we do, to the foundation of Jesus Christ and what he has done. Or of leaving our old life (our 'nets', Mark 1:18) to follow him. Check that they are ready to take this step.

Pray with them. Get them to say a prayer, preferably in their own words, or prompted by you, opening their lives to God, turning from their old ways of seeing things and doing things, receiving God's forgiveness and cleansing for all their sin, and inviting Jesus Christ to be their Saviour and Lord. When they have prayed, you, and perhaps others too, should pray for them, confirming their prayer, and perhaps laying on hands and asking for the infilling of the Holy Spirit.

Just what happens at this point is up the Lord, not you. But, whatever happens, continue to encourage them with the promises of Christ (John 3:36; John 6:37–40; Rev. 3:20) and the truths of God's word (Acts 2:21; 38–39; Rom. 10:8–11).

Set in place some structure that will enable the new Christian to start growing straight away. This could be joining a suitable small group meeting regularly to learn and grow together. Or it could be one-to-one mentoring, in which a close relationship is developed with a more experienced Christian who walks with them through their experiences and helps them to learn and grow.

Use the rich resources of booklets, courses and books for new Christians, available from any Christian bookshop.

See also **loss of faith**.

A widely used booklet on becoming a Christian

N. Warren, *Journey into Life* (Kingsway)

Books on knowing and sharing your faith

R. M. Pippert, *Out of the Saltshaker* (IVP)
N. Pollard, *Evangelism Made Slightly Less Difficult* (IVP)
J. Stott, *Basic Christianity* (IVP)

FEAR

Fear is in itself a healthy emotion. Fear of drowning or of being run over makes us careful when swimming or crossing the road; fear of failing an important exam motivates us to work hard in preparing for it, and tunes up our body and brain for action on the day.

We all experience fear in different ways and at different levels. Within reason, this is quite acceptable. A steeplejack has less fear of heights than dear old Mrs Matthews; John is more fearful of crossing the road than Fred because he was knocked down by a bus last year. Complete lack of fear, such as in a child who has no fear of fire, can be dangerous.

Fear becomes bad when it is excessive or unwarranted and produces unwanted or unacceptable results. We become so afraid of crossing the road that we stay at home all the time; or we feel terrified every time we see a bearded man. Such fear may be based on a fixation ('All bearded men are evil'), and be a form of paranoia. Excessive fear may take the form of panic attacks. Alternatively, fear may be experienced in the form of general anxiety.

We should not want to eradicate fear altogether. Rather, our aim should be to ensure that the fear we experience is appropriate to us and our circumstances, and leads to positive rather than destructive results. The level of appropriateness will vary from one person to another. It should be decided by a balanced assessment, and not determined just by our personal feelings (or the experience of the steeplejack).

Helping those who have a problem with fear

Never deride or minimize their fears. Accept that they are real to them, however foolish they may seem to you.

Help them get a balanced understanding of what fear is, how it is sometimes appropriate and helpful, and sometimes otherwise.

Talk with them about their fears. Help them decide how much of their fear is appropriate and how much is inappropriate. Help them to get to the point where they want to get rid of inappropriate fear.

It is not always necessary, but it can be helpful to understand where the inappropriate fear has come from. Was it something that was indoctrinated into them when they were children, such as 'All wasps will sting you'? Did it arise as the result of a bad experience, like being bitten by a dog? If it is easy to identify the source of the fear, help them to see the falsehood of the assumptions that underlie the fears. You could then set to work helping them to replace the false assumption 'All dogs bite' with the true understanding: 'Dogs are delightful creatures and only bite you if you upset them.' Unfortunately, changing a belief that has been ingrained for years, however wrong, often takes time and hard work; in some cases it may be necessary to encourage the person to get professional counselling in this area.

Encourage them to check out their lifestyle, health and relationships. Excessive fear can arise as a result of being run down, under stress and the like. We are less able to cope; things get out of proportion. The key to dealing with the fears may be in sorting these other things out.

Gently remind them of the relevant Bible teaching (see below). The greatest and best antidote to fear is God himself. Try and avoid making them feel even more guilty about their fears. It will probably be most helpful if you don't start with passages that condemn fearfulness. Start, rather, by stressing the nature and grace of God: his power and love; his promise to be with us and keep us through any situation. Enriching their view of God and strengthening their trust in him will help to get the things they are afraid of into proportion.

Where fear is a major or continuing issue it will probably be wisest to encourage the person to get help from a doctor or counsellor over the issue of practical steps to face and overcome it. But when dealing with people for whom fear is not such a big issue, try talking through with them possible steps they may be able to take, and then stand by them and encourage them as they try to take them. Basically, there are two approaches possible here; each can work – a great deal depends on the character of the individual and the nature of the fear. Let the person decide what approach to take; as a general rule, go for the first only if you are pretty sure of success!

- Face it head on. If you are afraid of water, jump in at the deep end – but don't forget to put your lifejacket on first! When you do so, you will find you don't drown – you may even enjoy the experience. As soon as you have left hospital after the motorway smash, get in the car and go for a long drive; that should deal with your fear!
- Alternatively, face it in a much gentler way. Start in the shallow end, or on a quiet country road, and only get deeper or busier as your confidence begins to build up. Your aim is to to learn to develop in small stages an appropriate reaction instead of the fearful one. Here the secret is to set yourself modest targets which are within your capabilities; reaching one will help give you confidence to move on to the next. The learning process may be a slow one; responses and reactions that have been ingrained in your system for many years may take a long time

to get rid of. But keep at it, and let even small steps forward encourage you.

Be patient. Encourage others to be gracious and non-judgmental.

Pray. Help those struggling with fear to pray through the wider issues, not just asking for help when confronted with the frightening situation, or the onset of the panic attack. Encourage them to make a point of praying for a broader understanding of God and his grace and power and goodness (Eph. 1:18–22), and for growing trust in his love and power to protect and keep them, giving them peace and wholeness and the right perspective on whatever it is that makes them afraid.

Some Bible teaching on fear

> I will fear no evil,
>   for you are with me;
> your rod and your staff,
>   they comfort me (Ps. 23:4).

> The LORD is my light and my salvation –
>   whom shall I fear?
> The LORD is the stronghold of my life –
>   of whom shall I be afraid?

> One thing I ask of the LORD,
>   this is what I seek:
> that I may dwell in the house of the LORD
>   all the days of my life,
> to gaze upon the beauty of the LORD
>   and to seek him in his temple.
> For in the day of trouble
>   he will keep me safe in his dwelling.
>   (Ps. 27:1, 4–5. The whole psalm is helpful.)

> In my anguish I cried to the LORD,
>   and he answered by setting me free.

> The LORD is with me: I will not be afraid.
>   What can man do to me?
> The LORD is my strength and my song;
>   he has become my salvation.
>   (Ps. 118:5–6, 14. The whole psalm is helpful.)

> This is what the LORD says –
>   he who created you ...
> 'Fear not, for I have redeemed you;
>   I have summoned you by name; you are mine.
> When you pass through the waters,
>   I will be with you ...
> For I am the LORD, your God,
>   the Holy One of Israel, your Saviour ...
> ... you are precious and honoured in my sight ...
>   I love you ...
> Do not be afraid, for I am with you' (Is. 43:1–5).

Peace I leave with you; my peace I give you. I do not give to you as the world gives. Do not let your hearts be troubled and do not be afraid (John 14:27).

God did not give us a spirit of timidity, but a spirit of power, of love and of self-discipline (2 Tim. 1:7).

See also **anxiety**, **changing thought patterns**, **low self-image**, **phobia**.

Useful books

N. T. Anderson, *Freedom from Fear* (Monarch)
R. Baker, *Understanding Panic Attacks and Overcoming Fear* (Lion)
T. Ward, *Taming Your Emotional Tigers* (IVP)

FORGIVENESS

Forgiveness lies right at the heart of Christianity. 'Forgive us our debts, as we have forgiven our debtors' is at the heart of the Lord's Prayer. The forgiveness of sins and the restoration of our relationship with God are the heart of the gospel.

We all sin frequently and need lots of forgiveness. The Christian community should be characterized by an atmosphere of forgiveness; we are all forgiven sinners, and, in contrast to the unforgiving servant (Matt. 18:21–35), we must be as ready to express forgiveness to others as God has been to express it to us. We need to fight any tendency to stand in judgment over others, or to make those who have fallen into sin feel they are not loved and accepted by the people of God. Even in a situation where some action of church discipline is taken, we should make it absolutely clear that our forgiveness, like God's, is free and unconditional once the person has expressed repentance; it is not earned by complying with the disciplinary action.

The only situation in which full forgiveness cannot be given is when the sin is continuing. But even then, it needs to be made clear that we are eager and ready to give our full and free forgiveness as soon as this is possible.

Many people struggle with guilt. Often we will need to help them (sometimes repeatedly) to a point where they come to God in repentance and receive the fullness of his forgiveness and cleansing. Sometimes it will be appropriate to do this in a prayer-ministry setting; it is often very helpful to have someone present who will clearly declare, on the authority of God's word, that the person's sins have been forgiven.

Some Bible passages on forgiveness

Wash me, and I shall be whiter than snow (Ps. 51:7).

If you forgive men when they sin against you, your heavenly Father will also forgive you. But if you do not forgive men their sins, your Father will not forgive your sins (Matt. 6:14–15).

Your sins are forgiven ... go in peace (Luke 7:48, 50).

Since we have been justified through faith, we have peace with God through our Lord Jesus Christ ... there is now no condemnation for those who are in Christ Jesus (Rom. 5:1; 8:1).

In [Christ] we have redemption through his blood, the forgiveness of sins, in accordance with the riches of God's grace that he lavished on us with all wisdom and understanding (Eph. 1:7–8).

He has rescued us from the dominion of darkness and brought us into the kingdom of the Son he loves, in whom we have redemption, the forgiveness of sins (Col. 1:13–14).

This is the message we have heard from him and declare to you: God is light; in him there is no darkness at all. If we claim to have fellowship with him yet walk in the darkness, we lie and do not live by the truth. But if we walk in the light, as he is in the light, we have fellowship with one another, and the blood of Jesus, his Son, purifies us from all sin.

If we claim to be without sin, we deceive ourselves and the truth is not in us. If we confess our sins, he is faithful and just and will forgive us our sins and purify us from all unrighteousness. If we claim we have not sinned, we make him out to be a liar and his word has no place in our lives (1 John 1:5–10).

Helping those who are seeking forgiveness

Point out that God longs to forgive, and has given us Jesus who died upon the cross specifically so that we may be forgiven. There is no sin that cannot be forgiven, except for that of hardening our hearts against the work of the Holy Spirit in us (Matt. 12:31). God has committed himself to give forgiveness and cleansing to anyone who asks for them.

Help them distinguish, where appropriate, three aspects of forgiveness they need to seek: the forgiveness of those they have wronged, the forgiveness of God, and self-forgiveness. The key one is God's forgiveness. This is the one that truly takes away our guilt and makes us clean, even when the other two do not operate.

Talk with them about the possibility of seeking forgiveness from those they have wronged. Where it is appropriate, encourage them to admit their fault, make suitable reparation, and ask their forgiveness. Even if that forgiveness is not given, assure them that they have done what they need to do at this stage; in God's eyes they are in the clear. They do not have to keep carrying their guilt or asking again and again for forgiveness.

Lead them through the second aspect of forgiveness, seeking and receiving the forgiveness of God. Remind them of the Scriptures. Lead them to the cross. Enable them to express true repentance. Help them to confess their sins to God, preferably out loud. Then, on the authority of the promise of God given in the Bible (1 John 1:9), assure them that their sin has been fully and totally forgiven. Pray for the infilling of the Holy Spirit, and for the peace and joy of God. But warn them not to rely on their feelings: their forgiveness is based on the promise of God, not on their feelings.

In some situations it may be wise to encourage individuals to seek the forgiveness of God with others present. Sometimes it will be appropriate to involve the elders or leaders of the church. At other times, where there has been a complex situation in which there are elements of guilt on all sides (for example, a church conflict situation), it could be very helpful if all those concerned could be present and share in seeking and receiving God's forgiveness.

Some find the third stage, forgiving themselves, the hardest of all. This could be the result of some form of pride, or arise from things like self-pity or low self-esteem. Gently insist on the foundational truth that once God has forgiven them, there is nothing left for which they should condemn themselves. They must not let their sense of shame or a false sense of humility stop them seeing themselves as God sees them. He has pronounced them clean; they must fight the temptation to question his word.

Where people have received forgiveness for a specific sin, but then repeat it and feel as a result that God will not forgive them, use the teaching of Jesus to Peter (Matt. 18:21–22) to show that however many times we return to God for forgiveness, where there is repentance, he will give it.

Helping those who find it hard to forgive others

Jesus clearly taught that refusal to let the Holy Spirit break down a hard, unforgiving attitude towards another person will prevent God forgiving us (Matt. 6:15; 12:31). Where we feel it is appropriate, we should point out the seriousness of this teaching and help people reach a point where they allow the power of the Holy Spirit to enable them to begin to forgive.

The teaching above, however, should not be taken to mean that someone who has been gravely wronged, and continues to have feelings of, say, anger towards the person responsible, cannot be forgiven by God. We need to distinguish between a fixed attitude, 'I will never forgive him; I am determined to nurse my anger and hatred', and the expression of deep emotion which makes forgiveness difficult: 'I know I ought to forgive her, and would love to be able to; but I get these strong feelings that just overwhelm me.' The latter God can work on, and will do so. It is a case parallel to that of the father in Mark 9:24: 'I do forgive; help me overcome my unforgiveness.'

Where individuals still have serious problems over forgiving those who have wronged them, a long time after the event, encourage them to seek help from a minister or Christian counsellor.

See also **failure**, **guilt**.

Helpful books

J. Arnott, *The Importance of Forgiveness* (Sovereign World)
V. Sinton, *How Can I Forgive?* (Lion)

GROWING OLDER

The media tend to stereotype older people as doddery, out of touch, unhappy, ugly, weak and useless. In fact, many older people are active and fulfilled in what for them is one of the richest periods of their lives. Even if there are negative factors such as the loss of a spouse, or physical or mental impairment, such as poor eyesight or forgetfulness, the quality of life does not have to be diminished, even though the pattern of life may have to be changed.

Many people cope with growing older very well indeed, and will not need any specific help in this area, at any rate not until their life becomes restricted by illness or frailty or the like.

Helping older people

The greatest contribution we can make to helping others grow older in a creative and positive way is to accept them and value them for who they are: their age, experience, memories, wisdom and so on. However contrary it may be to our current culture, we need to follow the biblical pattern of showing older people respect, simply because they are older. Even if they have a disability of some sort, we must never do anything that treats them as children or sub-human, such as shouting at those whose hearing is impaired as though they are stupid.

Avoid any patronizing elements, but make a special point of asking their views. Consult them on your gardening problems or whatever. Where appropriate ask for their help. Actively counteract the impression sometimes given that they have no contribution to make.

Try and empathize. How would you feel if you couldn't hear properly, and lived alone, and couldn't get about, and had lost most of your friends through death?

Make special allowances for them on the days when their arthritis is bad, or they are particularly missing their partner. Be patient with their fears of cancer, or of death, or of a break-in.

Maintain their independence. Allow them to be themselves. Encourage them to think and decide for themselves. Even when they are getting very frail, still try and maintain some areas in which they have privacy, independence and the right to choose.

Talk to them about the past, about their concerns for the present and the future. Encourage and help them. If you feel they need specialist advice and help (for example, over depression), encourage them to see a counsellor or a minister.

Encourage others of younger generations to get involved with them.

Additionally, some of the suggestions below may be relevant.

What could I say?

Thank God for who you are. Dismiss the idea that once you were a real person but now you are a has-been. You are more of a real person now than you have ever been, with sixty, seventy or eighty years of experience, and still a lot to do and contribute.

Don't vegetate. Keep your mind and body active. Maintain old hobbies and interests and keep trying new ones. If you are no longer able to get about, get involved in things you can do at home, such as writing letters to prisoners or lonely people.

Watch your mindset. It's easy to slip from 'I'm not the person I was' to self-pity and depression and believing all the falsehoods of the media stereotypes. Be grateful for God's gift of each new day, and that he has made you the person you are now.

Treasure the past. Relive old experiences. Remember friends and family from years gone by. But don't live in the past. Today and tomorrow are for living, not yesterday.

Make new friends. As you lose friends and family members through death, replace them with new and different friendships. Some of these will be of your own generation, but try also building bridges into other generations, including the youth generation; they may take a lot of understanding, but they are worth getting to know. If necessary, 'adopt' a grandchild or great-grandchild.

Use the extra free time you have for God's glory. There are all sorts of possibilities – praying, befriending the lonely, writing letters, helping in the church office, inviting people into your home, growing in your Christian understanding, and so on.

Work out and live the Christian answer to the fears that trouble many older people, such as the fear of suffering and of death.

If you can get out, get involved in clubs, organizations and church groups where you can meet other people, both of your own age and of other age groups. Wherever possible, make a contribution by taking on some responsibility in these groups. If you can't get out, consider the possibility of starting a small group in your home.

Have regular health checks. Be prepared to talk through any issues that may be troubling you with a wise friend or counsellor.

Clear out the junk of the past. You don't want to end your days harbouring old grudges, or carrying old guilt. Let the light of the Holy Spirit search your life. Forgive people who have wronged you, restore broken relationships, receive God's forgiveness and peace and healing.

Useful books

P. R. Clifford, *Expanding Horizons* (Lion)
W. Purcell, *Finding God in Later Life* (Lion Pocketguide)
T. Stafford, *As Our Years Increase* (IVP)

National resources

Age Concern, Astral House, 1268 London Road, London SW16 4ER. 020 8679 8000. www.ace.org.uk
Help the Aged, St James Walk, Clerkenwell Green, London EC1R 0BE. 020 7253 0253. www.helptheaged.org.uk

GUILT

There is a difference between feeling guilty and being guilty. We are guilty when we break a law or a principle or a relationship, but we may not *feel* guilty; many people break the speed limit, or tell lies, or stab someone in the back, and feel no guilt at all. In that case we are genuinely guilty, even though we don't feel it.

Conversely, some people feel guilt when in fact they are not guilty. Perhaps because of a strict, punitive upbringing, they are constantly condemning themselves when there is no reason to do so. This is unwarranted guilt.

In an exam the pass mark is 50%. Any student getting 50% or more will pass. Imagine someone who gets 80% and decides she is a failure because she didn't get 100%. Somehow or other she has a false belief that anything less than 100% is a failure. It is clear she needs to get rid of this false belief and get hold of the truth that the pass mark is 50%, and that, so far from being a failure, she is a brilliant success. Those who suffer from unwarranted guilt have been indoctrinated with a false belief that says they must get everything perfectly right; they must always score 100%. No-one can do that, and God does not expect it of us. We do not have to feel guilty for being human!

Getting rid of indoctrinated false beliefs that give rise to unwarranted guilt can take time. But it can be done; see the 'Ten steps' suggestions in **changing thought patterns**.

People can also suffer from exaggerated guilt, a mixture of warranted and unwarranted guilt. Any traumatic experience tends to leave the people involved with a sense of guilt. They feel that if they had said or done things differently, the disaster might not have happened. In a sense they may be right. The parents of the boy killed in a motor-bike accident could have done more to prevent him getting the bike in the first place. The children in a marriage break-up could conceivably have found some way of keeping their parents together. But very often the feelings of guilt are much stronger than the situation warrants. The parents may bear some responsibility, but there were plenty of other factors which led to their son's death. They do not have to carry the full load of guilt.

There is a close connection between anger and guilt. Bad experiences of any sort tend to make us angry. This in itself is a healthy anger; it is the right reaction to something that is evil; we dislike it and reject it. But most of us find it difficult to express anger at an abstract concept such as evil or loss or death. So we tend to vent our anger on any suitable person who may be around: people we feel are responsible for the bad experience, or God, or even those closest to us (see **anger**). But it may be that no suitable people are available for us to direct our anger at, or that, as conscientious Christians, we feel it would not be right to do so. So we turn our anger on the only person left: ourselves. And this produces feelings of guilt.

Guilt may also be closely linked with other emotions. In the case of the parents of the boy killed in the motor-bike accident, it will be interwoven with their feeling of sadness and grief, such that whenever they feel sad they will feel guilty as well. In this case we need to help them separate the two emotions, to be set free from the feelings of guilt, and to continue to express their love and loss in untainted grieving.

The answer to the problem of guilt is central to Christianity. The Bible teaches clearly that it is right to accept that we are guilty, whether we feel it or not, when we have done something wrong. Such guilt is right and good; it can be a constructive thing in that it leads us to repentance, to put right what we have done wrong, and to receive the grace and forgiveness of God.

Helping those who feel unwarranted guilt

Don't start by saying they shouldn't feel guilty. The fact is they do feel guilty, and we have to start with that and take it seriously. Telling them they shouldn't feel that way may cause them to go on the defensive and think out good reasons why they should; or it could add to their feelings of guilt: they feel guilty about feeling guilty when they shouldn't.

Point out that the ability to feel guilt is a positive and constructive part of human nature. Its role is to bring us to repentance and cleansing and thus to set us free from whatever we are feeling guilty about. Feelings of guilt are there to bring us freedom (see 2 Cor. 7:9–11). Once they've done that, we don't need them any more.

Explain the complexity of human emotions, and how positive and good feelings can get overlaid with guilty ones. For example, when we make a mistake such as dropping a cup of coffee over our mother-in-law's best carpet, we naturally feel annoyed with ourselves and sorry for what's happened. This annoyance and sorrow are healthy and positive, and ideally help deter us from doing the same again. They are worth hanging on to. The guilt that will generally be mixed in with these feelings, however, is not something we want to hang on to. We want to ask our mother-in-law's forgiveness, to receive it, and to be set free from the guilt. If we go on carrying the guilt when she has forgiven us, we are in fact calling into question the sincerity of her forgiveness. So although it is right for us to continue to feel sorry for what we've done, or annoyed with ourselves for being clumsy, it is not right for us to go on feeling guilty.

Help them think through the different emotions they feel. Help them distinguish between sorrow and guilt, between those emotions it is right for them to continue to feel, and guilt, which they need to off-load.

Talk with them about their feelings of guilt. Assure them that God doesn't want them to go on carrying them. Indeed, they may have asked his forgiveness some time ago, in which case he will have granted it. Help them reach the point where they wish to clear all remaining feelings of guilt out of their lives, even though they may continue to feel some of the other emotions.

It may be that by this stage it has become clear to them that the guilty feelings are in fact unwarranted guilt, and thus that no process of seeking forgiveness is called for; it has already been given. In this case you will need to help them accept this and hold on to it if and when guilty feelings try to return.

In many cases, however, it will be helpful at this stage to encourage the individual to bring the feelings of guilt to God, including a 'just-in-case' prayer of repentance and seeking forgiveness for any elements of true guilt that may remain (see below).

Encourage the person to tell you if any feelings of guilt return. When they do, remind him or her of the completeness of God's forgiveness and cleansing. If necessary take the feelings back to God again in prayer. If they continue to come, and remain a significant problem, it is likely that the person has some other deep-seated problem which is giving rise to these feelings of guilt, such as low self-esteem or depression. This problem must be tackled, very probably with the help of a professional counsellor.

Helping those who carry warranted guilt

Confirm that if they have done wrong, it is right and healthy to accept that they are guilty. This acceptance may or may not be accompanied by feelings of guilt. That does not matter; it is the acceptance of the reality of our guilt that matters.

Remind them that forgiveness and cleansing and freeing from guilt are at the heart of the Christian gospel. God has made these things possible, and has guaranteed that he will give them to those who ask for them.

Help them distinguish three aspects of forgiveness they need to seek: the forgiveness of those they have wronged, the forgiveness of God, and self-forgiveness. The key one is God's forgiveness. This is the one that truly takes away our guilt and makes us clean, even when the other two do not operate.

Talk with them about the possibility of seeking forgiveness from those they have wronged. Point out that it is not always possible or even advisable to admit our guilt to them and ask their forgiveness. For example, they may have died, or raising the issue with them would lead to unhelpful complications. But where it is appropriate, encourage them to admit their fault, make suitable reparation and ask their forgiveness. Even if that forgiveness is not given, assure them that they have done what they need to do at this stage. They do not have to keep carrying their guilt or asking again and again for forgiveness.

Lead them through the second aspect of forgiveness, seeking and receiving the forgiveness of God. Remind them of the Scriptures. Lead them to the cross. Enable them to express true repentance. Help them to confess their sins to God, preferably out loud. Then, on the authority of the promise of God given in the Bible (1 John 1:9), assure them that their sin has been fully and totally forgiven. Pray for the infilling of the Holy Spirit, and for the peace and joy of God; but warn them not to rely on their feelings: their forgiveness is based on the promise of God, not on their feelings.

In some circumstances it may be helpful for the individual to seek the forgiveness of God with others present, such as the leaders of the church or others involved in the specific situation that has given rise to the guilt. Repentance and forgiveness may then become a corporate rather than just an individual act.

Where people find difficulty with the third stage – forgiving themselves – gently insist on the foundational truth that once

God has forgiven them, there is nothing left for which they should condemn themselves. God has pronounced them clean; they must fight the temptation to question his word. See the section above on unwarranted guilt.

Some Bible passages on guilt and forgiveness

> Blessed is he
>> whose transgressions are forgiven,
>> whose sins are covered.
> Blessed is the man
>> whose sin the LORD does not count against him
>> and in whose spirit is no deceit.
>
> When I kept silent,
>> my bones wasted away
>> through my groaning all day long.
> For day and night
>> your hand was heavy upon me;
> my strength was sapped
>> as in the heat of summer.
> Then I acknowledged my sin to you
>> and did not cover up my iniquity.
> I said, 'I will confess
>> my transgressions to the LORD' –
> and you forgave
>> the guilt of my sin (Ps. 32:1–5).

Psalm 51.

Your sins are forgiven … go in peace (Luke 7:48, 50).

The story of the lost son (Luke 15:11–32).

Since … we have been justified through faith, we have peace with God through our Lord Jesus Christ … there is now no condemnation for those who are in Christ Jesus (Rom. 5:1, 8:1). This is the message we have heard from him and declare to you:

God is light; in him there is no darkness at all. If we claim to have fellowship with him yet walk in the darkness, we lie and do not live by the truth. But if we walk in the light, as he is in the light, we have fellowship with one another, and the blood of Jesus, his Son, purifies us from all sin.

If we claim to be without sin, we deceive ourselves and the truth is not in us. If we confess our sins, he is faithful and just and will forgive us our sins and purify us from all unrighteousness. If we claim we have not sinned, we make him out to be a liar and his word has no place in our lives (1 John 1:5–10).

Everyone who sins breaks the law; in fact, sin is lawlessness. But you know that he appeared so that he might take away our sins (1 John 3:4–5).

See also **changing thought patterns, failure, forgiveness, low self-image**.

Two useful books

J. Lucas, *Walking Backwards* (Scripture Union)
T. Ward, *Taming Your Emotional Tigers* (IVP)

HOMOSEXUALITY

The New Testament refers to homosexuality just three times. This is rather less than the number of references to pride, anger and telling lies, all of which are in double figures.

Despite the arguments of some, it is hard to read these three passages (Rom. 1:24–28; 1 Cor. 6:9–11; 1 Tim. 1:10) and avoid the conclusion that there is something about homosexuality that is not pleasing to God, and, because of the words used, that this something involves homosexual acts. Additionally, on the principle given by Jesus in Matthew 5:28, most Christians would add to this that the indulgence in homosexual lust is also sinful.

General homosexual feelings do not appear to be condemned in the Bible any more than general heterosexual feelings. Sexuality is expressed in different people in different ways. Despite many theories, no-one really knows why, for some, that expression is primarily directed towards people of their own sex. The cause may be a complex one, and include personality and physiological factors, childhood experiences and elements of personal choice. Though our culture is quick to put labels on individuals' sexual orientation, it seems likely that every person is somewhere on a scale of which one end represents exclusive homosexual orientation, and the other exclusive heterosexual, and it may be that comparatively few people are at either extreme.

Homosexual feelings, then, are probably fairly widespread, and are undoubtedly experienced by many Christians. This can be profoundly worrying, especially for those who believe that the Bible teaches that homosexual feelings are in themselves sinful, or that the very existence of such feelings necessarily brands that person as a homosexual.

It is probably best to reserve the noun 'homosexual' for those who have specifically chosen a lifestyle that expresses their sexuality in homosexual acts. On the principle that we don't label someone who thinks about killing another person a murderer until she or he has actually done the killing, we should not label someone who is not involved in homosexual acts a homosexual.

There is a close parallel between a Christian who has homosexual feelings and an unmarried Christian who has heterosexual feelings. Both have to face their sexuality and the fact that God asks them not to express it in the way our culture would assume is 'natural'. Both need to deal with specific sexual temptations, whether to sexual intercourse or to fantasizing lust. Both need to find ways of channelling their sexual energy that are creative and pure. It is, incidentally, worth remembering that the number of Christians (pre-marrieds, unmarrieds, divorcees, widows and widowers) who are heterosexual and would love to express their sexuality in marriage, but who in obedience to God choose to be sexually abstinent, is far greater than anyone's estimate of the number of homosexually inclined Christians. If God gives the one group the grace to live as sexual beings without breaking his guidelines, it seems strange to believe he will not do the same to the other.

Can homosexuality be 'cured'? Undoubtedly, some who have been involved in homosexual acts have broken free and moved over into a wholly heterosexual orientation. But they appear to be in the minority. Far more break free from homosexual acts, but have to learn to live with their continuing homosexual feelings, channelling them in ways that are glorifying to God, just as an unmarried Christian with heterosexual feelings channels them to God's glory. It may be helpful to look on this as a 'thorn in the flesh' issue (2 Cor. 12:7–10). Three times Paul asked God to take away his thorn; but God's reply was 'No'. But with the refusal came a promise of grace and power, such that Paul was able to say in effect, 'I rejoice in my weakness, because through it Christ's power rests on me.'

Homosexuality still excites a considerable amount of prejudice and fear both in society at large and among Christians. Among other things, this makes it harder for Christians struggling with this issue to ask for help. Our own attitude must be such that people feel instinctively that they can talk with us on this issue without being in any way condemned or rejected.

It is very sad that in our 'liberated' society it is almost impossible for two people of the same sex to have a close and deep relationship without others (including some Christians) assuming they are having sex together. But the Bible, in the stories of David and Jonathan, and of Jesus and John, 'the disciple Jesus loved', makes it quite clear that pure, same-sex friendships are not only possible but beautiful and glorifying to God. We have a responsibility to affirm and support people in such relationships, and to help counter prejudice against them.

Helping those who are concerned about homosexual issues

Some who seek help may be deeply involved in a homosexual lifestyle, including physical sex in casual or committed relationships. In this case our chief contribution will be to encourage them to get help from a specialist counsellor or Christian organization.

There will be others who are not deeply involved, but have participated in isolated or occasional homosexual acts. Some surveys have suggested that the proportion of such people is quite high. Adolescents, for example, go through a homosexual phase as their sexuality develops, and might choose to experiment with homosexual sex. Others might indulge in homosexual sex during a period of loneliness or depression. We may feel it is appropriate to encourage such people to get specialist help; or we may choose ourselves to help them to a point of full repentance and confession and cleansing, and a commitment to pure and holy living, perhaps using the 'Twelve steps to break free from sexual sin' in **sexual issues**.

Sadly, there will be those who are the victims of homosexual abuse, most often as children or adolescents, but sometimes as adults. Many of these will need the help of an experienced counsellor. Our contribution, perhaps through prayer ministry, will be to assure them of God's grace and cleansing from any defilement they might feel.

Others will not have been involved in homosexual acts, but will be struggling with homosexual feelings. Here, again, there is a wide range, from those who have just occasional homosexual feelings, through those who have a mix of heterosexual and homosexual, to those who are dominated by their homosexual feelings. We need to give such people the assurance that their feelings do not make them homosexuals, and that their commitment to remaining pure in the face of these feelings is something God will honour and bless. Where the problem is an acute one, we should recommend a specialist counsellor; in other situations we might feel we could help by our own support and encouragement, possibly using the suggestions in the 'Twelve steps'.

What could I say?

Your sexuality, whatever form it takes, and however strong it may be, is part of God's gift to you. It is part of what makes you the unique and special person he wants you to be. God has watched over you as your body was being formed and as your personality was being developed; he has allowed only those things to shape you and develop in you which he knows can be ultimately for his glory.

Having homosexual feelings is no more sinful than having hetero-sexual feelings. Sin only enters in when we allow these feelings to lead us to lust or illicit sexual activity.

Just as your sexuality is God's gift to you, you, as a Christian, must choose to give it back to God. You may ask him to change it, as Paul asked God to take away the thorn in his flesh (2 Cor. 12:7–10); but once you have given it to him, it is up to him to decide what to do with it. He may change you, or he may give you grace to live as you are, to his great glory.

You are not alone. All Christians are sexual beings; most Christians have to fight battles over sexual purity. The battle you will have to fight may be different in details from theirs, but it is the same basic battle that all unmarried (and even some married) Christians are fighting: to be the wholesome sexual beings God has made us without using our sexuality to commit sin.

Where appropriate, to help you in this battle, try using the suggestions in 'Twelve steps to break free from sexual sin' (see **sexual issues**).

With God's help, love with a pure love. Remember David and Jonathan, and Jesus and John, 'the disciple Jesus loved'. Develop deep friendships and relationships (both same-sex and other-sex) that are completely wholesome and pure and glorifying to God.

Get all the help you can. Don't struggle with this issue all on your own. Get help from close Christian friends, your minister, or from a counsellor. If appropriate, have someone to whom you can be accountable.

See also **changing thought patterns, lust, sexual issues**.

Helpful books

J. Howard, *Out of Egypt* (Monarch)
L. Payne, *The Broken Image* (Kingsway)

A Christian study video and book

A Question of Love (CWR)

Specialist Christian agencies

Courage, PO Box 338, Watford WD1 5HZ. 020 8420 1066.
www.courage.org.uk
True Freedom Trust, PO Box 3, Upton, Wirral CH49 6NY. 0151
653 0773. www.tftrust.u-net.com

ILLNESS

Illness, particularly if it involves a stay in hospital, tends to dehumanize us. We cease to be in charge of our own lives, and submit
to doctors and others who make us do things we would never
choose to do. We stop doing the things that normally make us feel
significant. We cease being a person, and become a patient or a
case. Our family and friends suddenly start treating us differently,
and talking about us behind our back. All this is disturbing and
threatening, quite apart from the pain and anxiety we may feel.

Caring for those who are ill

Counter the dehumanizing effect of illness. Relate to them in as
normal a way as possible. Never treat them as a case; talk with
them rather than about them. Reassert their significance and value.
Let the time of illness be a time when they discover how much they
are loved, and how much they mean to so many people.

Help give them motivation to fight the illness. Stand by them
and fight it with them. Give them encouragement and hope.
Wherever possible, enable them to channel their full energies into
fighting the illness by relieving them of any other responsibilities
or anxieties that may sap their limited energies.

Where possible, help them to accept the positive aspects of their illness. Counter any negative aspects, such as feeling guilt for being ill, or frustration at their weakness. Help them to accept that all people have to go through illness, and it can be a positive experience: a chance to be specially cared for and loved, for example, or a break from routine and a chance to see things in a different perspective.

Remember that small things can mean a lot – both negatively and positively. Because they are under physical and emotional strain, small things can upset them. Equally, a small act of kindness, or a child's drawing, can mean a great deal.

Allow them to express their feelings. When we are ill we go through a range of emotions; physical weakness may well mean we are less able than usual to cope with them. Be ready for anything; allow them to off-load their feelings, emotions, fears, anger, frustration, anxieties and so on, even if they project them on to you. Be understanding; make it easy for them; help them through it; accept it all with love.

Pray for them and with them. Let them know that others are praying. When praying for their healing, remember that the decision on how to answer our prayers is made by God alone. Nevertheless, let your prayers encourage them to a peaceful trust in God that he will use this time of illness as part of the working out of his gracious and good purposes.

What could I say to those going through illness?

Allow others to help you. Don't be ashamed of your weakness, or insist that you can cope. Others want to show love and kindness to you; don't stop them doing it.

Co-operate with your doctor. He or she is the expert.

Keep a good relationship with those who care for you. Be quick to say, 'Thank you.' Pain will sometimes make you feel irritable; your fear or anger or frustration at the illness may sometimes be expressed as anger at those who are caring for you. Try and avoid this, but if it does happen be quick to say you are sorry.

Concentrate your energies on fighting the illness. Lay aside other worries and responsibilities until you are better and can cope with them adequately.

Be open to the positive aspects of your illness. Our culture tends to think of health as an automatic right, and illness as in every way undesirable, negative and to be resented. But there are things to be learnt and even enjoyed in a time of illness. Nothing happens by accident to a Christian; God can and will use your illness for good (see **suffering**).

If you have to go through an extended period of illness or convalescence, consider using the opportunity to do something creative. Try a new hobby, sort out and classify your photographs, spend time in intercessory prayer. Most of all, use the opportunity to get closer to God; study a part of the Bible, read a good Christian book, spend time seeking God in prayer.

What could I say to family and close friends caring for those who are ill?

Most of the points above under 'Caring for those who are ill' are relevant. Additionally:

Yours is a great ministry. You are able to show love and encouragement and significantly influence the healing of the illness. See it as an opportunity to exercise the caring and healing ministry of Jesus. Ask specifically for his presence in you in all that you do.

Accept that the irritability and frustration felt as the result of physical weakness and emotional stress may at times be off-loaded on to you. This can be very upsetting, but do your best not to let it cause you hurt or to spoil your relationship with the person who is ill. It's not that they are really attacking you or complaining about you; rather, they need to off-load their feelings somewhere, and they feel safest doing this on those who are closest to them. If you can, take it as a compliment and an opportunity to show love: they trust you (probably unconsciously) to be able to take their hurt and still come back with grace and love.

Be aware of your own needs and emotions. It is important to care for yourself as well as for the person who is ill. This may involve giving yourself space, where possible sharing the load with others, and making the opportunity to talk through your feelings of fear, anger, hurt, loneliness and the like with someone you can trust.

See also **anger**, **carers**, **disability**, **fear**, **mental illness**, **suffering**, **terminal illness**.

Useful books

M. Bachelor, *A Way with Pain* (Lion)
F. Gamble, *Today's Grace* (CWR)
J. Woodward, *Finding God in Illness* (Lion Pocketguide)

INSOMNIA

Different people need different amounts of sleep. Some can live happily with just five hours a night. But those who need eight hours have a major problem if they go for a time with only five.

Sleeplessness is such that the sufferer may overestimate the seriousness of the problem. Those who have tossed and turned for two or three hours during the night may well feel they haven't had a wink of sleep, while in fact they have had six hours or more. Alternatively, though they have heard the church clock strike every quarter, they may have been dozing in a light sleep in between. The test of the seriousness of insomnia is whether or not it has an adverse effect on the person's waking life, leading to weariness, irritability, malfunction and so on.

Insomnia can have many sources. There may be external physical causes, such as a noisy church clock or a partner's snoring. There be medical factors, such as pain or some physiological condition. Or the source may be an emotional or spiritual one, such as worry or guilt. Or it may be a combination of factors.

Insomnia takes many forms. Some people take ages to get to sleep in the first place. Others sleep well for the first couple of hours but then wake up and toss and turn through the small hours. Others wake early and can't get back to sleep. Still others never get into a real sleep, managing at best a light doze all night.

Possible ways of helping those who suffer from insomnia

Insomnia is a worrying problem; worry about not sleeping can itself cause or aggravate insomnia. In the middle of the night, when bodily and mental functions are at a low ebb, the size of the problem may seem quite overwhelming. We therefore need to accept that this is a major problem for those affected, and to treat it with all the understanding and empathy it deserves. But, at the same time, we need to help them see that the problem is not insoluble, and help them work towards a solution.

In some cases we may need to help them see that their sleep-lessness is not necessarily impairing their lives. Human beings have a marvellous way of adjusting to changed circumstances; it may be they are able to adapt to getting less sleep. In that case, they can accept their sleeplessness, and use it creatively, spending, say, those sleepless small hours reading or praying.

People suffering from insomnia may struggle particularly with the issue of *why* they can't sleep. What makes them wake up at two every morning with their mind racing? Whether or not there is a ready solution, we can help them explore the possible source of their insomnia. Do they drink a lot of coffee? Is their bedroom stuffy or noisy? Is their bed too hard or too soft? Do they go to bed with their mind still fired up with all the day's pressures and wor-ries? In many cases, we might urge them to visit a doctor to see if there is a medical source to their problem. Helping them to analyse the cause of their sleeplessness helps to take away some of its terror, and may help them begin to see what they could do about it.

It is generally better to encourage people to find their own solu-tion to their problem, once we've helped them work out its source. But that doesn't stop us making suggestions. Would a lighter evening meal help? How about reading a relaxing book for the half-hour before going to bed? Instead of going over the day's events as you toss and turn, try praying (nothing like a lengthy prayer to send you to sleep!) or telling yourself a story, or recalling and living out the story you've read as your bedtime book? How about decaffeinated coffee? Or more exercise, early in the day? Or ear plugs? Or a clear and definite off-loading in prayer of all the things that are on your mind as you go to bed, giving all the problems over to God and asking him to carry them for the next eight hours, and then positively refusing to take them back before the alarm goes?

Where we suspect the source of the insomnia is something we don't feel able to tackle, such as a physiological condition or depression (sleeplessness in the small hours can be a classic symptom of depression) or serious stress, we should encourage the person to see a doctor or counsellor. We may have our own view on the advisability or otherwise of using drugs to cure the problem, but, again, individuals will have to make their own decision in this area.

Where there are specifically spiritual factors at work, such as guilt or anxiety, we may wish to refer the person to a minister or pastoral counsellor, or we may feel able to talk and pray through the issue with them, possibly including specific prayer ministry.

Some Bible passages that may be relevant

His delight is in the law of the LORD,
and on his law he meditates day and night (Ps. 1:2).

Answer me when I call to you,
O my righteous God.
Give me relief from my distress ...
Know that the LORD has set apart the godly for himself;
the LORD will hear when I call to him.

In your anger do not sin;
when you are on your beds,
search your hearts and be silent ...
I will lie down and sleep in peace,
for you alone, O LORD,
make me dwell in safety (Ps. 4:1, 3, 4, 8).

I will praise the LORD, who counsels me;
even at night my heart instructs me (Ps. 16:7).

On my bed I remember you;
   I think of you through the watches of the night.
Because you are my help,
   I sing in the shadow of your wings (Ps. 63:6–7).

Come to me, all you who are weary and burdened, and I will give you rest (Matt. 11:28).

Night and day I constantly remember you in my prayers (2 Tim. 1:3).

Cast all your anxiety upon him because he cares for you (1 Pet. 5:7).

LONELINESS

Loneliness may be short-term or long-term. Short-term loneliness arises from our immediate circumstances, for example when we lose someone particularly close to us, or we are cut off from our normal circle of friends and family through moving to a new area. Long-term or chronic loneliness is a more or less permanent condition and is not necessarily linked to circumstances. It has its roots in the personality or past experiences of the individual. Such a person finds it difficult to build meaningful relationships with others wherever they are.

Three major features of our current society are causing an increase in loneliness. The first is the decline in the significance of the family. In past generations, families tended to stay together more than today, and provided a strong source of belonging and caring.

The second is technological: the speed of life, high mobility, faceless city crowds, living with machines. Where people used to spend their time relaxing with others, they now withdraw into the unreal world of the TV or the internet.

A third factor is the large number of people who have been hurt in the past through the breakdown of a key relationship, such as a child whose parents go through a divorce.

People struggling with short-term loneliness need befriending and encouraging to make the effort to find new friends. But those who suffer from long-term loneliness will not be greatly helped by being urged to develop a busy social life. They can be lonely in a crowd. Their basic need is to deal with the factor that underlies their loneliness, that makes it difficult for them to make friends and build meaningful relationships. To do this they may well need the help of a counsellor. However, here are some suggestions that may be helpful if they try to tackle the problem without outside help.

Twelve steps to conquering loneliness

1. Accept that the basic source of your loneliness is not in others but in you.

2. Accept that loneliness as you are now experiencing it is not God's will for your life. He wants you to have rich and meaningful relationships with a whole range of people. Accept that it is possible for you, with God's help, to deal with the source of your loneliness. You do not have to stay as you are. Rightly faced and dealt with, even your loneliness can become a stepping-stone to a richer life.

3. Make a clear and definite choice that with God's help you will fight loneliness and win, even if you get hurt on the way. Specifically reject ideas such as, 'I will hang on to loneliness because it is safe', 'Things will never change', or 'It isn't worth the effort.'

4. Start keeping a daily journal. Observe and record your thoughts and behaviour over a period of time. Think through and analyse the factors in you (not in others) which prevent you having friends. For example, are you shy, or tongue-tied? Are you afraid of people? Do you find it difficult to trust people? Do you simply dislike them? Are you fearful they might get to know the real you? Do you feel you have nothing to contribute to a relationship? Are you afraid that any friendship will not last?

5. When you have made a list of these factors, try and discover

the underlying causes which give rise to them. There are all sorts of possible causes. Here are a few examples:

- You were constantly told when a child that no-one would want you as a friend. You believed it and it has become a self-fulfilling prophecy.
- Someone you loved and trusted, for example a parent, let you down very badly, hurting you so much that you can't trust anyone any more.
- You don't like yourself, and are unwilling to let others get to know the real you.
- You feel inferior to all the people you meet.

6. When you have decided the underlying cause or causes, imagine that someone comes to you for help with that particular problem. Use all your ingenuity to think of good advice and positive encouragement. Look up relevant Bible teaching. Think through what Jesus would say about it. Give the person hope and lots of good ideas. Write all these things down.

7. Use the suggestions you have written to work out a self-help programme for yourself. Pray over all the details. Write in your journal the basic principles you will follow, specific falsehoods you will need to reject, and truths you are determined to get hold of (see the 'Ten steps' under **changing thought patterns**). Work out specific actions you will take.

8. Take the whole programme to God. Ask for his strength and wisdom as you prepare to follow it. Accept that without his help you will fail, but that it is his will that you should not do so. Throw yourself on his grace, and expect him to act.

9. Implement your programme. Give yourself time. You may not make a lot of progress at first, and you may often fail. Keep a daily record, highlighting progress, and using failures to learn how to do it better next time.

10. Run some risks (small ones to start with!). Pray that God will lead you to one or two people who need your help; locate such people and get stuck into helping them for their sake, not yours.

11. Fight self-pity, apathy, defeatism, false indoctrinated beliefs and self-centredness.

12. Make sure you continue to operate at the two levels of changing inner beliefs and ideas, and of practical outward action. Don't give up on either front. Above all, keep looking to God to enable you to defeat loneliness in your life, and to become the means through which his love is able to flow into the lives of others.

A helpful book

G. Baker, *Friends* (IVP)

LOSS

Loss comes to us in many forms. For many of us its most threatening form is death, either the loss of our own life, or that of someone we love dearly. But other losses can hit us very hard, for example:

- The loss of youth or of health, or of freedom to do what we once used to be able to do.
- The loss of a limb.
- The loss of a home, through a fire or moving house, or the loss of a treasured possession.
- The loss of a job, either through redundancy or retirement, with the accompanying loss of status and purpose.
- The loss of a circle of friends.
- The loss of a pet.
- Divorce.

All loss is in a sense a bereavement, and will generally be accompanied by a grieving period parallel to that experienced in bereavement. It is generally not helpful to minimize the sense of loss, or to expect it to go away very quickly. It will be more helpful to encourage those who suffer loss to grieve, to talk about their loss, and to be open about their feelings and their need to off-load them.

If we should feel that a person's reaction to their loss is excessive, or the grieving process is continuing for an unreasonable length of time, we should encourage her or him to talk things through with a counsellor.

See **abortion**, **bereavement**, **divorce**, **illness**, **miscarriage**, **trauma**, **unemployment**.

LOSS OF FAITH

Though we tend to speak of loss of faith as a very specific point at which a person ceases to be a professing Christian, it is probably more helpful to think in terms of a scale that contains a wide range of points, such as strong opposition to Christianity, agnosticism, uncertainty, dormant faith, weak faith, assured faith and very strong faith. All of us move about on this scale, passing, say, from a period of strong faith to a period of uncertainty and questioning, and then back to a more secure position.

Whether those who 'lose their faith' cease to be Christians, in the sense of losing their salvation, has been a matter of debate among theologians. My own conviction is that once a person is a born again child of God, redeemed, forgiven, and possessing eternal life, it is not possible to be unborn or to cease to be God's child, or for eternal life to be cut short. That, of course, does not exclude the possibility that a person who appears to be born again in fact never was; so, whatever 'loss of faith' may be, for that person it is not loss of what the theologians would call 'saving faith'.

It is sometimes tempting to look on loss of faith as a matter of the intellect. Up to a specific point, we might feel, we have a certain set of beliefs which we accept; after that point we reject those beliefs and adopt a new set.

This is very much an oversimplification. Christianity is (or should be) much more than the acceptance of a set of beliefs. Far more than our intellect is involved. We could list at least six aspects of us, besides our intellect, that are involved in being a Christian: our emotions, our will, our principles or standards of behaviour, our relationships, our body, and whatever we may mean by our soul or spirit. If all of these are involved in being a Christian, then, presumably, when people say they have ceased to be Christians, something has happened in all or most of these areas.

Thus, in trying to understand why a person has stopped being a Christian, we don't have to assume it is primarily because they have stopped believing the basic Christian doctrines. Indeed, surveys of those who have 'lost their faith' indicate that most people actually give up the intellectual beliefs after they have decided, for other reasons, that they no longer wish to live Christian lives. Or, perhaps more accurately, the giving up of intellectual beliefs happens more or less concurrently with those other reasons, but arises from them, rather than their arising from it.

These 'other reasons' vary greatly, although there frequently seems to be an element of feeling let down, either by God, or by other Christians. They would include:

- The failure to obtain something we want and have prayed earnestly for. For example, some friends of mine 'lost their faith' as a result of disappointments in trying to move house.
- The feeling that Christianity is restrictive; for example, someone who became a Christian in childhood 'rebels' in adolescence.
- The feeling that God has become distant and unreal.
- Anger or resentment at the behaviour of another Christian.
- Specific rejection of a Christian moral principle. For example, a man decides to adopt a practising homosexual lifestyle.

Clear statistics are hard to come by, but it does appear that a substantial number of people 'lose their faith' basically because they are angry at God for allowing something to happen they feel should not have happened. 'If God's like that, I don't want to believe in him any more.' Such anger at God is often a projection of the anger they feel at what has happened. It is not easy to express anger at events or disappointments, so it is vented instead on God.

It is essential to do everything we can to maintain the strength of our relationship with those who 'lose their faith'. This will probably not be easy, since they will almost certainly stop coming to church and Christian activities, and may deliberately choose to try and cut themselves off from all their Christian friends. For our part, it is very possible that we will feel let down or hurt or even rejected, and will be tempted to let them go their own way.

The fact is, of course, that they need our love and help at this time, maybe more than at any other. So we need to swallow our hurt and do all that we can to show that we care for them as persons, not just as Christians or church attenders. Many people who give up living Christian lives sooner or later reach a point where their original hurt or anger or whatever has subsided and, given the opportunity, they would be willing to try again. Sadly, in many cases, they don't do anything about it, sometimes because it would mean loss of face, or because the effort to change back again would be too great. Such a big step will be made easier if we have maintained contact and friendship with them.

Helping those who 'lose their faith'

Keep in touch. Show concern and love just as much as you did when they were practising Christians. Let them see that you love them as people, not simply as professing Christians. Even if they reject your friendship, make it clear that your door is always open, and still do what you can to keep in touch, like sending cards.

Unless it is contrary to your theology, let them know that you believe that though they let go of God, God will not let go of them (2 Tim. 2:13), and that sooner or later they will hear his call to them again.

Be patient. It will take time, maybe years, for them to work through the issues that made them 'lose their faith'.

Where they raise issues of doctrine or intellectual problems, be ready to give them the best answer you can, or to refer them to those who are wiser than you, or to lend them suitable books. But do it all gently; don't get into high-powered arguments. Respect their position and allow them to state their views. Avoid the danger of pushing them to a more extreme position in the fires of controversy. It is often sufficient for them to see you graciously holding on to the faith, and maintaining your confidence in them that sooner or later they will come to the end of this spell of unbelief.

Where there are issues other than intellectual ones, be willing to talk them through if a suitable opportunity is given, but, again, ensure that this is done in a non-aggressive way. In particular, if there are moral issues involved, avoid the temptation to judge them by Christian standards. If necessary, state your view, though they will almost certainly know it already; and reiterate your love and concern for them, whatever they do.

Pray. Get others to pray. A spiritual battle is being fought over these people.

Remember the story of the lost son (Luke 15:11–32). Be prepared to model yourself on the waiting father.

Helping to prevent loss of faith

The most obvious safeguard against loss of faith is the development of a mature and strong Christian character that can withstand the pressures, intellectual or otherwise, that all Christians sooner or later have to face. But in addition to this, and in the shorter term, the following suggestions may be found helpful.

Counter the destructive effects of subjectivism. The last few decades have seen a huge swing from objectivism ('Truth and reality are outside of me; I don't create them; they are already there, and I have to submit to them') to subjectivism ('Truth and reality are in me, things I create. If I choose to believe something, then it is true or real for me. If I stop believing it, it ceases to be true or real'). As is so often the case, in reacting against the problems inherent in extreme objectivity, our culture has swung to the other extreme, unqualified subjectivism. The sensible position is, as you would expect, between the two extremes, holding the good points of both objectivism and subjectivism. My subjective experience is indeed very important and very real to me. But it doesn't exist in a vacuum. Certain things, like the world around me or other people, are still objectively given; I don't create them; they exist independently of me. Though my experience of them is *my* experience, with all sorts of subjective overtones, they are still real and true, quite independently of what I may believe or experience.

So with Christianity. My personal experiences of God, like my experiences of my wife, are *my* experiences, and contain subjective elements. But they are also experiences of God (or of my wife), who exists objectively, independently of any of my experiences or beliefs. If I were to choose to stop believing in my wife or God, I would change considerably subjectively, but it would make no difference at all to the objective reality and truth of their existence.

Recent decades have seen a healthy rise of interest in the personal and subjective elements of our Christian faith and experience. But these must not be allowed to push out the essential objective elements. Whatever I may experience or feel or choose to believe, the existence of God, the historical fact of the life of Jesus, the given facts of his teaching and so on, remain objective and unchanging, independent of me.

Encourage people to become multi-dimensional Christians. We are, after all multi-dimensional people, with intellects, wills, feelings, spirits, bodies and so on. So we need to resist the suggestion that Christianity is a spiritual issue, but has nothing to do with the intellect, or that it is a matter of the emotions, but not of the will, or, indeed, that it is all about experiences and feelings, but has nothing to do with facts. Help people see that Christianity has everything to do with every part of us, and help them to open up every part of their life to God and the power of the Holy Spirit.

Prepare people to cope with things like mood swings, depression, times of special satanic attack (see Luke 4:1–13, where the devil tempts Jesus to doubt, and Luke 22:31–32 where he seeks to destroy Peter's faith) and spiritually dry periods. Explain that all Christians have to cope with these things; they are not a sign that God has left them or ceased to exist. On the contrary, as in the two cases mentioned, they may well be part of a process of preparation for effective and fruitful ministry.

Encourage them to be honest about their intellectual difficulties. Where you are not able to give an adequate answer, direct them to others or to books that can. Remind them that there is no issue they can raise that hasn't already been thought of by many other Christians, and answered to their satisfaction.

Give wise and balanced teaching about prayer. Stress that prayer is not a way of forcing God to do what we want. However vehemently we pray, or with however much faith, God still makes the final choice – and he always chooses what is ultimately for the best. We are not able to see that at the time, but it is essential for us to leave that final decision to him, as Jesus did in the Garden of Gethsemane (Luke 22:42), and to be willing to accept it, even if we do not want it and cannot understand it. It may be helpful to point out that the cross was the most faith-shattering experience for the disciples; doubtless they prayed fervently that somehow Jesus should be rescued. But in God's purposes the cross was not only essential, it was the most beautiful and loving thing he had ever done.

Help people to get hold of the truth in Jesus' words, 'You did not choose me, but I chose you …' (John 15:16). There is a strong tendency today for people to feel that they choose to become Christians in the sense that the whole thing is up to them. If this is so, they feel, they can equally choose to stop being Christians. Help them to understand that God loved them and was at work in them long before they made any response; in a very real sense they have been chosen and called by God; it is he who has made them Christians; they didn't do it themselves. Whatever they may feel, the hand of God is on them; the choice to remove it is not theirs.

Teach them to cope with the weaknesses and failings of Christians. Teach clearly that we are still human, and that the devil, though he stands no chance of winning the war, still wins the odd battle here and there. Be honest about your own humanness. In the last analysis, the test of the truth of Christianity is not other Christians, but Christ.

Prepare them to face disappointments and tragedies and disasters. Help them to understand why God still allows bad things to happen. Help them to learn to use these things as spiritual growth points, and not to allow them to become faith-destroying experiences. Help them work through any anger they may feel positively and creatively, rather than direct it at God.

As far as you possibly can, within the limits of your own weakness and humanness, make the living reality of Jesus Christ in you so clear and strong that, even if everything else gives way, they are still able to hold on to Christ in you.

Useful books

F. Bridger, *Why Can't I Have Faith?* (Triangle)
D. Burke, *Struggling to Believe* (IVP)
R. Forster and P. Marston, *Christianity, Evidence and Truth* (Monarch)
P. Kreeft and K. K. Tacelli, *Handbook of Christian Apologetics* (IVP)
A. McGrath, *Doubt: Handling it Honestly* (IVP)
D. Wilkinson and R. Frost, *Thinking Clearly about God and Science* (Monarch)

LOW SELF-IMAGE

Many people in our culture struggle with feelings of inferiority, inadequacy, insecurity, lack of self-esteem, self-rejection and the like. These problems, which can be grouped together under the general heading of low self-image, have a number of possible sources, and can be at the root of a range of emotional and behavioural problems.

Sources of low self-image can include:

- The breakdown of structures of society, such as the family and accepted moral principles, which used to give security and worth to the individual.
- The competitiveness of our society, where to succeed you have to be clever, or good-looking, or with the 'in' crowd or fashion.
- An experience of rejection early in life, such as being an unwanted or wrong-sex baby.
- Lack of being affirmed or praised or encouraged as we grew up.
- A childhood experience of never being good enough, perhaps as

a result of over-ambitious parents whose expectations were unrealistically high.
- Being subject to continual criticism, or statements such as 'You're useless.'
- Physical, sexual, mental or emotional abuse.
- An experience such as redundancy and unemployment, which removes from us the structures that gave self-worth.

People with low self-image may:

- Find it hard to see anything but the negatives about themselves.
- Find it difficult to accept praise or compliments.
- Easily become discouraged or depressed.
- Have difficulty forming relationships with others, since they feel no-one would want to be friends with anyone as worthless as them.
- Seek to counter their feelings of inadequacy and insecurity by projecting the opposite image, and so become attention-seeking, or strongly assertive, or aggressive.
- Be judgmental and critical of others, in an unconscious effort to divert attention from what they see as their own weakness.
- Express their rejection of themselves in a physical form, such as anorexia.

Helping those with a low self-image

Our primary aim will be to help them see themselves as God sees them: created, loved, redeemed, valued, cared for and so on. But we need to remember that they will have more difficulty than most accepting the Bible teaching on this. So we need to make a special point ourselves of expressing love, acceptance and appreciation, and encouraging others to do so.

Give them hope. Assure them that it is possible for them to change their thought patterns.

Be patient. Be gentle. Keep affirming and encouraging. Counteract their tendency to major on failures and setbacks.

Help them see where the beliefs they hold about themselves are false or one-sided.

Gently emphasize the Bible's teaching on the value of each individual.

Help them come to a point where they commit themselves, with God's help and your support, to a process of moving to a healthier self-image.

Help them formulate goals for new thought patterns. Break down long-term goals into smaller short-term goals which are comparatively easy to attain.

Help them to be encouraged by the progress they make, however slow, rather than to focus on their failures.

If you have pinpointed the source of their low self-image, where necessary, encourage them to seek counselling over it, or help them work it through themselves.

Where appropriate, help them turn their attention away from themselves, for example by befriending a lonely person.

Help them to cope positively with current experiences of criticism or rejection.

Some Bible teaching on God and us

He sees us as we really are (Ps. 139:1–4).
He loves us as we are (Rom. 5:6–8).
He does not condemn us (Rom. 8:1).
He accepts us as we are (Rom. 15:7).
He calls us each to fulfil a key role (1 Cor. 12:7–27).
He sees us as brand new creations (2 Cor. 5:17).
He holds nothing we need back from us (Eph. 1:3).
He has forgiven us and lavished his grace on us (Eph. 1:7–8).
He has given us fullness in Christ (Col. 2.10).
He has done and is still doing fantastic things in us (Heb. 10:14).
He puts the highest value on us (1 Pet. 1:18–19).

What could I say?

Accept that you have a self-image problem. You may have thought that your problem was inadequacy, or loneliness, or fear of other people, or a need to be in control. But underlying these other things is the real problem, low self-image.

Be encouraged. It's possible to move from a low to a healthy self-image. Thousands of people have done it, and found a whole new dimension to life.

God wants you to believe the truth about yourself, not lies imposed on you by circumstances or other people.

Have a go at analysing what the source of your low self-image is. What experiences in the past have shaped your estimate of yourself? Can you trace the things you believe about yourself back to opinions imposed on you by someone else?

Accept that you don't have to keep on thinking the same way about yourself for the rest of your life. You can change your thought patterns. In particular, you can get rid of the negative and destructive false thought patterns that have been imposed on you by other people and by circumstances, and replace them with patterns that are true and helpful.

Start thinking God's thoughts about yourself. The truest and best way of viewing yourself is to see yourself as God sees you, since he alone sees things as they really are. Study and meditate on the Bible's teaching; learn the key verses; absorb them into your thought patterns.

Accept that some people will always criticize or reject you. Train yourself to cope with their criticism and rejection. It cannot hurt you unless you let it.

Work through the 'five sheets of paper' exercise (see below).

Remember that changing to a healthy self-image is like recovering from a long and serious illness. It doesn't happen all at once. It's a slow process, so slow that often you don't notice it happening. There will be setbacks as well as improvements. But overall, the progress is in the right direction. Keep going. Don't give up. Who wants to remain ill for ever?

The 'five sheets of paper' exercise

1. Get five sheets of paper.

- On the first, list the negative things that you believe about yourself, especially in your darker moments: things like 'I don't like myself', 'I'm useless', 'Nobody cares about me.'

- On the second sheet, list your failures. 'I didn't get that job', 'I tried playing the guitar, but couldn't get the hang of it.'
- On the third sheet, list your achievements and successes. Be honest here: don't let your low self-image blind you. 'I did get that other job', 'I can drive a car', 'I passed that exam.'
- On the fourth sheet, dream dreams. What sort of things would you like to be true about yourself? What sort of things do you feel God wants you to believe about yourself? Be reasonable here. Things like 'To feel at peace with myself', or 'To have two or three really good friends' are more realistic than 'To be perfect', or 'Never to have any problems.'

2. Have a good look at all four lists. Are the things on sheet 1 true, all of them, completely true? Or are they partly true, or exaggerated, or downright false? If they are not completely true, then you have got to stop believing them. You don't want to build your life on lies.

3. Compare lists 2 and 3. There may be lots more failures than achievements, but there are some achievements. You can succeed, because you have succeeded. What you have done once you can do again.

4. Look at list 4. Are these goals totally impossible? If so, could you adapt them a bit so that they manage to come within the bounds of possibility? Whether you can or not, take the fifth sheet and write out a list of part-way stages between list 1 and list 4. For example, a part-way stage between 'I don't like myself' and 'Feeling at peace with myself' might be 'Stop concentrating on my bad points and start focusing on God's positive truths about me.'

5. Look again at list 1 and list 5. Decide whether or not you want to change your low self-image for a more healthy one. Many people with a low self-image secretly rather enjoy being as they are. With a little bit of manipulation their 'problem' can have all sorts of useful spin-offs, such as the avoidance of responsibility, or the sympathetic attention they can attract. Decide once and for all that you are going to move away from the twisted image of list 1 towards the goals in lists 5 and 4, and, supremely, to the way God sees you.

6. Work through the 'Ten steps' in **changing thought patterns**. Pick out the steps you think will be helpful. Adapt them where necessary.

7. Take one or two of the goals in list 5 and think of ways you could begin to move towards them. Set yourself some easy goals for the next few days. Write them down on list 5. Pray for God's strength. Get others to pray for you. Check each evening how you are doing. Remember that, even if you only make a bit of progress, it is still progress.

8. When you feel that you have made reasonable progress towards these goals, try choosing a couple more. And when you've made some progress towards them, try some more. Don't make them too hard; better to move in small stages over a long period than to aim at a big goal and fail to hit it. Don't let any failures put you off; even ten failures and one success is progress. Remember, one day you may find that all your list 5 goals added together have made up one of your big goals in list 4.

9. Always remember Philippians 4:13, which tells us that in the God who empowers us we've got what it takes for any situation.

See also **alienation, anxiety, changing thought patterns, failure, forgiveness, guilt, rejection.**

Useful books

D. Ames, *A Humble Confidence* (Mission to Marriage)
T. Ward, *Taming Your Emotional Tigers* (IVP)

LUST

Lust is best defined in terms of Jesus' phrase, 'committing adultery in the heart' (see Matt. 5:28). General sexual feelings, including sexual attraction to someone, are not lust; but they become lust when we use them to fantasize to the point of imagined sexual acts. No normal human being can avoid sexual feelings; but using them to practise lust is specifically condemned in the Bible as sinful.

Perhaps at the root of the sinfulness of lust, as with other sexual sins from pornography to rape, is our use of someone else's body as an object to gratify our desires in a wholly selfish way.

In contrast to the Bible, the practice of lust is fully accepted and encouraged in our culture. Not just the pornography industry, but large sections of the media, art and literature are dependent upon it.

Given our culture, and the fact that lust can be kept hidden, we can be pretty sure that many Christians have problems in this area. We need to give clear teaching about its sinfulness, and be ready to minister graciously to those who turn to us for help.

Helping those who have a problem with lust

All forms of sin, when practised over a period, get a grip on our minds and lives, and are not easily shaken off. Pride, for example, can become a set attitude, and even though we realize it is wrong and repent of it, it still comes back to haunt us. This problem is especially acute with lust and other sexual sins, so we need to show acceptance and patience and be willing to help the person fight and win a long slow battle over lust.

In some cases, where lust has become a major problem, it will be necessary to urge the person to seek counselling from a trained Christian counsellor.

Give the person a copy of 'Twelve steps to break free from sexual sin' (see **sexual issues**), where necessary amplifying the suggestions made there.

What could I say?

Lust, that is, practising in the mind what would be sinful for Christians to practise with their bodies, is sinful. It needs to be repented of, forgiven and renounced.

To get free of it you need to be filled with God's goodness. Jesus' story of the returning demon (Luke 11:24–26) illustrates the point that it is insufficient to banish lust from our thoughts; we need to fill our minds with good things (Phil. 4:8) so that there is no room for lust to return. This can be done both in a general sense and more specifically; for instance, when someone comes to mind who excites our lust, we pray for God's pure blessing on her or him.

Keep giving yourself to God. Get into the habit of giving your eyes, your mind and your sexuality over to God every day, and particularly when you are vulnerable to temptation to lust. 'You are not your own; you were bought at a price. Therefore honour God with your body' (1 Cor. 6:19–20). A mind that is filled with the Spirit can't be filled with lust at the same time.

Be honest with God. Foster the habit of talking to God about your lust, especially in moments of temptation. Be straight with him; let him be straight with you.

Be tough. As far as is possible, avoid places, situations, people, TV programmes and so on that excite lust. Take seriously (though not literally!) the teaching of Jesus in Matthew 5:29–30.

If appropriate, consider the possibility of making yourself accountable to someone in this area. Having to be honest about your lustful thoughts can be a helpful way of discouraging them.

Scripture passages relevant to lust

You have heard that it was said, 'Do not commit adultery.' But I tell you that anyone who looks at a woman lustfully has already committed adultery with her in his heart. If your right eyes causes you to sin, gouge it out and throw it away. It is better for you to lose one part of your body than for your whole body to be thrown into hell. And if your right hand causes you to sin, cut it off and throw it away. It is better for you to lose one part of your body than for your whole body to go into hell (Matthew 5:27–30).

I tell you this, and insist on it in the Lord, that you must no longer live as the Gentiles do, in the futility of their thinking … They have given themselves over to sensuality so as to indulge in every kind of impurity, with a continual lust for more … among you there must be not even a hint of sexual immorality, or of any kind of impurity … For you were once darkness, but now you are light in the Lord. Live as children of light (Eph. 4:17, 19; 5:3, 8. See the whole passage, 4:17 – 5:20).

Set your mind on things above, not on earthly things … Put to death, therefore whatever belongs to your earthly nature: sexual immorality, impurity, lust, evil desires … (Col. 3:2, 5. See the whole passage, 3:1–8).

Be self-controlled and alert. Your enemy the devil prowls around like a roaring lion looking for someone to devour. Resist him, standing firm in the faith (1 Pet. 5:8–9).

See also 1 Thessalonians 4:1–8 and 1 John 2:15–17.

See also **sexual issues** and other articles referred to there.

MANIPULATION

Anyone who seeks to help others will sooner or later be faced with manipulation. Perhaps everyone who comes to us for help will have mixed motives; we hope that for the most part honest and helpful motives preponderate. But there will be those who consciously or unconsciously wish to use us and our helping relationship for their own devious ends. These could be things like:

- seeking to get our influence to back them over some controversial issue;
- using a problem, or even inventing one, to gain attention, or possibly with some more sinister motive;
- getting money out of us;
- using us to pretend to others that they are seeking help for a problem when all the time they have no intention of doing anything about it.

We shall also encounter manipulation in other situations, and find ourselves seeking to help victims of manipulation. Such situations might include:

- attention-seeking threats of suicide;
- someone using an illness to abscond from responsibility;
- individuals trading on the goodwill of Christians to indulge their own selfishness;
- someone using a weakness or disability to get his or her own way.

Confronting those who use manipulation

Because of the complexity of human motivation it is not always easy to decide when and to what extent manipulation is taking place. If we suspect it is, it is probably wise to start by being cautious; we do not wish to spoil our relationship with someone in need by making an unfounded accusation of manipulation. So we shall need to be specially gracious and choose to run the risk of being taken in, at any rate for a time.

If we do get to a position where we are pretty sure that manipulation is taking place, then we will need to act. The issue should be raised graciously, but reasonably directly. We could perhaps introduce it with a comment about the complexity of all our motives, and then clearly state whatever way it is we think the person is trying to manipulate us.

Most people challenged in this way will probably respond with a denial that that is their motive at all. This, in effect, puts us in a strong position. If, for example, a man we are trying to help has denied that he is trying to manipulate us on to his side in a family conflict, we can then make a special point of being scrupulously fair in our attitude to the quarrel.

Where individuals are willing to accept they are being manipulative, we need to help them agree procedures that will stop them doing it. If we feel able, we could talk through with them why they seek to use people in this way and help them to avoid doing it in the future. Alternatively, we may feel that this would be getting rather out of our depth, and it would be best to encourage them to get help from a more experienced counsellor.

Sadly, many of those who use manipulation, whether consciously or unconsciously, and are unwilling to admit it when challenged, will simply switch to another potential 'victim'. There is little we can do about this, except, where appropriate, to give a quiet (and gracious!) word of warning to the new person.

In some situations, of course, we shall need to be particularly careful. Unwisely calling the bluff of someone who is using threats of suicide manipulatively could conceivably push them to attempt suicide just to spite us. In this kind of situation we should consult with others before taking action.

MARRIAGE ISSUES

All marriages have problems. Good marriages are the ones where the problems are faced and dealt with constructively, so that as a result the relationship is strengthened and the marriage becomes all the richer and more beautiful.

Between a third and a half of all marriages in the UK break down. A few of these may fail because of a major factor which makes breakdown virtually inevitable. But in most cases there is no significant reason why the marriage should not have been a success. The couple start with love and commitment to each other, and a determination to succeed. But after a time the amount of work put in to building the marriage begins to get less. The level of communication declines. Boredom sets in. Problems cease to be faced and dealt with. Less and less effort is made to keep the marriage going. Difficulties and pressures build up. Perhaps more serious problems begin to appear, such as unfaithfulness and violence. And the marriage is pronounced dead, frequently without any serious attempt ever having been made to keep it alive.

One of the saddest things about helping those who have problems in their marriage is that far too often the help is called in or accepted far too late. We need to foster an attitude that everyone needs ongoing help and support with their marriage, just as everyone needs ongoing help and support in their career. We don't have an appraisal with our boss or go on a refresher or development course because our job is a failure; we do it because our job is going well and we want it to go better. So with marriage. Given the tremendous pressures on every marriage today, every couple should be willing to accept and use all the help they can get to make their marriage as strong as it possibly can be.

There are many ways such help can be offered. There are books, videos and training courses. There are marriage enrichment conferences. A local church or, perhaps better, a group of churches can put on courses or day conferences. Those who have been involved in preparing a couple for marriage can continue the relationship as friends and advisors (see **marriage preparation**). Churches can follow and extend the practice of holding regular services for the renewal of marriage vows, with specific teaching on marriage. House groups can make marriage a topic for study and discussion. To avoid letting singles (who may well be in the majority in a church) feel left out by such a programme, it should be made clear that, where appropriate, they should be included; they need to be aware of the issues married people face, just as marrieds need to be aware of issues singles face. A single person may well have significant insights to offer couples, whether or not she or he has previously been married.

What could I say to those who are married?

Here are some basic principles, with a few ideas of additional things you might say.

Go on working at your marriage. If you don't work at it, it will wither and die. Accept that if your relationship isn't getting stronger and richer, it is getting weaker. Be committed to doing everything you can to strengthen your marriage.

Enrich your love. Selfishness is one of the biggest destroyers of marriages, and some forms of love are pretty selfish, as when we love someone because they do something for us, or make us feel good, or fulfil our needs. Marriages built on that sort of love will soon be in trouble. Marriages need unselfish love, with Christian *agapē* love at its heart, the sort that Jesus showed in washing his disciples' feet (John 13:1–17), and described in the story of the good Samaritan (Luke 10:25–37). In this sort of love our primary interest is the well-being and enrichment of the other person, not ourselves.

Check the place that Jesus Christ has in your marriage. Be aware of the danger of letting him get pushed out by the pace of life, responsibilities, family, pressures and problems, or even busy church activities. Go back to your wedding-day promises when you asked him to be at the centre of everything.

Reassess your prayer life together. Is it living and vibrant? However good it is for parents and children to pray together, this should not be allowed to push out the practice of just the couple coming to God and praying together, perhaps at the close of each day.

Periodically make time to review and assess your marriage together. You could do this by attending a marriage enrichment course, or by working through the material in 'A marriage-check up' below.

Turn problems into growth points. Look on the stresses and disagreements and problems you encounter in your marriage as challenges to face that will draw you closer together and ultimately enrich your understanding of each other and build up your marriage. Remember that with God's help there is no problem that is too hard to solve one way or another. Other couples have faced the same problem as you and come through. God can and will turn it into a growth point for you.

Remember your vows. Read them through every now and then. Each time you go to someone else's wedding, use the repeating of the vows as an opportunity to renew your own. Periodically, perhaps at special anniversaries, share in a service of marriage re-dedication and renewal of vows, either at the church where you got married or in your local church.

Work hard at maintaining good communication with each other. Make opportunities when you can talk together. Go for walks, ban the TV, use car journeys. Be honest with each other, and allow each other to be open about your feelings. Make it easy for each to off-load. Listen; don't criticize or rush to your own defence.

Watch non-verbal communication. As you get to know each

other better, a lot of your communication will be by body language, tone of voice, facial expression, ways of putting things and subtle emphasis. Who you are speaks volumes.

Communicate honestly with each other. Avoid developing the habit many couples fall into of saying one thing and meaning another. He asks, 'Have you got a headache?' She (and he) knows that this is actually a criticism or complaint; it means 'You're grumpy this morning.' Better to have a relationship where he is able to be more open and say something like, 'Hey, sweetheart, I'm not finding you the cheerful charming person you usually are first thing in the morning'; or, better still, for her to admit that she's off colour before he has to comment on it.

Take special note of feelings. Feelings are very real, and very powerful. Never brush them aside. Make allowances for mood swings, especially when they come as part of the menstrual cycle.

When issues arise between you, don't waste time arguing over them. Get straight down to working out a constructive solution together.

Have your own consultant. Keep in regular touch with someone or a couple with whom you can talk together honestly about issues in your marriage. This may be the minister who took your wedding, or a trusted friend, or a wise married couple.

Keep your relationship exciting. Guard against getting into a rut. Remember that boredom is a marriage-killer. Find new things you can do together, such as new hobbies or a specific project.

Be generous with your marriage. Don't turn in on yourselves. Let your relationship enrich others. Be an inspiration to other couples. Befriend singles. Show the world what a great thing true Christian marriage is.

Maintain and develop your sex life together. Grow in your understanding of lovemaking. Learn to deal with the difficult times with patience and unselfish love. Be sure to get help if you have major sexual problems.

Be well prepared to cope together with the impact of major changes. These will include pregnancy, the arrival of a baby, a move, children leaving home or retirement.

Watch for any danger signals that could lead to unfaithfulness. Deal with them ruthlessly.

A marriage check-up

This is something for wife and husband to do together, perhaps once a year. You could make it a regular fixture in your diary, say round about your wedding anniversary.

Take time over it, and, while taking it seriously, let it be something you enjoy rather than find threatening. It would probably be best to write out your answers to the questions together.

Where you do list specific issues, always go on to decide what you are going to do about them. Keep a record of these decisions.

Where you don't agree over your analysis or theory, don't worry; simply write down both views. But try hard to agree when it comes to deciding courses of action.

1. In what areas has our marriage become richer since we last had a check-up? What problems have we faced and overcome?

2. Are there any areas, such as communication, lovemaking or the sense of excitement, where our marriage could be improved?

3. Are there any issues, personal or marital, over which we should get counselling help?

4. Do we spend enough relaxed time together and for each other? Are there ways, apart from sexual, in which we could show our love for each other more clearly?

5. What are the external pressures or stresses on our marriage at present and how are we coping?

6. Where is God in our marriage? Is Christ at the centre? Are we as in love with God as we were? Are we doing all we can to encourage each other to go forward as Christians? How could we strengthen the spiritual basis of our marriage? Do we pray enough together?

7. Have we got our priorities right?

8. Are we happy with the way we are working out our respective roles?

9. Are there any ways we could improve our parenting, or our relationship with others?

10. Are we managing our finances satisfactorily? Are there ways we could be managing them better?

11. Are there any specific issues we need to be facing and dealing with in the next few months?

12. What areas do we want to be concentrating on for growth and enrichment in the coming year?

What could I say to those who are having problems in their marriage?

Get help. Far too many couples ignore the problems, or hope they will go away, or adopt a fatalistic attitude. Problems rarely go away; they more often escalate. But with help they can be solved. Indeed, they can become the means of enriching a marriage. Talk to a counsellor, or to a minister, or to a wise and trusted couple.

Take action early. Marriage problems can be like a cancer. The longer you leave matters, the harder it is to sort them out.

Commit yourselves to doing everything in your power to deal with the problems and save your marriage. Pray together for God's grace and help. Give your marriage and relationship back to him. Ask for his guidance and strength in sorting out the problems.

Talk things through together. Listen; hear where your partner is at. Never jump to conclusions or brush things aside. If you have lost the art of communicating, or cannot communicate without it developing into a row, get a counsellor who will help you together, or apply the principles in the article on **communication.**

Work hard. Make saving your marriage your number-one priority. Be willing to do anything, and put your willingness into action.

Take feelings seriously. They are often more important than facts. Don't condemn one another for feeling the way you do; instead, work out constructive ways to deal with those feelings.

If appropriate, give yourselves a break. Use your savings (your marriage is more important than money in the building society) to have a holiday together. If things have become really serious, have a week or two apart, but make sure that each is committed to making this a constructive time, so that when you come back together you are ready to make progress.

Get specific help and counselling over particular problems that may underlie your marriage difficulties. These could include **low**

self-image, **depression**, **alcohol abuse**, **debt**, **anger**, **violence**, major **sexual issues**, **unemployment**, **parenting**, **work issues**, major **illness** and the like.

Find ways of turning points of conflict into opportunities for learning and growth together.

Aim for some goals. Together set agreed long-term goals, but also work out short-term goals, so that you can make progress in easy stages.

Give and receive forgiveness. Remember, anything can be forgiven. If you find it hard to forgive, ask for special grace from the Holy Spirit: 'Lord, I forgive; help my unforgiveness.' Seek and receive the forgiveness of God together.

Face and deal with any problems in your sexual relationships. Talk them through together, or with a counsellor or medical advisor. Learn to be understanding and patient. Commit yourselves to the expression of unselfish love. Remember that it is possible to share rich sexual experiences together without reaching orgasm every time.

Accept that your personalities and views differ. Remember that you are there to learn from and enrich each other, not to agree over everything, or to force change on each other. Find ways of disagreeing creatively.

Don't give up. Don't slacken off. Trust. Pray. Hope. Keep working at your marriage.

Where it has occurred, face and deal with unfaithfulness. With the help of a minister or wise Christian friend:

- Ensure that the unfaithful partner comes to a position of true repentance and not just remorse. It is essential to renounce the adulterous relationship, to be committed to taking very clear steps to ensure there can be no recurrence, and to seek and receive forgiveness from the partner and from God.
- Enable the other partner to work through the pain of betrayal and come to a point of forgiveness and acceptance. Accept that this may take time and may need to be done in stages.
- Locate and deal with anything, such as sexual frustration within the marriage, that may have been a contributory factor.
- Pray for God's healing on the broken relationship, and his

power and love on the building of a renewed relationship. Ask him to transform a disaster into a means of growth and blessing.

- When you are ready, make a formal rededication of your marriage and renewal of your vows to each other. If the unfaithfulness has been widely known, this would best be done openly in a church service. If others did not know of it, it could be done more privately, before, say, your minister and church elders.

- Set in place radical and effective measures to exclude any possibility of a recurrence. Remember the insidiousness of sexual temptation. Take very seriously indeed the teaching of Jesus in Matthew 13:43–45 about the seven evil spirits (see 'Beware of the seven evil spirits', p. 33), and Matthew 5:27–30 about gouging out our eyes and cutting off our hands in order to avoid committing adultery. These measures should include steps to avoid any contact with the person with whom adultery was committed, and a clear commitment to be honest if and when temptation returns and to seek help from a minister or Christian counsellor (see **sexual issues**, especially 'Twelve steps to break free from sexual sin').

See also, where appropriate, **change, childlessness, communication, conflict, decision-making, forgiveness, growing older, marriage preparation, miscarriage, remarriage, stepfamilies, stillbirth.**

Useful books

D. and M. Brown, *Breakthrough to Love* (CWR)
I. and R. Coffey, *Friends, Helpers, Lovers* (IVP)
W. F. Harley, *His Needs, Her Needs* (Monarch)
S. Hughes, *Marriage as God Intended* (Kingsway)
M. Kirk, *The Marriage Work-out Book* (Lion)

Video

Marriage God's Way (CWR)

Marriage guidance

Relate Marriage Guidance. Head office: Herbert Gray College, Little Church Street, Rugby CV21 3AP. 01788 573 241. www.relate.org.uk

Some Christian marriage resources

Family Alive! 1668 High Street, Knowle, Solihull B93 0LY. 01564 776 133. www.webcan.com/agape
Marriage Resource, 24 West Street, Wimbourne, BH21 1JS. 01202 849 000. www.marriageresource.org.uk
Mission to Marriage, Forge Cottage, Fishery Road, Boxmoor, Hemel Hempstead HP1 1NA. 01442 215 414.

MARRIAGE PREPARATION

Almost everyone spends time, sometimes years, being trained for their career. Yet most people slip into marriage, a relationship at least as demanding and, one hopes, longer-lasting than their career, with little or no training or preparation. Little wonder that so many marriages fail.

Equally, many people are supervised and appraised in their jobs and periodically go on courses and the like to improve their career skills. But, despite the existence of excellent marriage enrichment courses and marriage guidance counsellors, most people seem to think they know all they need to know about marriage, and carry on on their own.

The aim of marriage preparation is to provide as good a base as possible on which the couple can build their marriage. The old concept 'As long as they love each other everything will be all right' will not do. Love on its own is not enough. Wisdom and skills need to be developed, just as in a career. Chief among these are understanding of each other and of marriage, skills in relationships, communication and parenting, and the ability to cope with conflict, pressure and change.

Helping those who are preparing for marriage

Ideally, where a couple are getting married in church, the minister will arrange a series of marriage preparation classes. These may be anything from two or three sessions to a dozen or more, though most ministers, with the best will in the world, are not able to give all the time they would like to marriage preparation.

A sensible alternative is for the minister to share the responsibility with others in the church, particularly with suitable experienced couples. The minister would then have the responsibility of preparing the new couple specifically for the wedding service, and would perhaps take them through some basic principles, but would ask the other couple to take the main responsibility of getting alongside the new couple and helping them in a more long-term way in their preparation for marriage. Where there are several suitable, experienced couples available, each can have just one couple who are their specific responsibility, not just for the months leading up to the wedding, but for that key period of the early years of married life.

The first task of the experienced couple will be to make friends and win the trust of the new couple. This could be done in the context of meals together and other social activities. This friendship is key both to the time of marriage preparation and if the helping relationship is going to continue after the wedding day.

The experienced couple will need to make it clear that they don't see it as their task to prepare the others for marriage. Rather, they are helping the new couple in their own preparation for marriage. They are facilitators rather than instructors. If the relationship is good enough, they will doubtless have many opportunities of explaining how they view things and sharing their experiences, but these are not what they are primarily after; their main task is to help the new couple think issues through and sort things out for themselves in their preparation for their marriage.

Discussion about specific issues may well arise spontaneously. Alternatively, it may be necessary to spark off a conversation in a specific area. If such conversations are slow to get going, one way of stimulating discussion is to get both members of the couple (or of both couples) to write down their thoughts on the issue, and then read them out for the other(s) to comment on. Clearly, if significant differences of opinion emerge, these will need to be talked through, and the couple helped to work out how they can either resolve them or learn to live with them.

Issues that could be tackled in this way include:

- What is marriage?
- What is love?
- What are the distinctives of Christian marriage?
- What are the three (or five) most important things in life?
- What are the three (or five) basic ingredients of a successful marriage?
- What are the relative roles of wife and husband?
- What are the principles for good communication?
- What are the basic principles of good parenting?
- What do the vows 'for better, for worse ... forsaking all other', etc. (or their contemporary equivalents) mean?
- How will we keep Christ at the centre of our marriage?

There are many other issues, ranging from relationships with the in-laws to money and sex. Life will be too short to cover them all, but there should be sufficient time in the sessions to cover the ones that seem most significant, and, in so doing, help the couple to develop habits of formulating their ideas and sharing them with each other in helpful and creative ways. Again, it is much better to facilitate the development of skills of communication and resolving of differences than to fill their heads with masses of good advice.

One crucial area which needs to be covered is that of the individual's self-understanding, and understanding of the person he or she is about to marry. Linked in with this is the equally vital issue of knowing how to cope with the negatives and problem areas in each other. These issues can be tackled by inviting each of the pair to make out four lists:

- their own strengths;
- their own weaknesses;
- their fiancé(e)'s strengths;
- their fiancé(e)'s weaknesses.

This will normally give fuel for any number of discussions. The task of the experienced couple will be to help the others to a deeper understanding of themselves (whether or not they are able to accept that the lists are wholly accurate) and of the person they are going to marry, and, most importantly, to help them to talk through positively and creatively how they are going to deal with clashes of personality and weaknesses raised: how he will cope with her depression or irritability during her menstrual cycle, how she will cope with his dependence on his mother and so on.

Though the exercises are really for the new couple, and should focus mainly on them, it may make things seem fairer if the helping couple show willingness to do them too, particularly those that expose their weaknesses! But they need to be careful of the danger that their ideas and experience may dominate the discussion; that would not be helpful.

It is conceivable that as problem issues are raised, it becomes clear that the couple are not in fact suited, or are not yet ready for marriage, or one member of the couple is not yet ready. Great care should be taken before suggesting that the marriage be postponed (it is usually better to suggest an indefinite postponement than a clear cancellation). It is perhaps wisest to raise the issue very obliquely, and wait for the couple to come to the point of making the decision for themselves.

A number of organizations arrange marriage preparation weekends, some more didactic in style, some more interactive. The couple should be encouraged to attend one of their choice.

There are several good books on marriage, some of them specifically written for marriage preparation. It may be sufficient to recommend these books. A useful additional suggestion is to recommend that the couple read the books aloud to each other a few pages at a time, and discuss their individual reactions to them. The same principle applies to marriage preparation videos.

Even if the couple appear to know all about the sexual side of marriage, this is an issue they need to talk about before marriage, both to resolve, or begin to resolve, any issues (problems over sex are one of the major causes of marriage breakdown) and to help them to get over any inhibitions in talking about the subject. One way of encouraging them to do this is, again, to recommend a suitable Christian book that they could read to each other and talk through. It would be wise, however, to warn them against doing this in too intimate an atmosphere!

Encourage good habits such as praying together and consciously putting God at the centre of their relationship.

Key points that are worth emphasizing include these:

- Every couple (including Christian couples) have problems in their marriage. Having a problem is most definitely not a sign that the marriage was a mistake or that it is doomed. Rather, it is an opportunity to tackle an issue together, to learn together, to grow closer to each other, and to come through with the marriage tested and stronger.
- Almost all couples have sexual problems from time to time. Again, these can be solved with patience, grace and the ability not to take things too seriously.
- The wedding day is not the goal. It is the beginning, the moment when the couple start to build the marriage. Up to then they hardly know each other; from then on they begin to get to know the real person to whom they are married. That is the point at which they must consciously start to build a real, lasting relationship.
- Vows that are solemnly made before God are made to be kept; the commitment and the responsibility belong to the couple. But God is faithful and will do his part, giving the wisdom and strength to cope with every pressure and difficulty, as they allow him to work in their relationship.
- Make it a goal that on each wedding anniversary they can say, 'We have loved each other more this past year than ever before.'
- Marriages do not succeed on their own. A marriage will only work if the couple work at it. Love will die unless it is fostered. Husband and wife will get bored with each other unless they make the effort to be interested and interesting.

By the wedding day, all being well, the friendship between the two couples will be strong enough to last well into the future, and the relationship will be such that the new couple will be able to be open with their friends about any issues that arise. Equally, the more experienced couple will be able to keep a watchful eye on how things are developing and to raise issues if they feel it necessary.

See also **marriage issues** and the resources listed there.

A useful booklet

D. Ames, *Looking up the Aisle* (Mission to Marriage)

MASTURBATION

The Bible does not give direct teaching on masturbation. Some Christians conclude from this that masturbation, given careful safeguards, is not sinful, and provides one way of expressing and enjoying our sexuality and dealing with the build-up of sexual pressure in our bodies. Others feel that it is basically selfish self-gratification, and almost certainly entails elements of fantasizing and lust. Many would distinguish between occasional masturbation, which may be helpful and acceptable, and compulsive masturbation, in which the person has virtually lost control over his or her body, something unacceptable for Christians.

Perhaps the real test for the rightness or wrongness of masturbation comes in 1 Corinthians 10:31: 'Whatever you do, do it all for the glory of God.' If and when it can be done for God's glory, then it is good. When God is not glorified, and, in particular, when it is done from impure motives or accompanied by sinful thoughts, it is sinful.

Helping those who have a problem with masturbation

Masturbation is a lonely, secretive activity, tending to turn those who practise it in on themselves, and often accompanied by shame and guilt. The very fact that someone is willing to talk about the issue is a positive sign.

As in all situations involving sexual issues, take special prayerful precautions lest discussing these issues becomes in itself a source of sinful thoughts.

Where compulsive masturbation is a major problem, encourage the person to get help from a specialist Christian counsellor.

Whatever your views on masturbation, be gracious and accepting of those who struggle with it. Be very careful not to add to their sense of shame and self-rejection. Assure them of God's love and acceptance, and of his desire to bless them and use even this problem as a growth point in their relationship with him.

Those who ask for help over masturbation are generally ready to seek God's forgiveness for whatever sinful elements are involved. Assure them of the reality and strength of that forgiveness and of its inexhaustible nature, even though they may have to go back to him in repentance and confession again and again.

If the circumstances are such that you feel it is right to encourage an individual to make occasional use of masturbation to release sexual pressure and avoid lust or extramarital sex, make sure he or she knows at what points masturbation moves over into sinful sexual activity, especially in the area of fantasizing. Encourage the person to be very open with God. Whatever he or she does, it must be in the awareness of God's presence and in the spirit of 1 Corinthians 10:31.

If you feel it right to encourage the person to stop all masturbation, be ready to help to provide all the prayerful support he or she will need, very possibly over a long period.

Give a copy of 'Twelve steps to break free from sexual sin' (see **sexual issues**), where necessary amplifying or applying the suggestions made there.

See also **addiction, failure, lust, sexual issues**.

MENTAL ILLNESS

As with physical health and illness, there is a sliding scale between full mental health and serious mental illness. Most people at one time or another suffer, say, a bout of depression, and so are less mentally healthy than they would like to be. But it is probably wisest to reserve the term 'mental illness' for its serious expressions, such as severe depression, psychosis and major neuroses. All such illnesses can be cured or controlled, generally by drugs. There is still much debate over their causes; it seems most likely that these include physiological, emotional and environmental factors.

Care of those who are mentally ill must be given by professionals and specialists. If we suspect someone we are involved with is suffering from a mental illness, we should refer them to their doctor. However, as with any illness, we, and others in the church, can still exercise a significant caring ministry alongside that of the professionals.

Caring for those who are mentally ill

Do all you can to avoid the stigma and fear of mental illness that are often expressed by our society and even by Christians. Help people to see that it is an illness, not the plague, or a judgment from God for sin. Sufferers are hurting and bewildered; they need love and acceptance and encouragement.

If they have to spend a time in hospital, visit them there, and encourage others to do so. Staying away because of fear of a psychiatric ward is an expression of selfishness, not of love. Encourage people to write and send get-well cards, just as much as they would if the sufferers had had a road accident.

Accept them as they are. You may find aspects of their behaviour difficult to cope with, though contemporary drugs generally succeed in preventing most abnormalities. Talk to them as normally as possible; express the love of Jesus in the way you approach and respond to them.

Some will be aware that they are ill; others will insist that they are all right, and that they shouldn't be receiving whatever treatment they are being given. It will almost always be appropriate to encourage them to submit to the treatment, even if we have to play along with them to some extent: 'I know you feel fine; but just carry on doing what they say to please them, and they'll soon send you home.'

Pray for them and with them. Get others to pray. If people feel that deliverance ministry of some sort should be attempted, consult very widely, including talking with doctors or psychiatrists, before you do anything. Remember, you don't have to have the person there to pray for them (Matt. 8:5–13); it would be perfectly possible for a prayer-ministry team to pray against any demonic influence they may feel is involved in the person's mental illness without her or his being present.

Information and help

MIND (National Association for Mental Health). Head office: 15, Broadway, London E15 4BQ. 020 8519 2122. Information line: 0345 660 163. www.mind.org.uk

Miscarriage

The loss of a baby at any stage can be a devastating experience, involving the pain of bereavement heightened by a sense of failure, anger, bewilderment, and the shock of something that should be characterized by joy and new life suddenly changing to sorrow and death.

Technically, the twenty-fourth week of pregnancy is the dividing-line between a miscarriage and a stillbirth; until then, the death does not have to be registered or the body buried or cremated. However, the loss can still be very severe, and should never be ignored or minimized.

Helping those who suffer miscarriage

Recognize that even an early miscarriage can be a shattering experience. Show understanding, love and support, as you would in any bereavement situation, and encourage others to do so.

The proportion of couples who have had a miscarriage is surprisingly high (one in five normal pregnancies ends in miscarriage); you will almost certainly find some in the family of any reasonably sized church. Try talking with them, and, if suitable, encourage the newly bereaved couple to talk with them.

Be aware that there are likely to be elements of bewilderment, anger, jealousy of those who have babies, and fear of a repetition. Help the parents to talk about their feelings; if necessary encourage them to seek the help of a minister or counsellor.

Though a funeral service is not required, it may be helpful to suggest holding a simple private memorial service, in which prayer for the bereaved parents can have a part.

Most miscarriages are followed in time by successful pregnancies. However, it is worth encouraging the parents to talk about the causes of the miscarriage with their doctor or medical staff.

Remember that although another pregnancy will help them to come to terms with their loss, it will not necessarily remove its pain. Grieving may well last a considerable time.

What could I say?

I'm sorry. As with any bereavement, our attitude and actions are more significant than our specific words. A simple expression of sympathy and love should be followed up with support and understanding and prayer.

Allow yourselves to grieve. However other people may view miscarriage, you have lost your baby; let your tears and grief express your love and sorrow.

Talk to each other, and to others who will be able to help you with your feelings. They won't have all the answers, but they will be able to help you in your sadness.

A helpful book

N. Kohler and A. Henley, *When a Baby Dies* (HarperCollins)

Support organizations

The Miscarriage Association, c/o Clayton Hospital, Northgate, Wakefield, W. Yorks WF1 3JS. 01924 200799. www.miscarriageassociation.org.uk
SANDS (Stillbirth and Neonatal Death Society), 28 Portland Place, London W1N 4DE. Administration: 020 7436 7940. Helpline: 020 7436 5881. www.uk-sands.org

PARENTING

Sooner or later the majority of people do it. Many of them find it the toughest job they ever do. But plenty would also say it's the most rewarding. It gives us the incredible privilege of doing and being something very Godlike. We create; what we create is in our own image. We love; we nourish; we care. We weep; we laugh; we rejoice; we are hurt. We watch our children grow in love and understanding; our relationship with them deepens and grows – or it does the opposite. We work, we give, we long, we teach, we encourage, we give ourselves. In all this we are experiencing something that is at the heart of the Father God.

If there's any issue in which we need to remember that every situation is different, it is the issue of parenting. Parenting a baby is radically different from parenting a teenager; parenting a hyperactive child is nothing like parenting a placid one; parenting youngsters who are secure and responsive is quite different from parenting insecure rebels. So, in seeking to help parents, we need to be very hesitant about saying, 'This is how it worked with my kids', or 'Here are the quick answers to your problem.'

Helping parents is not, of course, limited to helping them when they've got problems. Parenting is a huge task, and all parents need understanding, encouragement and support in it. We should be praying regularly and specifically for those in our house groups and the like who are parents; this is a ministry in which those who are not parents can share fully.

Almost all parents find parenting tough at some time or another. But some cope less well than others with its challenges, and some have to face particularly difficult situations. Where we are confronted with parents who are experiencing major difficulties, we should almost always encourage them to get specialist help. They may do this through contacting their child's school or doctor, or consulting a specialist counsellor or child psychiatrist or family therapist.

Helping parents who are finding the task difficult

Stand by them. Don't criticize them, even if you feel they've made mistakes. Make it a matter of 'Where do we go from here?' rather than 'How did you get into this mess?' Encourage them; support them; pray for them.

Help them to clarify their thinking about parenting and the principles they are following. All too often, parents just muddle along without really knowing why they do what they do. Talking issues through can help to highlight the principles they should be applying in the specific situation. Relevant principles may include:

- Be consistent. Don't say one thing one day and the opposite the next. Don't allow the children to play off one parent against the other. Even if your approaches differ, as they generally will, always back the other up.
- Show lots of unconditional love. Children need to be constantly reassured that their parents love them. Tell them verbally, in your attitudes, and in your actions. When you have to discipline them, or do something they find difficult to accept, be sure to surround it with love. Pattern your love on the love of God.
- Pray for your children. Put them in God's hands. Trust God with them.
- Empathize. Put yourself in the child's position; seek to understand how he or she feels.
- Accept them for who they are. Don't expect your children to react like adults. Respect them as persons. Study them; seek to understand them as far as you can.

- Talk with your children. Make it your aim that they will spend more time talking with their parents than watching TV. Talk about their day and their concerns. Explain to them why you do things. Take their questions seriously, and give them good answers. Do this from childhood, and right through adolescence.
- Affirm them. Praise them. Thank them for what they do. Tell them and show them that they mean a lot to you.
- Give them clear structures within which to operate. Children need to know the rules; they need the security of a structure which they can understand. They will, of course, try going outside the structure, or pushing the boundaries to test your reaction. Show wisdom, love and grace in dealing with this, but continue to keep the boundaries in place.
- Be specially sensitive to potentially traumatic experiences, like the death of a pet or a grandparent. Children may appear to get over things very quickly, but guard against, and watch for, delayed or disguised reactions (see **bereavement, loss, trauma**).
- Trust your children. Demonstrate that you trust them. Let them be themselves. Be prepared to let them go. Run risks with them. Your aim is to enable them to grow into whole people, not to remain children for ever.

Where appropriate, encourage the parents to talk about the issues and possible practical ways forward. As a general rule it is better for them to decide what specific steps should be taken, rather than for you to tell them what to do. But encourage and support them as they take them, and, as necessary, help them to continue and develop the process.

Encourage them to use all the resources available, from books and seminars on parenting to the power of prayer.

See also **single parents, stepfamilies**.

A useful book

J. Dobson, *The New Dare to Discipline* (Kingsway)

A Christian resource

Care for the Family, Garth House, Leon Avenue, Cardiff
CF4 7RG. 029 2081 0800. www.care-for-the-family.org.uk

PHOBIAS

Fears can be appropriate or inappropriate, helpful or unhelpful.
By contrast, phobias are almost always inappropriate and unhelpful. They are normally long-term conditions where the sufferers
have a debilitating and sometimes paralysing fear that appears in
itself to be irrational and unjustified by whatever triggers it.

   The source of a phobia may be complex, often going back to
the sufferer's childhood; it will not necessarily bear an obvious
relationship to the nature of the trigger event or the form in which
the phobia is expressed. Those who experience phobic reactions
to, say, closed-in spaces, bearded men or fog may well be reacting
to bad experiences in which one of these was an attendant feature,
but not the main one; the phobic reaction has been transferred
from the main one to the attendant one. This kind of complica-
tion makes phobias particularly bewildering and hard to cope
with. Sufferers should almost always be referred to trained counsellors for help.

Helping those who have phobias

Some of the material in the section on **fear** will be appropriate. In
situations where the sufferer is receiving counselling it will be
important to offer general support to what the counsellor is doing.

What could I say?

You are not going mad. Though it may be hard to understand,
there is a rational cause of your feelings. It may well be that some-

thing has happened to you, maybe a long time ago, which causes you to react in this way.

Phobias can be cured. Many sufferers have been completely liberated from them.

Make up your mind that you are going to get rid of your phobia. See a counsellor; be willing to face the source of your problem and deal with it.

Along with the counselling, get people to pray for you. If the counselling locates a particular bad experience or series of experiences that has given rise to the phobia, it may be appropriate to arrange a time of specific prayer ministry in which that experience is brought to the Lord for his healing and grace.

Try not to worry too much about other people's reactions to your phobia. If they fail to understand the nature of a phobia, that is their problem, not yours.

A helpful book

R. Baker, *Understanding Panic Attacks and Overcoming Fear* (Lion)

PORNOGRAPHY

Never has pornography been so readily available and widespread. Half the profit from the video industry is from porn; 90% of the material available on the internet is pornographic. Huge financial interests underlie the porn industry. No Christian is exempt from its pressure.

There are perhaps six main reasons why Christians should have nothing to do with pornographic material in any form.

The first is moral. Pornography stimulates lust, and lust is sinful. Much pornography depicts acts that are expressly forbidden in Scripture.

The second is an issue of truth and falsehood. Pornography presents a false picture of sex and of people. In real life very few people look like those it portrays. Real sexual activity is far more complex and rich than it pretends. It shows sex without love, intercourse without relationships. It has a distorted view of sexuality and humanity. Life is not like that.

Thirdly, pornography contains a huge amount of unacceptable add-ons, such as violence and the debasing of women and children.

In the fourth place, it takes human sexuality, something that is very beautiful, that God has given us to use to his glory, and that is the basis of one of the deepest and richest forms of human relationships, and turns it into a cheap, self-gratifying amusement.

Fifthly, it has a subtle but profound effect on those who use it. However much they claim it is a harmless diversion, studies show that it has far-reaching effects, sometimes physiological, and certainly psychological and sexual.

Finally, it is hugely addictive. Many of those who get involved with it find that it controls them. They have to keep using it, and very possibly keep moving to harder and harder porn.

Helping those who have a problem with pornography

We need to be very clear about the unacceptability for a Christian of any form of pornography. 'Would you expect to find Jesus using it?' is a good question to ask.

Those seriously hooked on porn may need the help of a trained counsellor to enable them to break the habit (see **addiction**).

Those who have used porn need to reach a point where they repent and confess their sin to God and receive his forgiveness. They need to renounce their use of porn and seek God's infilling of their mind and the power of his Holy Spirit to conquer this sin. Prayer ministry, probably on a number of occasions, may well be appropriate.

If the use of pornography has been over a period, it is likely that it will take time for the person to break free from its hold. There may well be lapses; remember, God can cope with these and renew and restore again and again. Be patient, give hope, hold the person to a commitment to break free, keep praying.

Use the suggestions in 'Twelve steps to break free from sexual sin' under **sexual issues**.

Take the parable of the driven-out spirit seriously (Luke 11:24–26). Help the person find ways of replacing the role pornography has played in his or her life with things that are good and pleasing to God.

Encourage the person to be drastic. Emphasize the teaching of Jesus in Matthew 5:29 about gouging out your eye if it causes you to sin. If they are using the internet for porn, get them to come off the net or to block the channels.

Stress the central Christian teaching that other people are given to us by God to be respected and loved in deep, self-giving relationships, not to be used as objects on which we can indulge our sexual lusts.

See also **addiction, failure, forgiveness, lust, sexual issues**.

PRAYER MINISTRY

As Christians we are able to use not just the 'natural' resources, such as the skills of doctors and counsellors, to bring help and healing to those who are in need. Jesus specifically gave his followers commands to use the resource of God's supernatural power to bring healing and help. When he sent out the Twelve in Matthew 10 he gave them the authority and commanded them to heal the sick, to raise the dead, to cleanse those with leprosy and to drive out demons – all as an expression of the truth of their message, 'The kingdom of heaven is near.' Later, others were sent with the same commission, and the early church clearly believed that it was the privilege of all believers to push back the frontiers of the kingdom of darkness, whatever form it might take, through the power of prayer and the working of the Holy Spirit (Eph. 6:12–18; 2 Cor. 10:3–4).

The mistake has sometimes been made of seeing a strong contrast between using 'natural' and 'supernatural' means in helping people. Some Christians have even felt that using natural means shows a lack of faith, and have been suspicious of the contribution of doctors, hospitals or counsellors. At the opposite extreme, some have argued that God does not intervene supernaturally these days, and expects us to use only 'natural' ways of helping.

The truth is, of course, that everything God does, whether through us or without us, is supernatural. When we as Christians are seeking to let the love and grace of God flow through us to someone in need, whatever form our helping takes it is going to be anointed by the Holy Spirit and done in his power, and so in that sense is as supernatural as a spectacular miracle. Even if we have used human wisdom and skills, at the end we want to say, 'It wasn't me; it was the presence and power of God working through me.' So all our ministry is supernatural; what we need to say is that sometimes the power of God works through 'natural' human gifts and skills, and sometimes God works more directly. Further, God isn't limited to using Christians to do his work in the world; many times he will work through a doctor or a counsellor, even though they do not acknowledge him.

So prayer, our asking God to intervene, is certainly relevant when a person is being helped by means of an operation or by a counsellor. Very often, a Christian surgeon or a Christian counsellor will be seeking God's wisdom and strength as they do their work. Certainly, whether the surgeon or counsellor is a Christian or not, we and others should be praying for those they are trying to help.

Prayer ministry, then, which we could define as specifically asking for the supernatural inbreaking of God's grace and power into a situation, is not to be contrasted with other ways of helping people. Rather, it is one way among several in which we seek to minister Christ. Everything we do in helping others is done in a spirit of prayer; every intervention of God in the lives of those we are helping is 'supernatural', whether or not it happens in a prayer-ministry situation.

However, there may be occasions when our prayers will best be expressed through holding very specific times of prayer, using the particular approach of prayer ministry. This can take a variety of forms. Many churches have a trained ministry team; sometimes it is right for the ministry to be exercised by the spiritual leaders or elders of a church; at other times a person's house group or other similar group will be the most suitable people to exercise the prayer ministry. Normally such ministry is done in a small group, but it can be by just one person, or in the context of the whole church. It may be accompanied by anointing with oil, the laying on of hands, or the breaking of bread in communion. According to the preferences or traditions of the participants, it can be a quiet and peaceful time, or develop into a very lively affair.

At heart a time of prayer ministry is the bringing of a specific situation or person to the Lord for him to work in the way he chooses. The expectation is that there will be a two-way process: we come near to God and he comes near to us (Jas. 4:8); we bring to him the things that are on our hearts, and he speaks to us. We respond to his voice, and he answers our prayers. The element of openness to whatever God may say or do is essential; it is not a case of demanding that our will be done and not giving up until we get what we want. Rather, we wait on him and let him do his work, whether or not it is what we have asked for or were expecting.

The range of issues that can be brought before God in a time of prayer ministry is, of course, unlimited. Some of the general themes would include:

- prayer for physical healing;
- prayer for the renewing of the mind (Rom. 12:2);
- prayer for emotional healing after a traumatic experience;
- confession and cleansing from a specific sin;
- renouncing and being set free from the hold of a sinful or unhelpful relationship or habit;
- recommitment and renewal after a period away from the Lord;
- prayer for deliverance from the powers of evil.

Suggestions for a time of prayer ministry

Encourage those who are going to be involved to prepare themselves before they come, ensuring there is nothing hindering their relationship with the the Lord. Both prayer and fasting may have a place.

Explain to all concerned what you are doing. Stress that the session is open to God, and that anything may happen. If prayer for deliverance is likely to be included, explain what this is, and prepare those present for any manifestations or unusual occurrences.

Stress the element of listening to God. According to the theology and traditions of those involved, explain about words of knowledge, prophecies, a message or prayer in tongues or the like.

It may be helpful to explain that though the person has come for a specific reason (say, prayer for healing of an illness), our openness to God means that he may lead us to deal with other issues as well as or even instead of the illness. So, in the story of the man let down through the roof, Jesus responds to the request for healing by ministering forgiveness of the man's sins (Mark 2:1–12).

It may also be necessary to explain that, as in any prayer situation, God may choose to answer our prayer immediately, or he may choose to answer it partially, or he may answer it in a way we do not expect, or the answer may be delayed.

Allow yourselves time. Be unrushed. Ensure there will be no interruptions.

Be relaxed. Be comfortable. There are no rules about standing, kneeling or sitting. Do what feels right.

There are no set procedures. Some find symbolic actions like anointing with oil or the laying on of hands helpful; if necessary, explain why we do these things.

Allow for times of silence. Since most people find silence difficult to cope with, explain how to use these times to wait upon God.

Be God-centred. Don't focus on the illness or the problem or the powers of darkness. Focus on God, our sovereign Lord and Father, on Christ, our risen and victorious Saviour, and on the Holy Spirit, at work in each heart and life.

Listen. Give plenty of opportunity for listening: to the person, to each other, but most of all to God.

God can speak in any way he chooses – to our hearts, through the Bible, in a word of knowledge, and so on. Except when giving a direct and obviously applicable passage from Scripture, avoid claiming, 'God is saying ...' Say rather something like, 'I think God might be saying ...', thus allowing the others present to test and confirm the message.

Never force something on those to whom you are ministering. Even if it is true that their backache is caused by their bitterness over the way they've been treated, they still have the right not to admit this, and we must allow them that right.

Fully involve those who are receiving the ministry. It is not so much a matter of their having something done to them, as their coming, with the help of others, to God for his grace and power. This should be something active, not passive. It may be appropriate to ask them questions, and to invite them to share what God is saying to them or how they are feeling.

Take any issue that arises to the Lord; there is nothing that can come up that is beyond his wisdom and power.

If nothing particular happens, don't worry. An hour or two spent in prayer and drawing near to God is never wasted.

In many situations it will be appropriate towards the end of the ministry time to pray for a specific infilling of the Holy Spirit, particularly in the area on which you have been focusing.

Make sure the time of prayer ministry is followed up. Continue to talk through any special issues that have arisen or are ongoing. Continue to give support and further prayer where necessary.

Prayer for 'inner healing'

All sorts of approaches to the healing of inner hurts or past traumas have been tried, some of them depending heavily on secular psychological theories, and some using rather questionable techniques. Nevertheless, the cleansing and healing power of God can extend to events long past and into the inner recesses of the human person and memory. Some form of 'inner healing' ministry may be appropriate in situations such as:

- deeply ingrained feelings of rejection and worthlessness, in which a person's self-acceptance has been destroyed by drastic or constant rejection;
- the defilement and pain of sexual abuse or rape;

- the inner defilement arising from pornography, lust and other sexual sin;
- deeply rooted anger or bitterness or hatred;
- irrational fears or phobias;
- the ongoing wound inflicted by a severe trauma such as a bad car crash.

Beware of looking on such prayer ministry as a short-cut. It should always be done in the context of a wider process of counselling. It should be seen as a part of that process. The counsellor is able to locate certain issues as lying at the root of the person's problems. The prayer ministry brings these issues very specifically to God for his power to work on them. Counselling then continues to follow up and build on the prayer ministry.

Again, avoid any slick techniques or fixed procedure. In a relaxed, prayerful and God-centred atmosphere, bring the issue to God. Wait upon him. Listen to anything he might have to say. Respond. Receive his grace and goodness and healing. Pray for the infilling of the Holy Spirit.

'Deliverance' ministry

Again, there is a range of views among Christians on the extent to which Satan or the powers of darkness can gain influence in a Christian's life. The details of the debate are not that important; suffice it to say that most Christians would agree both that those who have the Holy Spirit in them cannot also be possessed by satanic powers in any absolute way, and that, however we describe it, from time to time the powers of darkness do seem to get some sort of a foothold in some Christians' lives. This might be linked to problems such as:

- compulsive sin in a specific area, such as lying or lust;
- involvement in the occult or paranormal experiences;
- excessive and inexplicable anger or violence;
- powerful and overwhelming evil thoughts or temptations.

It is often difficult to decide if a situation is one that calls for deliverance ministry or not. The decision is not one to take on your own; consult prayerfully with your church leaders and especially with those who are experienced in such things. You may feel it sometimes acceptable to exercise a 'just-in-case' prayer ministry in this area, however, praying that if Satan has managed to get some foothold in the person's life or mind or emotions, God will break that hold. My own conviction is that God is wise enough and gracious enough to do what needs to be done even if we do happen to pray for it in the wrong way, so I see no need to get hung up over just what approach to prayer ministry we adopt.

This kind of ministry should always be done by a team, which should include at least one person experienced in this area, and, preferably, someone with medical or psychological training.

As in other prayer-ministry situations, there should be prayerful preparation by those involved, perhaps taking special note of Jesus' words, 'This kind can come out only by prayer [and fasting]' (Mark 9:29).

Where necessary, explain both the theology and the practical implications of what you are doing.

Where individuals have been involved in deliberate sin or, say, dabbled in the occult, allow them to confess and renounce that sin, and receive cleansing from God. Get them also to renounce any powers of evil, perhaps using the words of the old baptismal formula: 'I renounce the devil and all his works.'

You may choose to speak directly to the evil spirit or powers of darkness in the person, commanding them to go in the name of Jesus. Alternatively, you may pray directly to God and ask him to drive them out and set the person free. You may find a specific form of words helpful, or you may use your own. Whatever you do, do in faith, in humble confidence in God, calling upon his authority (not yours) and his victory over the powers of evil. Take as much time as you feel is needed over this part of ministry – don't rush it.

Encourage the person to join in the casting out of the powers of evil.

If there are manifestations such as Jesus encountered at times in this kind of ministry, take them as they come and give each over to God in prayer. Don't be frightened by them; God is in control.

Remember that not all manifestations have a demonic cause. They may be the result of the work of the Holy Spirit, or even the expression of pent-up emotion.

Give those you are ministering to opportunity to say what is happening to them and how they feel. Continue to listen for anything that God wants to say.

In the light of Luke 11:24–26, be sure to pray for the infilling of the Holy Spirit.

As with other prayer ministry, continue with counselling and further prayer as necessary.

A useful book

J. Woolmer, *Thinking Clearly about Healing and Deliverance* (Monarch)

PREJUDICE

Prejudice can take many forms, some of which are more socially acceptable in our culture than others. But, for Christians, any form of prejudice would seem unacceptable, on at least two grounds. In the first place, prejudice involves rejection, and, if we follow the example of our God, we will not wish to reject anyone. Secondly, prejudice involves making sweeping judgments which are often false or only partly true, breaking the principle Jesus gives us in Matthew 7:1.

Though it is easy to see prejudice in others, it is harder to admit it in ourselves. If we spot prejudice in someone for whom we have some pastoral responsibility, and feel it is necessary to raise the issue, we should be very careful how we go about it. Remember the plank and the speck (Matt. 7:3–5; see 'Watch out for planks!', p. 18). The following suggestions assume that the person we are trying to help has already accepted that she or he does have a problem with prejudice.

What could I say?

Go for the whole truth. Prejudice arises from generalized beliefs that are at least partially false, such as 'All motorcyclists drive dangerously' or 'Traditional churches are dead.' Help the person to accept the injustice of such beliefs and to reject their falsehood.

Think the way Jesus thinks. With the person, work through how any relevant Bible teaching applies in the specific situation (see below). In particular, ask 'What attitude do you think Jesus would adopt?'

Go the second mile. Even where we feel our 'prejudiced' beliefs are true and our attitude is fully justified, it is our Christian duty nevertheless to lay aside our 'rights' and demonstrate forbearance, forgiveness, grace and love.

Be full of grace. Grace, particularly, is something we are called to exercise. John 1:16 could be translated, 'We have all received from his fullness, grace piled upon grace.' Given that, we need to do the same. What's more, he promises to give us what it takes (See James 4:6).

Let the Holy Spirit renew your mind (Rom. 12:2). If appropriate, encourage the person to work through the 'Ten steps' in **changing thought patterns**.

Plumb the depths of love. Removing prejudice against a person is only the start of the story. God wants us to go on to learn to love them positively, and to show that love in appropriate ways. Point out that love of enemies (in this context, love of those we are prejudiced against) is one of the highest forms of love (see Matt. 5:43–46), so here is a God-given opportunity to be a great lover. Additionally, real love has to be practical as well as in the mind. Challenge the person, where appropriate, to find ways of showing the love of Christ to the people in question.

Bible teaching relevant to prejudice

Do not judge, or you too will be judged. For in the same way as you judge others, you will be judged, and with the measure you use, it will be measured to you.

Why do you look at the speck of sawdust in your brother's eye and pay no attention to the plank in your own eye? (Matthew 7:1–3; see also verses 4–5).

The story of the good Samaritan (Luke 10:25–37).

Love each other as I have loved you (John 15:12).

Accept one another ... just as Christ accepted you, in order to bring praise to God (Rom. 15:7. See the whole passage, Rom. 14:1 – 15:8).

To the Jews I became like a Jew, to win the Jews ... To the weak I became weak, to win the weak. I have become all things to all men so that by all possible means I might save some. I do all this for the sake of the gospel (1 Cor. 9:20, 21–23).

As God's chosen people, holy and dearly loved, clothe yourselves with compassion, kindness, humility, gentleness and patience. Bear with each other and forgive whatever grievances you may have against one another (Col. 3:12–14).

My brothers, as believers in our glorious Lord Jesus Christ, don't show favouritism. Suppose a man comes into your meeting wearing a gold ring and fine clothes, and a poor man in shabby clothes also comes in. If you pay special attention to the man wearing fine cothes ... but say to the poor man, 'You stand there' or 'Sit on the floor by my feet,' have you not discriminated among yourselves and become judges with evil thoughts? ...
    Speak and act as those who are going to be judged by the law that gives freedom, because judgment without mercy will be shown to anyone who has not been merciful. Mercy triumphs over judgment! (James 2:1–4, 12–13. See the whole passage, 1–13).

The story of Jesus and the woman at the well in John 4 makes a trebly strong statement about Jesus' attitude to the prejudice he would have been expected to show; she was a woman, a Samaritan, and living in sexual sin.

RAPE

Rape can be defined as sexual intercourse involving any form of penetration forced on a non-consenting person, generally with the use or threat of violence. The victim is usually (though by no means exclusively) female; a high proportion are in their teens; only a minority are raped by strangers; a considerable number of rapes occur within marriages.

As a technical definition, sexual assault covers any form of invasion of sexual privacy. Frequently, in its effects it is the equivalent of rape without penetration. The suggestions below can be applied equally to victims of rape and of serious sexual assault.

Powerful elements of our culture, including some music, some aspects of the media, and pornography, tend to link violence and sex and give the message that a man has the right to gratify his need for dominance and sexual intercourse. In contrast, rape and sexual assault are a denial of the basic Christian principle of love, that honours and puts first the other person, and they are rightly seen as serious criminal activities.

There is a lot of pressure on a victim of sexual assault or rape to remain silent. She may be afraid that she will not be believed, or be blamed for leading the rapist on. There may be threats from the rapist, or he may be a friend or family member whom she wants to protect. There will be fear of publicity and all the complexity of possible consequences, including becoming involved in a criminal trial. Sometimes pressure is applied by close family members who wish to avoid scandal. However, there are three strong reasons why she should not remain silent: she needs help in getting over the experience; a serious crime has been committed and she is required by law to report it; and failure to take action will only encourage further rape.

Helping a rape victim

Listen. Accept her. Make it easy for her to tell you. Even if her story is incoherent and inconsistent and doubts arise in your mind, still accept it. Details can always be checked out later if necessary.

Encourage her to see a doctor, the police and a counsellor, and if possible contact a specialist rape centre. Go with her where appropriate.

Take what comes. In the first few days of shock this may be a sense of unreality, emotional outbreaks, inability to concentrate, excessive fear, or emotional dullness (see **trauma**). Encourage the expression of her feelings such as anger or fear. Help and support her through it all.

Help her to resist the self-blame and self-rejection that many victims feel (see **guilt, low self-image**). Where the rapist was someone known to her, help her deal with the sense of betrayal, and the issue of her future relationship with him.

Where necessary, take steps to support the family as well as the victim. Remember that the parents of a teenage girl who has been raped may well respond with denial or excessive anger. Help them through these things.

Watch for any effects that develop in the long term, such as low self-image or obsessive cleanliness, and encourage her to get help from a counsellor.

If a pregnancy should develop, stand by her and help her as she works through the issue of an abortion (see **abortion**).

What could I say?

Contact a doctor immediately.

Inform the police. Have someone with you, perhaps a solicitor, as you talk with them. Do not be put off by the highly publicized cases where the process of taking a rapist to court has been more traumatic for the victim than the rape itself. The attitude of the police and the courts towards rape victims is increasingly sympathetic; you have a duty to report what has happened; you will not necessarily have to press charges.

Accept that for a few days you will be in a state of shock. Everything may seem unreal; you can't believe this is happening to you. Go easy on yourself; accept all the help you can get from others. Don't try and pretend everything is normal; this experience is not normal.

Don't worry about expressing your feelings. All sorts of things are bottled up inside you, and need to be let out. Cry when you feel you need to. Talk to someone about your anger or fear or hatred or feelings of helplessness or panic.

Be prepared for a possible reaction. As with any traumatic experience (see **trauma**), a couple of weeks or more after the event a reaction may set in. This may take the form of depression, or something else such as nightmares, excessive fear, or a phobia. Again, don't hesitate to get help if such a reaction occurs.

Don't blame yourself. Rape victims often blame themselves for what happened. Don't do this. Even if you were unwise to put yourself in a vulnerable position, it was the rapist who committed the crime, not you.

Don't worry about what other people are thinking. You may feel embarrassed and self-conscious and wonder what others are thinking. In fact, the large majority will be very sympathetic and helpful. If there are those who are not, remember that that is their problem, not yours.

Get all the help you can. Find a Christian counsellor or wise minister. If you can, get involved with a local support group for rape victims.

Talk things through with your counsellor. Be honest about your feelings about the rapist, and allow the counsellor to help you move from negative and destructive feelings to something more positive and helpful. Like most victims, you will probably feel that both your body and your inner person have been defiled. When you feel able, talk about this with your minister or counsellor.

Be prepared to begin to work towards forgiveness. As a Christian, you will know that you ought to forgive the rapist, but you are unlikely to find it easy. Don't worry too much about this. Forgive him as far as you can, and give the rest over to God. 'Lord, I forgive; help my unforgiveness.' If, after several months, you are still a long way from being able to forgive, seek help from your minister or Christian counsellor.

Pray. Throughout the process keep praying for God's grace and strength. At an appropriate time, ask the minister and perhaps some of the church elders to help you through a time of prayer ministry in which you put the whole experience into the hands of God, seeking his grace and cleansing and healing, expressing your forgiveness of the rapist as far as you are able, and seeking the infilling of the Holy Spirit into every part of your body and mind.

Live in hope. Rape is a terrible experience. But it doesn't have to spoil you. Many rape victims have recovered from their experience, and have lived a full and rich life. Be determined that with God's help, and the help of good friends and counsellors, this will be true of you.

See also **anger, forgiveness, fear**.

Rape counselling organizations

Rape Crisis Federation. 0115 934 8474. www.rapecrisis.co.uk
Victim Support, Cranmer House, 39 Brixton Road, London SW9 6DZ. 020 7735 9166. www.victimsupport.com

Helping a rapist

Whatever our personal feelings, those who have committed rape or sexual assault urgently need help. In giving it we are in no way condoning what they have done. Indeed, we are taking it so seriously we feel we have to take action to prevent it ever happening again.

What could I say?

Face up to and admit the seriousness of what you have done. Don't try and evade responsibility; what you did you chose to do. Alcohol or the attitude of your victim may have made some contribution, but it was still your act.

Pray. Ask God for mercy and grace to help you to face the consequences of your act and to come out of the experience forgiven and healed and closer to him.

Get help. If the police have been informed, get a solicitor or parent or trusted friend to be with you when they interview you. Find a specialist counsellor and continue to receive counselling until you and your counsellor are sure you have sorted out all the issues.

Take drastic action. Put in place stringent measures to avoid any temptation to do it again. If alcohol was involved, give up drinking. Work through 'Twelve Steps to break free from sexual sin' (see **sexual issues**).

Get right with God. When appropriate, with the help of a minister and perhaps a group of church elders, go through a time of prayer ministry, in which you express your full repentance, and seek God's cleansing and renewing. Be willing to accept special prayer for the breaking of the power of the sexual or violent desires in your mind and body.

Stay right with God. Keep handing your life over to him; in particular, give your sexuality to him, and ask him to fill your body and mind with the Holy Spirit.

Face the results of what you have done. Accept that you will have to face anger and rejection from those who know what you have done. Ask for God's help in taking this on board without resentment or anger on your part. Show by your attitude and your life that you have truly repented.

If appropriate, express your repentance. Talk through with others the possibility of writing briefly to your victim expressing sorrow for what you have done. Don't try and excuse yourself; don't ask for forgiveness – leave that to her.

See also **failure, forgiveness, sexual issues, violence**.

REJECTION

God is love, and in making us in his image he has put in us the ability to love and the need to be loved. God values each one of us highly, and we too have the ability to value others and to be valued by them. God also communicates, and has put in us the ability to communicate with others, and the need to receive communication from them.

For a person to be whole, he or she needs to be functioning in all these areas, both giving and receiving, relating both to God and to others. Where this fails to happen, problems will inevitably arise.

Among our basic needs are the needs to be accepted and affirmed, and to belong and feel secure. Ideally, in our early years these are met through the love of our parents and the security of the family and home. Later, friends accept us and affirm us; we belong to peer or activity groups or a church and so on; structures around us give us security. Achievements help our self-worth; a clear belief system helps our understanding and gives us meaning; faith in God gives us confidence and security.

For many, however, the story is different. Perhaps they were conceived by accident and unwanted even before they were born; it may be that a child in the womb is able to sense its mother's feelings of rejection towards it. At birth they may be rejected because they are the wrong sex, or have some 'defect', or because their parents cannot cope or choose not to. As they grow up, rejection may come as the result of family break-up, or failure to be accepted by their peers. It may be the outcome of being different in some way from the 'norm': of different appearance, differently dressed, poorer or richer, and so on. Later there may be other forms of rejection, such as:

- failure in exams or inability to get a job, or the right kind of job;
- the collapse of a romance; some single people feel wholesale rejection by the opposite sex;
- loneliness;
- failure to live up to the high standards we or others set for us (ambitious parents or school staff can be very cruel here, as in a recent case of a child who got nine 'A' grades at GCSE but who was condemned because only eight of them were starred);
- being passed over for a promotion;
- redundancy.

Such rejection from others can lead to self-rejection, and, in its turn, to further rejection. If others have rejected us, we feel there must be something about us that is bad and warrants their rejection. So we reject ourselves, and build up a barrier against the pain of further rejection by assuming that everyone else will reject us.

This in turn means that we make it harder for people to love and accept us; so they do end up rejecting us, confirming our low view of ourselves, and pushing us further down the rejection spiral.

Helping those who suffer from rejection

Clearly, their greatest need is acceptance, affirmation and love. These are things that we must give personally and faithfully over a long period. We must also encourage others to do the same.

People who have suffered a lot of rejection may be so sure that the pattern of rejection will be repeated that they will, consciously or unconsciously, seek to push us to the point where they are more or less forcing us to reject them. They may do this through annoying or bizarre behaviour, or by seeking to shock us or upset us or the like. We need to be aware of what is happening and do all we can to avoid being pushed to the point of rejecting them.

We shall want to remind them of the accepting grace of God, but in doing so we need to remember that their concept of God will be strongly influenced by their experiences of people; for example, a woman who suffered rejection by her father will not find it easy to think of God as a gracious accepting heavenly Father. Again, this can greatly be helped if they see the expression of the love and acceptance of God in us.

Where the experience of rejection is deep-rooted and serious, we should encourage them to seek further help in dealing with it. This will probably be from an experienced counsellor, and it may also include specific prayer ministry.

Besides individuals demonstrating love and acceptance, a family or small group such as a house group can provide a healing, accepting and secure atmosphere for people hurt by experiences of rejection.

Some Bible teaching on God's grace and acceptance

The Lord did not set his affection upon you and choose you because you were more numerous than other peoples, for you were the fewest of all peoples. But it was because the Lord loved you, and kept the oath he swore (Deut. 7:7–8).

The story of the lost son (Luke 15:11–32).

The Word became flesh and made his dwelling among us ... full of grace and truth (John 1:14).

God demonstrates his own love for us in this: While we were still sinners, Christ died for us ... Where sin increased, grace increased all the more (Rom. 5:8, 20).

If God is for us, who can be against us? ... Who shall separate us from the love of Christ? Shall trouble or hardship or persecution ... ? ... No, in all these things we are more than conquerors through him who loved us. For I am convinced that neither death nor life, neither angels nor demons, neither the present nor the future, nor any powers, neither height nor depth, nor anything else in all creation, will be able to separate us from the love of God that is in Christ Jesus our Lord (Rom. 8:31, 35, 37–39. See the whole passage, verses 28–39).

My grace is sufficient for you (2 Cor. 12:9).

Be strong in the grace that is in Christ Jesus (2 Tim. 2:1).

See also **alienation, changing thought patterns, conflict, loneliness, low self-image**.

REMARRIAGE

Remarriage after divorce

It is a sad fact that the failure rate of second marriages is higher than that of first marriages. There are a number of reasons for this, but it does not have to be so. Second marriages can be very successful, especially where commitment is high, and mistakes and hurts of the past are used as a source of wisdom and strength for the new marriage rather than being allowed to undermine it.

On the positive side, those marrying for the second time have the advantage of maturity and experience. They have a realistic concept of marriage and are aware of many of the problems they are likely to face. Very often they will enter their new marriage with a strong determination to make it work, and to avoid the mistakes of the past.

On the negative side, their task is often made harder by the continuing presence of the hurts, guilt, anger, grief, and the like from their previous marriage, the weaknesses in their own personalities that contributed to the first break-up, and continuing pressure arising from the relationship with the previous spouse and with children.

Clearly, those who are entering a second marriage after a divorce need a lot of help and support in the major task they are undertaking. Though we may have reservations ourselves on the issue of divorce and remarriage, we should not let these prevent us from doing all that we can to help them make their new marriage a success.

What could I say to those remarrying after divorce?

Face squarely the issues that led to the break up of your previous marriage. Accept your responsibility – in very few marriage failures is the blame wholly on one side.

If you have not already done so, bring these issues to God. Ask for his grace upon your own weaknesses and failures, however large or small, and his forgiveness and cleansing. Remember, there is nothing too hard for him to forgive and heal, provided we are willing to let him.

Talk through these issues. Discuss them with a counsellor or with the minister who is going to take the wedding service. Then talk them through with your fiancé(e), preferably with the counsellor or minister present. Work out ways of coping with them in your new marriage. Remember, even weaknesses, rightly handled, can be a means of strengthening a marriage; they don't have to destroy it (see **failure**, **forgiveness**, **marriage issues**).

Work on healing your emotions. Talk through with the minister or a trusted Christian friend any feelings of hurt, anger, grief, bitterness, guilt, fear, or other strong emotion you are feeling from the break-up of your previous marriage. Seek healing for them as far as is possible at this stage, while accepting that full healing may take a long time.

Let your previous marriage go. Consciously and deliberately, as far as you can, accept that it is a thing of the past. Let it go; from now on your interest is in the future, building a new marriage and a new life that you will live to the glory of God. Your old marriage is not going to overshadow your new one, whether with its good points or its bad points. Be determined to make a really new beginning.

Follow through a programme of marriage preparation. Even though you may have gone through one before, it is essential to prepare thoroughly for this new relationship.

Be very sensitive to the needs of any children involved. This is important whether or not they are going to become part of the new family. As far as you can, talk with them and help them to understand and feel a part of what is going on. Remember, they will probably have conflicting and very strong emotions. Allow them to express their feelings; take what comes; do not respond negatively to things like anger or rejection of the new parent. Accept that these are expressions of the hurt they feel from the break-up of the previous marriage. Help them through these feelings. Show extra love and support for them. Where necessary, make it possible for them to receive counselling help (see **step-families**).

Prepare for problem areas. Talk through and agree with your fiancé(e) basic principles for difficult issues such as finances or the relationship with a previous spouse and with children. Clearly, you can't envisage all eventualities, but agreed principles can provide the foundation for further decisions in due course.

Tap into all the resources available. Together, commit yourselves to extra back-up resources to strengthen your marriage, such as attending marriage enrichment weekends, annual 'check-ups', and agreeing to see a counsellor as soon as any problems begin to arise.

Make your wedding service very special. In consultation with the minister, plan the church wedding (or service of blessing on your marriage) so that it will be personally relevant and significant for you. You may, for example, choose to include a section specifically giving the past over to God and acknowledging his grace and forgiveness. If you have children who will be part of the new family, you will wish to include them in the ceremony in a way that is meaningful for them. If they are old enough, this could involve an act of commitment by them and special prayer as they accept their place and are accepted in the new family.

What could I say to those remarrying after a bereavement?

With gratitude and love, give your previous marriage over to God, and put it behind you. This may not be an easy thing to do, but it is vital that you do not let it overshadow your new marriage. However much you will treasure the memories, God is leading you forward into a new relationship that will be different from the old one; you need to lay aside every aspect of the old so that you can be wholly committed to the new. Firmly resist the temptation to build expectations for the new marriage on the old one, or even to make comparisons. Be committed to building a marriage relationship that is tailor-made to the uniqueness of you and your new husband or wife.

Where necessary, allow yourself to continue grieving. Even though you deliberately put the old marriage behind you, you may well need to continue the process of grieving for your previous wife or husband. Even if you feel you have reached the end of the process, getting married again may well stir up memories and cause grief to return for a time. Don't worry about this. Talk about it with your new partner, and explain that this is grieving for someone you have loved (like a son or a daughter) and not a rejecting of the new relationship in favour of the old.

Where necessary, get help in coping with your emotions. Should you find that feelings of grief or even anger and guilt become very strong, seek help from a trained counsellor.

Be sure to go through a process of marriage preparation for your new marriage. Even if you have gone through one previously, and feel you are well experienced in all the issues, you and your fiancé(e) still need to prepare yourselves specifically for your new relationship.

Where there are children, be sure to involve them in all ways that are appropriate in the process of preparing for the new marriage. Remember they too will be grieving a parent, and that the process of being given a new parent will not always be an easy one (see **stepfamilies**).

In consultation with the minister, plan your wedding service very specifically for the new marriage. Resist the temptation to have a re-run of your previous wedding day. If you have children, make a point of including them in the ceremony in a way that is very meaningful for them.

See also **bereavement, divorce, marriage preparation, marriage issues, stepfamilies**.

Useful books

G. Forster, *Healing Love's Wounds* (Marshall Pickering)
M. Williams *Stepfamilies* (Lion)

SEXUAL ISSUES

God has made us sexual beings. Rightly expressed, our sexuality is good and beautiful. Perverted, it can destroy us.

Our culture is obsessed with sex, constantly presenting us with erotically stimulating material, and showing minimal concern for moral standards. It is fair to assume that those we are trying to help are both swept along and confused by this material. A vital first step, then, is to help them understand and accept the Christian principles taught in the Bible (see below).

It is helpful to distinguish in our thinking between sexuality and the way we choose to express our sexuality. Our sexuality is always good: our masculinity or femininity, our sexual feelings, the outworking of our sexuality in our bodies and emotions and relationships – these are all parts of the good and wholesome power of sex God has put in us. However, we can choose to express our sexuality in a range of ways, some of which are good (such as wholesome friendships), some of which are sinful (such as lust), and some of which are questionable (such as masturbation). We need to reject very clearly the foundational assumption of our culture that the only way to express our sexuality is in physical intercourse, and to help people live as fully sexual beings without breaking God's guidelines.

It is worth remembering that though the Bible takes sexual sin seriously, it does not single it out for special condemnation. 'Sexual immorality' and 'impurity' rub shoulders with 'discord', 'jealousy' and 'selfish ambition' in Paul's list of the 'acts of the sinful nature' (Gal. 5:19–21). In seeking to help people struggling in this area, we must offer the same degree of acceptance and grace as we would to someone struggling with, say, pride or anxiety.

There is, however, one area in which we need to take special care. Talking about sexual issues, especially in a one-to-one situation, can itself be sexually stimulating. Tragically, far too many Christians who have set out to help someone over a sexual problem have themselves ended up falling into sexual sin. Here, more than anywhere, it is essential to observe the principle of avoiding getting too closely involved in a helping situation with someone of the opposite sex. Even in same-sex situations, we need to guard against taking an unhealthy interest in the issues involved.

Some of the Bible's teaching on sex

Sexuality is God's gift and is very good (Gen. 1:27, 31).

Sexuality (our maleness and femaleness) can be expressed in a range of ways, many of which are good and glorifying to God (1 Cor. 6:12–20). See the life of Jesus, and his relationships with both women and men.

Sexual intercourse is God's gift for the marriage relationship (Gen. 2:24, Heb. 13:4).

Sexual intercourse outside of marriage is sinful (Prov. 5:1–23; 1 Cor. 6:13–20; Eph. 5:3).

Sexuality can be used sinfully in situations where no physical intercourse takes place (Matt. 5:28; Eph. 5:3).

Helping those who are struggling with sexual issues

Given that the biblical principles are so different from those practised in our culture, we shall need to state the Christian principles clearly, and help the person to understand and accept them.

For some, understanding the biblical principles may be a liberating experience, freeing them from unjustified guilt over their sexual feelings, and releasing them to be the sexual beings God has made them. We would need to give such people guidelines on how to express their sexuality in a creative and pure way, and perhaps lead them through an act of rededication of themselves and their sexuality to God, seeking the infilling of the Holy Spirit into this aspect of their lives.

Where those we are trying to help have broken God's guidelines, we need to help them come to a point of repentance and confession of their sin. On the basis of Scripture (1 John 1:9) we can assure them of total forgiveness and cleansing, and then, as above, help them commit themselves to following God's guidelines in the power of the Holy Spirit. In doing this we and they may be only too aware that they may well fall into sin again; the power of sexual temptation over someone who has, say, been hooked on pornography for years, is very great, and is rarely broken overnight. But here, as in any area, we can stress the inexhaustibility of God's grace, maybe using Jesus' teaching in Matthew 18:21–22 to emphasize the availability of God's forgiveness, even though we fail again and again.

Whatever our own feelings may be about sexual sin, the basis for our attitude towards those who have fallen into it must be that of Jesus in his reaction to the woman caught in the act of adultery (John 8:1–11).

What could I say?

Live as a sexual being without breaking God's guidelines.

Be the person God has made you. Express fully your masculinity or femininity in your ordinary living. Find ways of expressing it that are personally right for you; you don't have to be a macho man or a sweet, petite woman. Rather, be the man or the woman God has made you, delighting in the aspects of your personality and living that arise from your masculinity or femininity and give wholesome expression to it.

Be a great lover – without losing your purity. Jesus, who was a fully sexual being, loved people deeply, both male and female, and expressed that love fully without falling into sin. The sexual aspect of our loving is not something to be afraid of or to be isolated from other aspects of our loving, such as *agapē*, but something to open up to the Holy Spirit, and to use, along with those other aspects, to form positive and beautiful loving relationships.

Use the physical, sexual energy in your body for the glory of God. Find ways of doing this that are right for you, such as a creative hobby or physical exercise.

Train yourself in saying 'No' to the devil. Fight all sinful ways of expressing your sexuality. Practise self-control. With the Spirit's help you can be different from those around. Regularly rededicate your sexuality, your body and your thoughts to God, and ask the Holy Spirit to fill them.

Use all the help you can get. If appropriate and helpful, make yourself accountable in this area to someone who will help to hold you to God's standards.

Where you have fallen into sin, take decisive action. Talk with a minister or Christian counsellor. Seek and find the forgiveness and cleansing of God. Work through the 'Twelve steps' below.

Twelve steps to break free from sexual sin

Not all these suggestions will be relevant in every situation. Take the ones that are helpful for you, and adapt them if necessary.

1. Admit once and for all to God, yourself, and someone you can trust that what you are doing is sinful.

2. Make a clear decision, suitably recorded and shared with someone else, that you are committed to a process in God's strength of ridding your life of this sin.

3. Pray. Not just 'God, solve this problem for me', but a good, long conversation with God over the issue, in which you are very honest with him, and you allow him to be very straight with you.

4. Pray again. And again. Pray each morning for sexual purity through the day. Pray when you are feeling particularly vulnerable. Keep open a hotline to God.

5. Give yourself totally to God, specifically including your mind, your eyes, your maleness or femaleness, and your sex organs. Ask the Holy Spirit to fill every part of your body and your being. Ask him to make you as holy as he is. Do this daily, and repeat it when the pressure is on.

6. Make yourself accountable to a suitable Christian friend or counsellor with whom you have to be totally honest and who will hold you to your commitment. Talk through with him or her the suggestions made in this list.

7. Take very specific steps to avoid situations, places, people and so on which push you towards sexual sin. If necessary be drastic (Matt. 5:30). In particular watch your eyes (Matt. 6:22–23). Be drastic over what you look at. You will not be able to avoid seeing sexually titillating things, but you can avoid looking at them. Turn off the TV; look the other way. 'If your right eye causes you to sin, gouge it out and throw it away' (Matt. 5:29).

8. Be aware of your specially vulnerable times or feelings, such as when you are lonely or down. Work out ways of dealing with these things other than resorting to sex.

9. Train yourself to take immediate action as soon as the first thought of sexual sin begins come into your mind. Don't play around with the serpent – kill it! Have escape routes, things to which you can switch your thoughts. Wear a WWJD (What would Jesus do?) bracelet or use some other helpful device.

10. Study the New Testament teaching on holiness. Model your living and thinking on that of Jesus.

11. When you do fail, be very quick to get back to God and receive his cleansing and forgiveness.

12. Work continuously at getting your mind and life so filled

up with good and wholesome and Christ-centred things there is no space left for sexual sin to get in.

See also **changing thought patterns, child abuse, failure, forgiveness, guilt, homosexuality, lust, masturbation, pornography, rape**.

Two helpful books

S. Ayres, *Sex and Sexuality* (IVP)
N. Pollock, *The Relationships Revolution* (IVP)

SINGLE PARENTS

There have always been single parents in the community, chiefly as a result of the death of a spouse. But the rise in the number of divorces, and the decreasing pressure to get married when the woman finds she is pregnant, have meant that the number has grown very considerably. There are well over a million single parents in Britain; nine out of ten of them are women.

Single parents face the usual range of problems encountered by all parents. To these are added several more:

- The attitude of society, which tends to lump together all single parents and stereotype them as parasites and scroungers.
- Where single parenthood arises from the death of a spouse, parent and children will be struggling with the process of grieving.
- Where it arises from a divorce, all the complicating factors of a post-divorce situation will be present, such as feelings of anger or guilt, relationships with the former partner, and the relationship between the children and their other parent.
- Many single parents have major financial problems. Despite the efforts of the Child Support Agency, many get no money from

the fathers. State welfare payments are small and tend to prevent mothers from earning more than a pittance for themselves.
• Loneliness is often a problem. Social habits and structures often do not fit the needs of single parents.

Nevertheless, despite all the problems they face, many single parents have been able to care well for their children and have succeeded in making an excellent job of their parenting.

In many divorce situations, although one parent has the main task of caring for the children, the other parent will continue to fulfil the role of parent in a limited way. This can bring extra stresses and strains, though it does not have to. For the sake of the well-being of the children, divorced parents may be able to agree a policy that enables the children to benefit from remaining in contact with both their parents.

The needs of single parents give the church a whole range of opportunities to show the mercy and love of God in action. The biblical teaching is very clear; widows, the disadvantaged, the poor and others like them are a special concern of God; he calls his people to care for them and share their resources with them. See, for example, Deuteronomy 24:19–21 and James 1:27.

In particular, the New Testament tells us about the establishment of a new type of family, replacing, where necessary, the traditional, natural family. This is the family of the community of God, which can be expressed in the local church, or, where churches are large, in a unit of the church like a house group. Here, in the company of the Lord Jesus, we find our 'real' family (Mark 3:34–35), whether or not we belong to a natural family as well. So single parents and their children should be able to find in the church or small group all the elements of family that they might otherwise lack. In seeking to help them, one of the most significant things we can do is to ensure that this New Testament vision is being fulfilled in our own local situation.

Helping single parents

The task single parents face is huge; it seems all the greater when they feel they have to face it alone. Though you may not understand it all, let them know you appreciate the size of the challenge, and want to stand with them as they face it.

Ensure that the church or house group is aware of the needs and committed to helping to meet them. Encourage the single parent to take specific steps to counter the sense of loneliness and isolation.

Where appropriate, encourage the development of suitable role models in the church to help replace the missing parents.

Give special prayer support. God is specially concerned for the needs of 'the fatherless and the widows'.

Be aware of complicating factors such as grieving over a bereavement or a divorce. Give them opportunity to express their feelings. Make counselling help available where necessary.

Offer or arrange what practical help is possible and productive. Use the skills that are present in the group, for example in financial counselling or coping with housing or legal issues.

Where possible, arrange for the parent to have an occasional break from the children.

Watch for reactions such as self-pity, guilt, bitterness and fear of the future. Encourage the parent to talk these things through with a minister or counsellor.

Be aware that it is not uncommon for single parents to develop a relationship with their children that is excessively dependent, in which they find it very hard to let them go. Do what you can to help them avoid this.

Surround the children with the love and security of their Christian 'family'. Pray for their protection and well-being.

See also **parenting**.

A Christian support organization

The Christian Link Association for Single Parents (CLASP), 'Linden', Shorter Avenue, Shenfield, Brentwood, Essex CM15 8RE. 01277 233 848.

Other organizations

The Gingerbread Association, 35 Wellington Street, London

WC2E 7BN. 020 7336 8183. www.gingerbread.org.uk. A network of local self-help groups for single parents and families. *The National Council for One-Parent Families*, 255 Kentish Town Road, London NW5 2LX. 020 7428 5400. www.oneparentfamilies.org.uk. Advice for single parents on a range of issues.

SINGLENESS

In many church congregations, singles are in the majority. Some of these will be young people, not yet married. Others will have been married, and have lost their partner through divorce or death. Others will, to all appearances, be committed to a life of singleness. Some will have chosen singleness. Some will feel they have had it forced upon them. Some will be content with their present lot. Some will be eager to find the right person and marry. Some will live rich and wholesome lives, exploiting, with Paul, all the advantages of singleness. Others will spend all their lives struggling to come to terms with it.

The Bible teaches both the centrality of marriage and the significant place of singleness in God's purposes. Jesus brings the two together in the first section of Matthew 19, where he states that for some it is right to remain single for the sake of the kingdom of God (Matt. 19:12), a theme Paul takes up in 1 Corinthians 7. Both marriage and singleness are gifts and callings from God, and should be given back to him to be used for his glory.

In one highly significant respect, Jesus took singleness and gave us a radical new perspective on it. He himself is the archetype for the new kingdom of God, the new humanity, the new people of God, the one in whom all Christians live and whom we all follow. And he is single. In the kingdom there will be no marriage (Matt. 22:30). Each of us, as we live in Christ, is personally complete as he is complete. No longer does God have to look at Adam and say, 'It is not good for the man to be alone' (Gen. 2:18). Jesus is the new Adam; he is single, and God sees that that is very good. In Christ, a person who is single is complete. Whereas before Christ marriage may have been seen as providing the answer to loneliness and the needs for relationships and self-giving and love, in Christ and in the new community of God's people these needs are fully met. Being single and in Christ is a foretaste of the kingdom of heaven.

Rightly or wrongly, many singles feel churches put so much stress on the importance of marriage and the family that the interests and needs of single people are neglected. Clearly, care has to be taken that this does not happen; there must be no suggestion that one group in a church is of more importance than another (Jas. 2:1–13). Some churches have developed specific teaching and activity programmes for singles in answer to this need. But, ideally, churches should not need to be making significant differentiation between the groupings of people in the congregation ('This week we'll have something for marrieds, next week something for singles'). Singles and marrieds, like young and old, black and white, new converts and mature saints, should be closely integrated into the one body. If there is a time of teaching about, say, parenting, it shouldn't be designed for and attended by marrieds alone. Singles need to know the pressures of parenting; many of them will be involved with other people's children, and need to develop skills parallel to those of parents, and so on. Similarly, if there is teaching on issues of particular relevance to single people, marrieds should be concerned enough about their single sisters and brothers to want to share in it.

Helping those for whom singleness is an issue

There are perhaps four basic ways in which we can help those who find their singleness difficult to cope with. The first is to give real friendship and love, to accept them as they are and for what they are, to encourage, affirm, support and help them to be the people God wants them to be.

The second is to do all we can to make the local church or house group or cell group a true Christian community that fulfils and transcends the role of the natural family for all those in it, and, in particular, enables single people to know that they belong and are accepted and can be themselves, living the lives and exercising the gifts God has given them.

Thirdly, we can help them and others in the church to develop a biblical understanding of singleness.

These three things in themselves may be sufficient to enable them to face the many issues that their singleness raises. But a fourth way we can help them is to be ready to talk such issues through with them. In some situations, where the issues are major, we may feel that we should suggest they get the help of an experienced counsellor.

What could I say?

Acceptance and love in a true Christian community are basic; without them our words will sound pretty hollow. But, against the background of our friendship and a welcoming and affirming church fellowship, here are some things we may be able to offer them when appropriate occasions arise.

Four Bible truths to build your life on

1. As a Christian, you are an individual person who has been specifically designed and shaped by the love and power of God. You are not an accident or a freak. All the events of your life leading up to this day and every aspect of your developing personality have been in the hand of God; you are who you are because he has planned and made you. Even the things that you see as disasters he can transform into something beautiful and creative.

2. Jesus was perfect, whole and complete. He lived a perfect life, fulfilled and full of God's grace to others. And he was single. He sets the pattern for our lives. He lives in us and gives us his completeness and fullness (Col. 2:10).

3. In Christ, God has brought into being a new type of community, something richer and more lasting than the natural human family. Natural families are good, and one of his gracious gifts to the human race. But they are not permanent, they may break down, and they may clash with our loyalty to Christ (Luke

14:26). So, alongside and in some ways replacing the natural family, God has given us a new family, the community of his people in the local church or small group, with Jesus at the centre (Mark 3:34–35).

4. There is a cost to following Jesus and to allowing God to work out his purposes in our lives. But Jesus promises that each sacrifice and every price paid will in his time be rewarded a hundred times over (Mark 10:28–31).

Four things to resist

1. Resist the tendency to turn in on yourself and feel sorry for yourself. You may find you are alone a lot; but that doesn't have to make you lonely. You will probably need to make a special effort to build friendships and maintain an active social life. Self-pity is a killer; fight the insidiousness of 'if only'. Work at being thankful and rejoicing in the Lord always (Eph. 5:20; Phil. 4:4).

2. Resist the feelings of envy and bitterness. Remember that what God has given you is his best for you, and that, in his way of seeing things, it is far better than those things you envy in others or feel bitter about.

3. Resist the pressure to adopt the attitudes of those around you. Plenty of people, including parents and well-meaning friends, will try to impose their way of seeing things on you. 'There must be something wrong with you if you're not married', 'Are you still single? What a pity!', 'It must be awful being alone.' If they think that way, that is their problem; but don't let them make it your problem. Shape your thinking and attitudes according to the way God sees you, not according to their prejudice and stereotyping.

4. Resist the tendency to drift. Don't spend your life hanging around and waiting for someone to turn up. True, you don't have the predetermined structure to follow that many marrieds have: courting, wedding, mortgage, new home, jobs, first baby, second baby, larger home, and so on. But in many ways that's an advantage. As Paul found, it opens up the possibility of doing some really effective things with your life (1 Cor. 7:32–35). After all, you are you; you don't have to wait until you've got a partner to live for God's glory.

Six steps to take

1. Deliberately and decisively give yourself to God. Give him your concerns, your fears, your body and sexuality, your future, your relationships – everything you can think of. When you find yourself taking these things back, give them over to him again. Tell him that by his grace you choose to accept his purpose for your life.

2. Where you are aware of particular areas of pressure (such as the pain of seeing all your friends getting married and having children, or loneliness, or self-pity, or sexual issues), ask for an extra gift of his special grace (Jas. 4:6; 2 Cor. 12:9). Accept this gift, and let it shape your reaction.

3. Be thankful (Eph. 5:20). Cultivate an attitude of thanksgiving. Focus on the good things in your life. Thank him for the special freedoms and opportunities singleness brings. Thank him for trusting you with something that many others can't cope with. Thank him for his grace.

4. Build, cultivate, and grow. Build deep friendships; cultivate interests; grow as a person; become more like Jesus. Have a wide circle of friends; develop your career; seize opportunities; be adventurous; exploit the benefits of singleness. Show the world how wrong they are if they suggest you're a might-have-been or a reject.

5. Learn how to be a healthy sexual person without having to have intercourse. Allow God to channel your love and relationships and creative powers in ways that are wholesome and pleasing to him. God's gift of loving does not have to be repressed; express it as fully and as richly as Jesus did.

6. If you find specific issues such as bitterness or self-pity hard to deal with, get help. Find a wise Christian friend or a counsellor and talk things through together. Where appropriate, ask others to pray for you, maybe in a time of specific prayer ministry.

A helpful book

A. Hsu, *The Single Issue* (IVP)

SOLVENT ABUSE

Each week two youngsters somewhere in the UK die of 'solvent' abuse. Each day tens of thousands get high or drunk on substances such as glue, correction fluids, petrol, butane gas, thinners and antiperspirants. There are said to be over thirty such products in the average home. Mostly these substances are sniffed, with or without the use of a plastic bag; some aerosols are sprayed direct into the mouth. Most of them are not addictive in the strict sense, but some youngsters become dependent on them to give them kicks or to keep them going.

Abusing these substances is not illegal, although it is illegal for shopkeepers to supply them to people under eighteen if they are fairly sure they will be used for sniffing. The peak age for sniffing is thirteen or fourteen. Evidence of sniffing, apart from the presence of empty containers and plastic bags, is mood swings, drunken behaviour, loss of appetite, headaches, a sore throat and runny nose, and spots on the nose and mouth.

Children frequently try sniffing for fun, or to be in with the crowd. They continue to do it because they like the effects or because it provides a means of escape from real life and its pressures.

There is no requirement to inform the authorities of cases of solvent abuse, but where youngsters are involved we may feel it right to discuss the issue with their parents.

Helping those who abuse solvents

Resist the temptation to judge or to condemn them, or to tell them how silly they are. Adopt the view that experimenting with these things is a phase they are passing through and need to move out of.

If they have been using them for a time, persuade them to have a medical check-up.

Most youngsters who try sniffing give it up of their own accord. Those who continue to practise it generally do so because of other factors such as personal needs or external pressures. To help people like this, we shall need to locate and tackle the underlying issue.

Where boredom is a factor, if possible find positive things for them to do.

Help Christian youngsters develop their understanding of the implications of the fact that their body belongs not just to them but is a temple of the Holy Spirit (1 Cor. 6:19–20).

Youngsters need affirmation. Boost their self-esteem. Provided you are not critical or condemning, the very fact that you are showing interest in them will help towards this.

What could I say?

Watch out. Sniffing seems harmless but it can be dangerous; it kills, and it can cause permanent damage to your body.

You don't have to do it just because others do. You can resist the trend. Better still, you can set the trend in the opposite direction.

You'll only ever get one body. Don't mess it up now just for the sake of a quick high.

There are plenty of better things to do when you feel bored. Do something constructive you enjoy doing. Go for a ride on your bike. Phone a lonely friend and have a chat. Do something for the old person across the road.

Give your body over to God. Let him fill it with his goodness. He's big enough to give you all it takes to live a great life, with all the kicks you could ever want.

See also **addiction**, **drug abuse**.

Christian organizations that offer help to abusers

Hope UK, 25(f) Copperfield Street, London SE1 0EN.
020 7938 0848. www.hopeuk.org
Life for the World Trust, Wakefield Building, Gomm Road,
High Wycombe HP13 7DJ. 01494 462 008.
www.doveuk.com/lfw
Yeldall Christian Centre, Yeldall Manor, Hare Hatch, Reading
RG10 9XR. 0118 940 1093. www.yeldall.org.uk

STEPFAMILIES

Parenting (and being children) is no easy task. When it is overlaid with all the extra complications of a stepfamily it becomes a huge task. Step-parents and stepchildren need all the help and support they can get.

What could I say to those becoming step-parents?

Welcome your new children. Be sure that you reach the point where you can accept them as a beautiful gift from God; firmly reject any thought that they are a rather unwelcome part of the new marriage package. Make prayer for them and for your relationship with them a priority.

Be sensitive to your special position. Accept that your role is going to be different from that of a natural parent, especially in situations where the children are in touch with their original parent, or where they are in their teens. Talk through your role with your partner, and with the children if they are old enough. Work out basic principles on things such as discipline, and stick to them.

Present a united front. Ensure that the signals that you and your partner give to the children are consistent in all areas. You will probably not agree totally on all issues, but it is vital to sink any differences and present a united front to the children; if there are weaknesses they will soon find them and use them to play one parent off against the other.

Commit yourself to continuing to work at building your relationship with the children. It takes a lot of time, effort and grace, and often there are major barriers to be overcome. Be patient, careful and gentle. Be especially sensitive to the fact that they will continue to feel hurt at the loss of the parent you are replacing, or even betrayed by her or him.

Be sensitive to the special needs of the children. Remember that, even if the natural parent is still living, the children will probably be going through a grieving process for their lost parent which may take years to run its course (see **bereavement**). View things like outbursts of anger or bouts of depression in this light, and do all you can to help them through the process.

Love and love and love. It is a statistical fact that stepchildren receive less parental attention than natural children, while in fact they almost certainly need more. So make a special effort to show them extra interest, love, affirmation and support. Make a point of spending time with them, doing things together, and being interested in what interests them.

Get help where needed. For example, where there is still a strong attachment between the children and the parent you have replaced, you may find that consciously or unconsciously they are rejecting you as an expression of their loyalty to him or her. In this and in other problem situations, specialist family counselling may be needed. It is vital to be aware that they are not basically rejecting you, and to avoid reacting in a negative way.

Be very sensitive to the issues that will arise over the arrival of a new baby. Stepchildren will almost certainly find this a threatening and difficult time. Do everything you can to help them through it. Keep a careful watch on yourselves as parents to ensure that you continue to give the same amount of love and attention to the stepchildren through this time.

Beware. Sadly, sexual abuse is much more common in stepfamilies than in natural families. Take stringent measures to avoid any risk in this area.

Talk with other step-parents. Learn from their experiences, and even from their mistakes. Get all the help you can. Join a local stepfamily support group, or attend a conference run by the National Stepfamily Association.

What could I say to stepchildren?

Talk to someone about how you feel. You may have all sorts of feelings about your new parent and new family. If you can, talk about these with someone you can trust, such as a youth leader or a school counsellor.

Do all you can to make the new family a success. Taking on a new parent and family is a big step. It is rarely easy, but in many cases it works well. Whatever your feelings about it, give your new family the best chance you can of being a success. After all, it is your family, and you'll be much better off if it is a happy family. Work hard at welcoming and getting to know and love your new parent. If you find it hard to accept him or her as a parent, try treating him or her as an uncle or aunt or special adult friend.

Pray for your new parent and new family. God has a great way of picking up broken pieces and making something new and good out of them. Ask him to do this for you. Ask him to help you play your part in this.

Be especially careful if you feel hurt and angry at the loss of your old family. There's no point in letting this spoil your new one. If you can, talk about these feelings with your parents or an adult you can trust.

If you can and wish to, keep in touch with your parent and grandparents and so on who are not in your new family. Look on these as your extra family, so that you actually have two families to enjoy.

See also **parenting**, **remarriage**.

A useful book

M. Williams, *Stepfamilies* (Lion)

Resource

Parentline Plus, 520 Highgate Studios, 53–79 Highgate Road, Kentish Town, London NW5 1TL. 020 7284 5500. Helpline 0808 800 2222. www.parentlineplus.org.uk

STILLBIRTH

In some ways the death of a baby at birth can be the hardest form of bereavement. Months of expectation and anticipation end in sorrow and bewilderment. The moment that should bring joy and new life brings pain and death. The awfulness of loss cannot be offset by treasured memories and the sense of a life well lived, as when an older person dies.

There is also a special element of loneliness for the parents. For most other people the unborn baby has not really started to exist, and thus they may tend to minimize its loss. For the parents, and especially the mother, the child is very real, and the loss is very great.

In the UK the dividing-line between a miscarriage and a stillbirth is the twenty-fourth week of pregnancy, but this is an arbitrary definition, and the emotions at miscarriage and at stillbirth will be very similar (see **miscarriage**).

Suggestions for helping those who lose a baby by stillbirth

Show that you realize that stillbirth is a shattering experience. Counter the tendency to minimize the loss. Encourage others to offer special love and support to the parents and close family.

Encourage the parents to get all the help they can, from medical staff, minister, counsellor, others who have gone through the same experience, and organizations like SANDS (Stillbirth and Neonatal Death Society; see below).

Encourage them to talk about the baby by name, to treasure her or him as a person and part of the family. It may be helpful to compile a simple record of the baby's life, with details of the pregnancy, photographs, handprint and footprint, possibly lock of hair, documentation, record of the funeral, and so on.

It is still not always possible to pinpoint the cause of a stillbirth. Be aware that not knowing what has caused the death will put an extra strain on the parents, and on their decision whether or not to go for another pregnancy. Encourage them to talk with medical staff about these issues.

Encourage the parents to talk about their feelings, either to you or to a trained person such as a minister or counsellor. Be aware that the shock and pain of losing a baby will cause a range of emotions in the parents and close family, towards themselves, the medical staff, other parents and their babies, and God. Be understanding; make it easy for them to off-load and work through such things as anger, guilt, jealousy, bitterness and fears.

Be especially sensitive over situations that may trigger the expression of grief, such as seeing someone else's baby, or an anniversary.

Be aware that the loss of a baby can put a considerable strain on a marriage. Sadly, a significant number of marriages break up following a stillbirth. Be alert to any danger signs, such as blame or anger directed against a partner, and encourage the couple to get help.

Keep an eye on other children in the family. They too will go through a process of mourning, and will need extra love and assurance.

Remember that the grieving process may well be a long one. Be patient and understanding, especially when an event such as seeing someone else's baby triggers an expression of grief. If you feel concerned that the process of grieving is too slow or moving in an unhelpful direction, talk with someone skilled in bereavement counselling, and, if necessary, encourage the parents to see a trained helper.

What could I say?

As in any form of bereavement, your love and acceptance and support will often be much more meaningful than your words. But, at appropriate times, these suggestions and those under **bereavement** may be helpful.

Resist the pressure to minimize your loss. Even if others treat it as a small thing, accept that it is a major bereavement.

Get as much help as you can. There are those who can help you as you work through the range of emotions you will experience as you grieve for your baby: medical staff, a specialist counsellor, your minister, help groups, friends, others who have lost a child, and so on.

Talk about the baby. Use his or her name. He or she is a person, a member of the family. Remember the Christian belief that children who die at birth are now in the presence of God in heaven. We have the hope that this is only a temporary separation; you will meet your child again, perhaps as a perfectly mature adult, in heaven.

Some things not to say

'It's not as bad as losing someone older.'
'I know how you feel.'
'Don't worry, you'll soon get over it.'
'Have another baby soon, and you'll forget this one.'

Helpful books

M. Rank, *Free to Grieve* (Bethany House)
E. Storkey, *Losing a Child* (Lion)

A support organization

Stillbirth and Neonatal Death Society (SANDS), 28 Portland Place, London, W1N 4DE. Administration: 020 7436 7940. Helpline: 020 7436 5881. www.uk-sands.org

STRESS

There are two factors in stress: external pressure or pressures, and our personal response. We can all cope with a certain amount of pressure without feeling stressed. Indeed, a degree of pressure generally has a good effect: the approaching exam makes the student work harder. But as pressure increases or continues for a long time, we pass a threshold, and we begin to cope less well. The extra resources we have called on to meet the pressure are used up. We no longer have what it takes to meet it, and instead of stimulating us it destroys us.

It is possible to feel stress at almost anything, from traffic noise to cancer, and from debt to demanding children. For some people a thing that is minor in itself may trigger a stress response because they associate it with something more serious. Someone who was injured in a house fire, for example, may feel stress at the sound of flames in the living-room fireplace. Others appear to have the kind of personality that can take almost anything without any sign of a stress response.

City life and the pressures of a high-speed technological society are contemporary pressures which have caused increases in stress. But it is generally accepted that in our present culture the biggest increase in stress is in the area of our daily work.

Symptoms of stress vary widely. Since stress is basically the fail-ure of body and mind and feelings to cope, they can be physical, mental and emotional, including headaches, indigestion, other aches and pains, poor resistance to infection, sleep problems, inability to concentrate or think clearly, loss of perspective, for-getfulness, lethargy, frustration, irritability, loss of control over anger or tears, or loss of vision.

Stress unrelieved over a long period will lead to burnout, a con-dition marked by physical and emotional exhaustion, and total inability to cope.

What could I say to those subject to stress?

The best way to deal with stress is to prevent it building up in the first place. Here are some suggestions you might make to those who are subject to stress.

Reduce the number of stressful factors in your life. None of us can get rid of them completely, nor would we want to. But some pressures we can do without. Draw up a list of all the pressures you face. Classify them as 'unavoidable', 'possibly avoidable' and 'avoidable', Select some from the last two categories and take positive steps to remove them from your life.

Build more relaxation and exercise into your living.

Find ways of switching off. If your mind keeps going back to stressful issues and churning them over, learn to take positive steps to divert it to something else. Get absorbed in a hobby. Plan a holi-day or a new project. Read a book. Pray.

Get in touch with nature. Spend time with plants and wildlife. Get in tune with the rhythm of the seasons. Gaze at the glory of the Milky Way. Walk regularly in the country or a park. Stop and look at things. Plant a garden. Talk to the trees.

Be thankful. Thank God for each new day, and for all the good things in life. Appreciate the world. Make a point of thanking other people.

Opt out of the consumer rat-race. Ignore the adverts. Throw away the junk mail. Let the trendsetters do what they like. Live simply.

Reassess your priorities. Live for the things that really matter, and let the others look after themselves. Spend more time with God. Train yourself to look at things as he sees them.

Keep your job in its rightful place. Don't let it dominate your life or your family. Give it its forty-five hours, or whatever, and keep the remaining 123 for yourself, for your family, for God, and for others.

Where you have to face unavoidable pressure, meet it as a positive challenge. Pressure is not stress. Stress only comes in if you make a stressful response. Commit yourself to respond without getting stressed. Let the pressure stretch you, excite you, bring out the best in you, and push you to heights of achievement you've not reached before. But refuse to let it stress you.

What could I say to those who are stressed?

Where the person we are trying to help is already showing signs of being stressed, we may wish to make further suggestions:

Accept that you need to take firm action. Your stress response is destroying your effectiveness, and if not checked will lead to burnout.

Get help. See a doctor or a counsellor.

Give yourself space. Take a break. If you find yourself arguing that you are indispensable, reply that if you go on as you are going you'll be seriously ill in a few months' time and will have to take a much longer break.

Be gentle with yourself. You have drained your physical and mental and emotional resources and are running on empty. You need time for the damage to be healed and the system refilled.

But also be firm with yourself. When your mind reverts to the old, stressful thought patterns, shut it up. Divert it into patterns that will heal and help. Work at developing wholesome interests and activities. Discipline yourself to take exercise – gentle at first, but developing.

Begin to work at sorting things out. When you feel able, with the help of someone who knows you well, list the pressures that underlie your stress. Wherever possible, find ways of relieving these pressures. Seek to get the others into a realistic perspective. Hand them all over to God.

Get down to the root issues. With the help of a counsellor or wise friend, analyse why you have made a stress response to these pressures. Is it simply a matter of bad self-management? Or is there some factor in you that makes you susceptible to a stressful response? If so, get help in dealing with it. Think through ways of making a non-stressed response to these pressures in the future.

Do a stock-take on your life. Reassess your priorities. Assess your coping threshold and plan a lifestyle that is within it.

Take time to rediscover God's purposes for your life.

Jesus on stress

I tell you, do not worry about your life, what you will eat or drink: or about your body, what you will wear. Is not life more important than food, and the body more important than clothes? Look at the birds of the air; they do not sow or reap or store away in barns, and yet your heavenly Father feeds them. Are you not much more valuable than they? Who of you by worrying can add a single hour to his life?

And why do you worry about clothes? See how the lilies of the field grow. They do not labour or spin. Yet I tell you that not even Solomon in all his splendour was dressed like one of these … So do not worry, saying, 'What shall we eat?' or 'What shall we drink?' or 'What shall we wear?' For the pagans run after all these things, and your heavenly Father knows that you need them. But seek first his kingdom and his righteousness, and all these things will be given to you as well (Matt. 6:25–29, 31–33).

See also **burnout**.

Some Christian books on stress

S. Chalke, *Managing your Time* (Kingsway)
G. Davies, *Stress* (Kingsway)
C. and F. Munro, *A Place of Rest* (CWR)
C. Powell and G. Barker, *Unloading the Overload* (Gazelle)

SUFFERING

Our culture finds the issue of suffering a huge problem. The presence of pain and evil in the world is used by atheists as a major argument against the existence of God. Christians struggle to keep their faith when confronted with setbacks or illness or death. Books are written on why bad things happen to good people.

Former generations did not find suffering such a problem; nor is it a problem in some non-western cultures today. In biblical times the issue was faced and explored, and a number of insights gained; but, again, in the New Testament in particular, suffering was not seen as a major, intractable problem, but rather as something to which God has provided the answer and which we can therefore accept and cope with in a positive way.

Perhaps underlying our culture's attitude to suffering is the assumption that we each have a right to unbroken health, happiness and well-being throughout our lives. Anything that infringes this right must be an evil, and it is the responsibility of a good God to remove all evil from us. If he fails to do so, something has gone seriously wrong.

It is interesting that this attitude has developed in a culture where, it could be argued, much suffering has been virtually eliminated. We have dentists to deal with our toothache, pills to take away our pains, hospitals to cure our illnesses. While in former generations gruesome death was a familiar visitor to every home (all parents expected at least half their children to die in childhood), many people today live for decades without experiencing bereavement, and even when death comes it is generally carefully packaged to cover up its nastiness.

Underlying the Bible's teaching on suffering are two great truths. The first is that God is God. In the last analysis we have to allow that he may do whatever he chooses to do. He is not required to shape his purposes according to what we might think will give us personally the maximum amount of happiness. Rather, he shapes the details of the universe, including the events of our lives, according to his ultimate and perfect purposes. If, in the short term, these appear unacceptable to us, it is we who have to give way and say, 'Not my will, but yours', not the other way round. God is God, and before him we have to bow.

The book of Job, a great theological poem which faces the issue of suffering in its starkest form, ends up with wonder and worship at the greatness and glory of God, whose ways are beyond our understanding. This is not an admission that there is no meaning or answer to suffering; rather, it is an affirmation of the perfect goodness and greatness of God's purposes, even though they may puzzle or hurt us. And these purposes, though worked out on a huge canvas, include personal love and care for every individual.

The second great biblical truth is the message of the cross. So far from remaining apart from the hurt and darkness of our world, God has come and taken it upon himself. He has suffered, and through his suffering the power of evil over us has been broken; suffering is no longer evil.

Some of the New Testament teaching on suffering

> Blessed are you who are poor
> for yours is the kingdom of God.
> Blessed are you who hunger now,
> for you will be satisfied.
> Blessed are you who weep now,
> for you will laugh.
> Blessed are you when men hate you,
> when they exclude you and insult you
> and reject your name as evil,
> because of the Son of Man.

Rejoice in that day and leap for joy, because great is your reward in heaven (Luke 6:20–23).

As he went along, he saw a man blind from birth. His disciples asked him, 'Rabbi, who sinned, this man or his parents, that he was born blind?'

'Neither this man nor his parents sinned,' said Jesus, 'but this happened so that the work of God might be displayed in his life' (John 9:1–3).

Every branch that does bear fruit he prunes so that it will be even more fruitful (John 15:2).

We rejoice in the hope of the glory of God. Not only so, but we also rejoice in our sufferings, because we know that suffering produces perseverance; perseverance, character; and character, hope. And hope does not disappoint us, because God has poured out his love into our hearts by the Holy Spirit, whom he has given us (Rom. 5:2–5).

… our present sufferings are not worth comparing with the glory that will be revealed in us … trouble or hardship or persecution or famine or nakedness or danger or sword … in all these things we are more than conquerors through him who loved us (Rom. 8:18, 35, 37).

Where, O death, is your victory? … thanks be to God! He gives us the victory through our Lord Jesus Christ (1 Cor. 15:55–56).

… we do not lose heart. Though outwardly we are wasting away, yet inwardly we are being renewed day by day. For our light and momentary troubles are achieving for us an eternal glory that far outweighs them all. So we fix our eyes not on what is seen, but on what is unseen. For what is seen is temporary, but what is unseen is eternal (2 Cor. 4:16–18).

… there was given me a thorn in my flesh, a messenger of Satan, to torment me. Three times I pleaded with the Lord to take it away from me. But he said to me, 'My grace is sufficient for you, for my power is made perfect in weakness.' Therefore I will boast all the more gladly about my weaknesses, so that Christ's power may rest on me. That is why, for Christ's sake, I delight in weaknesses, in insults, in hardships, in persecutions, in difficulties. For when I am weak, then I am strong (2 Cor. 12:7–10).

I want to know Christ and the power of his resurrection and the fellowship of sharing in his sufferings, becoming like him in his death, and so, somehow, to attain to the resurrection from the dead (Phil. 3:10–11).

Endure hardship as discipline; God is treating you as sons (Heb. 12:7).

Consider it pure joy ... whenever you face trials of many kinds, because you know that the testing of your faith develops perseverance. Perseverance must finish its work so that you may be mature and complete, not lacking anything (Jas. 1:2–4).

Helping those who are struggling with suffering

Never minimize the pain or pressure they feel. Even if we sense they are overreacting, we need to accept that the issue is a major one to them. Our task is to help them face the suffering and allow it to be transformed by God, not to act as though it is not there.

Talk with people about what they are suffering. Encourage them to express their feelings. Provide a listening ear and a shoulder to cry on.

The primary need of those who are suffering is love and support, not theological explanations of why they are suffering. The explanations have a place, but we need to give ourselves first, and demonstrate the reality of the love of God through our lives and the lives of God's people.

Point out that God knows and understands what they are going through, and shares in its pain and hurt. Point them to incidents in the life of Jesus where he went through a parallel experience.

Assure them that God's love is constant. Our feelings and experiences come and go, but God has promised he will never fail us. Broaden their vision of the breadth and length and height and depth of the love of Christ (Eph. 3:18). Gently help them to put their trust in God's faithfulness and love rather than in their experiences or feelings.

Should they feel that their suffering is a punishment from God for their sins, or a sign that God is upset with them in some way, some of the following suggestions may be helpful:

- Gently ask them if they have specific sins in mind. If they have, check that they have brought these to God in repentance and received his forgiveness. If they have not, help them to do so.
- If there are no specific sins, but just a general sense of sinfulness, help them to bring that to God, perhaps in a time of prayer ministry.
- Help them to grasp the Bible's teaching on grace and forgiveness, stressing the completeness and totality of the cleansing God gives. You might use verses like Romans 8:1, Ephesians 1:7–8 or Isaiah 44:22.
- Stress the constancy of the grace and love of God; he does not have 'off' days; he doesn't change according to our circumstances.
- Point out that Jesus and Paul both suffered greatly, and that their suffering was in no way a sign of God's displeasure or neglect.

When appropriate, talk with them about the nature of suffering, and the Bible's view of it. Help them to accept that as Christians we should view it biblically, rather than accept the mindset of our culture that sees it as an unacceptable infringement of our right to total happiness.

Help them to begin to grasp the Bible's view of suffering. Points you might mention include:

- God is sovereign. Jesus is on the throne of the universe, and all things, including evil things, are under his feet (Eph. 1:22). Nothing happens to Christians by accident, or without God's knowledge.
- Christ's victory on the cross has not removed suffering from the

world, but has broken its power to harm us (Col. 2:15). For the Christian, the powers of evil cannot use suffering to destroy; on the contrary, God now uses suffering to enrich.

- Just as Easter Day transformed the disaster of Good Friday into the most wonderful thing the world had experienced, so the cross and resurrection transform suffering for the Christian. Christ's redeeming power buys it back from evil and makes it good.
- God is totally committed to the ultimate good of all his children and has promised that he will work everything to this end (Rom. 8:28).
- Not everything he does will be pleasant or even welcome to us (Heb. 12:5–7); the pruning-knife can be painful (John 15:2).
- Everything we suffer God has suffered in Christ (Is. 53:4). He knows and understands and is with us in the pain and hurt.
- God could take any suffering away from us, and he will do so if that is for the greatest good. Where we feel it right, we should pray that he will do this, but always with the proviso, 'Not my will, but yours.'
- Where he doesn't remove the suffering, we can be sure he has some special purpose in it, either for us specifically, or for others through us. Given that fact, if at all possible, we should accept the suffering as a privilege, and even rejoice in it (Rom. 5:3; 2 Cor. 12:10; Jas. 1:2).
- Where he calls us to experience suffering, he promises us his grace and strength to go through it for his glory. See, for example, Psalm 23:4; Isaiah 43:1–3.

A major problem for many is that their particular suffering seems pointless. They could accept it if it was clearly suffering for the sake of the kingdom of God and producing some obvious good. But much of our suffering does not produce obvious good, and is not clearly for the sake of the kingdom. We can see no point in it. The Bible's answer to this is that for the Christian no suffering is ever pointless; it can all be used by God for good, and everything that God is doing in our lives is for the sake of his kingdom; God does not recognize a religious/secular or Christian life/ ordinary life divide in us. He is at work in all the circumstances and situations of our lives, allowing us to be tested and refined and shaped and made more like Jesus through every experience, whether good or bad. The story of Joseph, culminating in his comment in Genesis 50:20, is a useful illustration of the way God uses apparent meaningless disasters for good. Among other examples are the cross, as viewed by the disciples on Good Friday evening, and the death of Stephen and the persecution that arose as a result.

Help them to apply the biblical teaching to themselves and their own suffering. Stress that it is impossible for us to know for sure just what good thing God is going to bring out of this particular experience. Sometimes, however, we might have an idea ('God is letting this happen to me to teach me patience' or 'to give me an opportunity to show love to my enemies' or 'to enable me to show how Christians respond to suffering'), and it may be helpful to hold on to this. But the point remains that most of God's purposes are unknown to us, and many of them will be so throughout our lives.

Enable others to share in the sufferings, in both their pain and their privilege. See 1 Corinthians 12:26, Galatians 6:2 and Romans 12:15. Corporate carrying of the burden not only makes it lighter, but all learn together from the experience and help each other to grow.

Use the power of prayer. Mobilize prayer support by individuals; pray with the sufferer; pray as a group. View prayer not as an escape hatch, but as a means of furthering the gracious and creative work of God in the situation. Take Jesus in Gethsemane and Paul's 'thorn in the flesh' as models for praying (see Luke 22:39–46 and 2 Cor. 12:7–10). Ask clearly and in faith that, where possible, the suffering will be taken away. But leave the decision to God, and, where he so guides, accept that his answer is 'No' and that he is working out some special purpose through it.

Watch for signs of negative results of suffering, such as bitterness or loss of faith. If possible, deal with these things before they develop and become serious (Heb. 12:15).

Two books on suffering

S. Cassidy, *Why Suffering?* (Lion Pocketguide)
S. Chalke, *The Truth about Suffering* (Kingsway)

SUICIDE

Every day 275 people in Britain attempt to end their lives. Not all of them succeed, but many of them do. Every day a far greater number consider the possibility of suicide. Many of these never go on to attempt it, but some of them do.

The knowledge that someone we know is thinking about suicide places a heavy responsibility on us. Even if we suspect that there is little possibility that he or she will reach the point of attempting it, we must never ignore the possibility. Preventative action must be taken.

But, equally, we need to remember that in the last analysis those who take their lives are responsible for their own actions. We do not have to carry the burden of responsibility for their death. We should never allow them to blackmail us emotionally, either before or after the deed.

There are many reasons why people attempt to take their lives. Perhaps the main one is because they have lost hope; they can see no other way out of an intolerable situation. But people can also kill themselves to spite others, or in a last pitiful attempt to gain attention or to manipulate a situation, or out of a desire to rejoin a loved one who has died. Often a suicide attempt is a 'cry for help', with no real intention to go the whole way; tragically, such 'cries for help' do often end in death.

Although some people, such as those prone to depression, are more at risk, anyone could reach the point where they think of taking their own lives. Never classify someone as a non-suicidal type; it can be that those we would least expect, without any warning, will take their lives.

The possibility of suicide depends on the availability of means. In the 1960s there was a significant drop in the number of suicides due to the introduction of natural gas. Up to then the typical British way of killing yourself was to stick your head in a gas oven. Unlike 'town' gas, the new gas was non-toxic. There has been a parallel drop in numbers since the introduction of catalytic converters in many cars; the exhaust fumes are considerably less toxic. Clearly, a jar of pills on the bedside cabinet or a gun in the drawer will make it more likely that at a moment of deep darkness the attempt will be made.

Helping those you think might be contemplating suicide

Do something. Don't just leave it. Contact their relatives, or someone suitable at their school or place of work. If they are seriously depressed or exhibiting disturbed behaviour patterns, contact a doctor; there may be need of help in a psychiatric unit.

Talk to them about the problems and pressures that have driven them to think of suicide as the way of escape. Demonstrate to them that it is not the only answer and certainly not the best one. Point out that suicide is a very permanent answer to problems that, though large, are only temporary. Show what a devastating effect their suicide would have on their family and friends. Offer help and hope.

If you can, remove any possible means of suicide, such as tablets.

Be available, or make sure someone else is, at any time. Give them the Samaritans' phone number (0345 90 90 90). Encourage them to contact you or someone else when they are feeling particularly low. Assure them they can always talk to someone at any hour of day and night.

Be a patient listener. Keep offering love, acceptance, support and reasons for living. Many suicidal people urgently need the security of a stable relationship in which they feel accepted and loved.

Pray for and with the person. Get others to pray, and tell the person they are praying. Suicidal people often feel unable to pray for themselves, but the knowledge others are praying offers them hope. Regularly place them through prayer in God's keeping; you don't have to carry the burden of anxiety over what they may do – hand it and them over to God (1 Pet. 5.7).

If necessary, ensure they are not left alone.

Do all you can to ensure that the issues that have driven them to think of suicide are dealt with as far as is possible. This may involve getting help over external factors like school bullying or a highly stressed job or marriage problems. Or it may be a matter of arranging professional counselling to deal with emotional or personality needs, such as fear, self-rejection or depression.

Make a special point of affirming and encouraging them. Speak to them of God's care and love for them; demonstrate that love in your own life. Give them hope. If their faith is low, carry them on the shoulders of your faith. Gently build up their self-confidence. Teach them coping skills. Help them to form balanced and mature judgments.

What could I say?

Accept that as you are at the moment, you are not the best person to decide the way out of your problems. The pressure you are under means that you are not really able to think straight. You need someone to advise and help you.

Find someone you can trust and talk to them about how you are feeling. It doesn't matter whether it is someone you know or a stranger, such as a counsellor or the Samaritans.

There is an answer. However big your problems seem to you, remember that with help you will be able to find an answer. Many people with the same problems have found answers. God, in his love and grace, is ready to show you his way through.

I'm going to pray for you. Without breaking any confidences, I'll get others to pray for you. Even if your faith is very small, we have strong faith in a strong God, and are going to ask him to keep you, especially in your darkest moments, and bring you through.

Choose life. At a time when your mind is clear, make a definite decision that you wish to live and not die. Get rid of any means by which you have thought of taking your life. If you feel you can't really trust yourself, get someone to stay with you so that you are never left alone.

Use the lifelines others offer you. Make a contract with those who are standing by you that you will always be honest and contact them when the pressure to take your life begins to mount up.

When you feel ready, with the help of your friends or your counsellor, set yourself to begin to crack the problems. Accept that it will take time and may be hard work. But with God's help you will do it.

Helping those who have been bereaved through suicide

Our culture still tends to attach a stigma to suicide. To counter this, and because of the awfulness of the experience they are going through, those who have been bereaved will need special love, acceptance and support, as well as all the normal help and support we would give to any bereaved person (see bereavement).

Encourage them to be honest and express their feelings. These will range widely, and may well be bewildering and distressing. For example, they will almost certainly feel anger, and may find that it is directed not only at the circumstances that have caused the suicide, but also at the person who has committed suicide. Help them to understand what is going on as they face the shock and pain of their loss; assist them in off-loading their emotions; be patient and very gracious.

Urge them to use all the resources for help they can find, including their doctor, minister, counsellor, and specialist help and support groups. Because of our society's attitude to suicide, they may tend to try and hush the thing up, to withdraw and hide themselves away. While respecting their right to privacy, we must discourage any withdrawal that is in effect a refusal to face up to what has happened.

Just as many bereaved people go through a period of denial, those who have lost a loved one through suicide may go through a period where they are able to accept the death but deny that it was suicide, insisting, say, that it was an accident or a 'cry for help'. Unless such denial has damaging repercussions, we may well feel that it is in fact a helpful way of lessening the awfulness of their loss, and so we should not be quick to try and correct it.

Those close to a person who has committed suicide, especially parents of a young person, often carry a heavy burden of guilt. This may well be an expression of anger turned in upon themselves; but, very often, there is an element of warranted guilt: they could have done more to prevent the suicide. Where this is so, we should encourage them to talk things through with a minister or Christian counsellor (see **guilt**).

As with any bereavement, encourage them to talk about the person who has died and to treasure memories of her or him. Help them not to let the fact of the suicide overshadow everything else; that was one brief action; there is a whole life to remember and treasure.

The grieving process is likely to be more intense and longer than in the case of a normal bereavement. As far as you can, keep in close touch throughout. Watch for any danger signs, such as acute depression, and ensure appropriate help is given. Be aware that once there has been one suicide in a family or close circle of friends, the chances of another are considerably increased.

What could I say?

You are facing bereavement in one of its darkest forms. All the signs and stages of grief and loss and hurt are likely to be intensified. You will need all the help you can get. But, remember, others have walked this dark road and come safely through.

Get help. Get in touch straight away with a trusted friend, minister or counsellor, with whom you can be open about your feelings, and who will stand by you and help carry the load.

Make the most of all the support that is available to you. Find a local support group for those bereaved through suicide. Make the most of all their resources. Ask your house group or circle of Christian friends to stand by you and support you in prayer and in every way. You may feel tempted to withdraw, perhaps because of a sense of shame. Don't do this. At this time, of all times, you need the help of others.

Try not to worry about other people's reactions. Some people cannot cope with the concept of suicide and may show this in their attitude to you. Try to ignore this; it is their problem, not yours.

Go gently on yourself as your body and emotions react to the awfulness of what has happened. You will probably go through a period of shock and unreality, which could last for weeks. Don't worry about this; it is a fairly normal reaction.

Don't be too concerned if you find yourself feeling considerable anger. This is basically anger at the awfulness of what has happened; try not to let too much of it be turned on to people or on to the person who has died. This can be very destructive. Talk to your minister and counsellor about your feelings of anger and let him or her help you off-load them in a constructive way.

In the same way, deal wisely with feelings of guilt. You may well find strong guilt feelings arising. But remember that you do not have to carry the responsibility for other people's actions; what they do is, in the last analysis, their choice and their responsibility. But if you feel that you bear part of the responsibility, talk with your minister or a wise Christian friend who will help you find God's forgiveness and healing.

Take special care when you feel down or stressed. Those who have lost someone close to them through suicide may themselves be more likely to attempt to take their lives, and parents who have lost a child through suicide are more likely to suffer a marriage break-up. Guard yourself carefully against such things.

See also **anger, bereavement, guilt.**

A helpful book

G. L and G. C. Carr, *After the Storm: Hope in the Wake of Suicide* (IVP)

Resource

Samaritans, 10 The Grove, Slough SL1 1QP. Administration: 01753 216 500. Helpline: 0345 90 90 90. www.samaritans.org.uk

TEENAGE PREGNANCY OUTSIDE MARRIAGE

Perhaps one quarter of all teenage girls become pregnant. Some of these are married; most are not; many are under age. Some of the pregnancies are deliberate; many are accidental. Some of the girls will have their baby and care for it; others will have their baby and reject and neglect it; others will have an abortion; a few will arrange an adoption.

Unmarried teenage girls get pregnant for a number of reasons. They may be sexually uninformed or misinformed. They may have been seduced. They may have had unprotected intercourse, possibly under the influence of alcohol or drugs. They may have used contraceptives that failed; the failure rate of condoms among teenagers is said to be over 10% over a one-year period.

But very often they deliberately choose to get pregnant. Again, there may be a number of reasons for this. It could be an expression of adolescent rebellion. Or a way of getting out of school. Or an attempt to demonstrate that they are adults. Or a way of holding on to a partner. Or the result of a desperate need to love and to be loved.

Though it is generally accepted that parenting requires maturity and that children of teenagers are likely to face more pressures than those of older parents, there is no reason why teenagers should not make excellent parents. Indeed, teenage marriages, and particularly teenage brides, were common in biblical times; Mary the mother of Jesus was very probably a teenager when she became pregnant.

In seeking to help unmarried pregnant teenagers, and their partners, our main concern will be the well-being of the baby and of the parent(s) in the weeks and months ahead. This does not mean that we cannot express our sadness and disapproval at what they have done; but we need to do this in a way that does not increase their guilt and feelings of rejection towards the baby. Ideally, we need to help them come to a point of true repentance and confession and of receiving the forgiveness and grace of God. They can then go forward with the pregnancy, freed, as far as is possible, from remorse, guilt, feelings of rejection, and the like.

Helping unmarried teenagers with a pregnancy

Be aware of the many conflicting feelings and emotions the girl will be feeling. Pregnancy is in any case a time of emotional upheaval; to this may be added feelings of guilt, fear, shame, anger and so on.

Ensure that she has someone to talk to with whom she can be really honest, and who will help her cope with her feelings. Remember that it is possible for a baby to suffer damage if the mother is seriously stressed or emotionally unstable during pregnancy.

Pray with her, praying especially for the baby. If possible arrange a time when some of the leaders of the church can pray with the girl and her partner, putting the whole situation into God's hands, and asking him to work out his own purposes of grace in each life.

If there is pressure on her to consider an abortion, do what you can to ensure she gets wise and balanced advice.

If the girl and her partner decide to get married, do all you can to ensure that they get adequate marriage preparation.

If the girl plans to keep her baby and be a single parent, help her to set in place structures to support her in such a major undertaking.

Watch for signs of continuing guilt or the like, and if necessary encourage her to talk things through with a counsellor.

Where the girl is very young, remember the additional pressures of her changing emotions as she goes through adolescence and copes with issues of education.

Be aware of the needs of her parents. They are likely to feel anger, guilt, profound disappointment and shame. Make sure there are people standing by them and giving them the needed support.

See also **abortion**, **anger**, **guilt**, **marriage preparation**, **single parents**.

TERMINAL ILLNESS

Very few people escape the experience of caring for a loved one who is terminally ill. Many of us will ourselves have to face death as a result of a period of illness. This is one of the darkest roads we have to walk, yet even in the darkness, love and faith and hope can bring light.

Both the terminally ill person and those closest to her or him will go through a range of reactions to the prospect of death and all that it means. This is not a fixed process, though there is often something of a pattern. It is helpful to realize that these are normal reactions to the prospect of death that almost everybody in this situation goes through.

1. Denial. Our bodies and minds are so made that our first reaction to the prospect of death is to deny it: 'This can't be happening to me', 'The diagnosis must be wrong.' Such denial in the short term has a helpful cushioning effect: the news is so bad we can't take it all on board at once, so we absorb it by stages. If it goes on too long, however, such denial is unhelpful; when we are ready, we need to face up to the prospect of death.

2. Anger. We are naturally hostile to the evil of death and all the suffering it brings. But since it is not easy to express hostility to an abstract concept like death, our anger frequently comes out in other ways. We feel anger at the doctor for not diagnosing the cancer sooner, or at God for allowing this to happen to us, or we lash out inexplicably at those who are nearest to us. Such expressions of anger can be very disturbing, especially if they are out of character. It is important to understand why they arise, and to do what we can to ensure they are channelled positively rather than destructively.

3. Fighting. Denial and anger are both expressions of our basic rejection of the prospect of death. So is a fighting spirit: 'I'm not going to let this thing beat me.' Again, this can be very positive if channelled rightly.

4. Fear. Understandably, there will be anxiety and fear about a whole range of things: pain, surgery, hospitals, how our loved ones will cope, losing control over our lives, and the experience of death itself.

5. Despair. As we work through the various stages of the rejection of death, we begin to emerge into the acceptance of its inevitability. Frequently this is marked by moods of depression and despair.

6. Acceptance. For many, the darkness of despair leads on to a period almost of peace, where the inevitability of death is accepted, and the last weeks or days of life take on a special value and beauty.

In our ministry to those who are terminally ill, we must be especially aware of the needs of their closest family members and friends. In some senses it is harder for them than for the person who is dying, and they will need just as much support. They too will go through a range of reactions and mood swings, but will feel they have to keep going for the sake of their loved one. The stress of caring may build up and lead to a major reaction when the person eventually dies.

The issue of prayer for healing is a huge one (see **prayer ministry**). Here are some points to bear in mind.

- In any of our prayers, we must not tell God what to do. Rather, we tell him what we would like him to do, and leave the doing to him.
- Some people may not want us to pray for healing; they may want to 'depart and be with Christ, which is better by far' (Phil. 1:23). If so, we should respect their wishes.
- Sometimes a strong faith in healing is a form of denial, a refusal to face reality, which deprives the person of the opportunity to reach the stage of acceptance and peace and of preparing for death. There is no contradiction in praying for healing while at the same time encouraging those concerned to face the possibility and implications of death.
- However great our faith, we should avoid telling people that they definitely will be healed. We are fallible human beings and may be mistaken. If we are convinced God is going to heal, it is much better to say, 'I believe you're going to be healed, but, of course, only God knows for sure.'

Confronted with the question, 'Why has God let this happen to me?', it is generally wisest to be honest and admit we don't know. But use the opportunity to assure them of both the power and the love of God, and to affirm that he will not only give the strength to face each day at a time, but will somehow ensure that even the suffering and pain will play a part in his gracious purposes.

Our culture makes us reticent to speak about death. Don't pressurize people to do so, but be willing to respond positively if they do. The reading of a passage like Philippians 1:20–24 can raise the issue in a sensitive way, or we can touch on it when we are praying with them.

Remember that those who appear to be unconscious may still be aware of what is going on and being said. Never talk about them at the bedside; always assume they can hear. Hold hands, speak as you normally would, and pray with them, even if there is no response.

Don't worry about being there at the moment of death; it is rarely an experience to be feared. If it is appropriate, walk with them and their loved ones through the dark valley. Again, read appropriate scriptures, such as Psalm 23, and pray with them, committing them into the hands of the Lord.

Some Bible passages on death

> Even though I walk
>   through the valley of the shadow of death,
> I will fear no evil,
>   for you are with me;
> your rod and your staff,
>   they comfort me (Ps. 23:4).

None of us lives to himself alone and none of us dies to himself alone. If we live, we live to the Lord; and if we die, we die to the Lord. So, whether we live or die, we belong to the Lord (Rom. 14:7–8).

… we know that the one who raised the Lord Jesus from the dead will also raise us with Jesus … Therefore we do not lose heart. Though outwardly we are wasting away, yet inwardly we are being renewed day by day … We fix our eyes not on what is seen, but on what is unseen … if the earthly tent we live in is destroyed, we have a building from God … Therefore we are always confident and know that as long as we are at home in the body we are away from the Lord. We live by faith, not by sight. We are confident, I say, and would prefer to be away from the body and at home with the Lord (2 Cor. 4:14, 16, 18; 5:1, 6–8).

I eagerly expect and hope that I will in no way be ashamed, but will have sufficient courage so that now as always Christ will be exalted in my body, whether by life or by death. For to me, to live is Christ and to die is gain ... Yet what shall I choose? I do not know! I am torn between the two: I desire to depart and be with Christ, which is better by far; but it is more necessary for you that I remain in the body (Phil. 1:20–24).

[Jesus] shared in their humanity so that by his death he might destroy him who holds the power of death – that is, the devil – and free those who all their lives were held in slavery by their fear of death (Heb. 2:14–15).

See also 1 Corinthians 15; 1 Thessalonians 4:13–18; Revelation 21:1–22:6.

What could I say to those who are terminally ill?

Go gently on yourself. Accept that you will experience a wide range of emotions in your reaction to your illness, the prospect of dying, pain and so on. These are the natural responses of your body and your emotions to what you are going through. Seek to take them in your stride; don't be afraid of them; God will give you the strength you need for each new situation.

Do all you can to ensure that this period is a beautiful one in your relationships with your loved ones and those who care for you. Aim to make it the richest ever.

Take the opportunity to put right all you can think of from the past. Restore broken relationships, write letters of apology, make reparation, draw very near to God.

Remember and relive and enjoy the good things of the past. Look through old photograph albums and diaries. Don't worry if it upsets you; there's nothing wrong with having a good cry.

Find and do something really worthwhile in your last days. Write a poem or a journal incorporating what you've learnt from life. Paint a picture. Befriend a lonely or hurting person. Help somebody to faith in Jesus.

Remember that this is a very tough time for those nearest to you.

Do everything you can to encourage and help them.

When appropriate, talk about your feelings and fears with a minister or counsellor or someone who will understand. Be honest, and be willing to receive help in facing these fears and feelings and the prospect of death. You don't have to walk this path alone; let others walk it with you and carry some of the burden.

Keep trusting in the power of prayer. If you find your faith runs low and you can't pray for yourself, let us know. We will carry you on the shoulders of our faith and praying.

When you feel you can, talk through plans for the future with those closest to you. These may include funeral arrangements, but remember too to help equip your loved ones to face the future without you.

Hold on to the promise of God: 'Never will I leave you; never will I forsake you' (Heb. 13:5).

What could I say to family and close friends of those who are terminally ill?

(See the suggestions above, and under **illness** and **carers**.)

Accept that you will probably feel shock and emotional reaction to the illness as much as the person who is ill. Don't feel bad about this; it is a natural reaction and an expression of your love for them.

Don't feel that you must always put on a brave face in front of the person. There may well be some times when the best thing is for you both to have a good cry together.

Go easy on your own emotions. If you do feel it is right to be brave and cheerful in front of the person and the family and so on, do remember that you will still need to off-load the emotional stress somewhere. Have somebody – a close friend or a minister or a counsellor – with whom you can be really honest about your feelings, your fears, your questions and so on.

Get people to pray for you as well as for the person who is ill. You need the support and grace of God, too.

Be ready to receive help from all who offer it. You need the help, and for them it is their way of showing love.

Make it your aim that, despite all the pressures to the contrary, these few days or weeks will be full of the beauty and grace of God.

Put each day and each need into his hands.

Be especially careful that minor things don't get out of proportion.
This is a time to major on the big things like love and mercy and
goodness and the presence of the living God.

See also **bereavement, carers, illness, suffering**.

Helpful books

D. Clark and P. Emmett, *When Someone you Love is Dying*
(Bethany House)
M. Stroud, *Cancer Help* (Lion)

Resources

There are several help groups for those suffering from specific
illnesses. Details of these may be found in local phone books
(*Yellow Pages*) under 'Helplines', or from doctors or hospitals.
One of the best-known is: *Macmillan Cancer Relief,* 15 Britten
Street, London SW3 3TZ. www.macmillan.org.uk

TRAUMA

Trauma is a general term describing major disturbing experiences
that shock and hurt us deeply, covering personal disasters such as
a road accident, bereavement or rape, and high-profile public disasters such as Zeebrugge, Hillsborough, Lockerbie or Dunblane.
Besides unexpected or sudden disasters, particularly painful
processes such as a war or a divorce can also be traumatic. Trauma
can be experienced not only by those directly involved in the disaster, but by those closely linked, such as relatives, spectators, or,
say, someone who just missed catching a plane that subsequently
crashed.

Any trauma will produce a reaction, as the individual copes

with the shock physically and emotionally. In effect, the traumatic experience is a shattering blow both to our body and to our feelings; everything is bruised and thrown out of gear, and it needs time and space for it all to get back into balance and to begin to function properly again. This reaction is frequently painful and can be embarrassing. Sadly, in our culture, we often try and hide the reaction ('I'm fine, thanks'), but failure to allow the reaction to take its course, and the bottling up of emotions, almost always lead to complications and more serious reactions, known as post-traumatic stress disorders.

Everyone will react differently. Some will experience little or no disturbing reaction. Some will be fine for a time, and then go through a reaction weeks or more after the event. The size of the reaction is not necessarily directly related to the seriousness of the disaster, but can be influenced by factors such as personality and background.

Helping those who have gone through a traumatic experience

Stand by them. They have been knocked sideways. Their world has fallen apart. They feel they can't cope. They need someone who is secure, whom they can lean on, who is dependable, who brings normality.

Pray for them. Get others to pray. Let them know you are praying for them. Accept that they may not themselves feel able to pray, but assure them that that is a common experience during such times and God understands.

Help them to talk about the experience, to express their feelings and fears, to share the pain. Make it easy. Never belittle the hurt they express. Accept that they need to off-load it, and that the simple act of expressing it is part of the healing process.

In the darkness of the traumatic experience, it is rarely wise to try and give a full answer to the question, 'Why has this happened to me?' It is often best to say something like, 'We don't understand why, though one day maybe we will.' In the long run your love and support will count for far more than a carefully argued answer.

Be prepared for, and accept, mood swings, irritability, anger, tears and irrational feelings. Gently help them cope with them.

Watch for any danger signals, such as serious depression or excessive focusing on the disaster, and make sure they get professional help.

What could I say?

Expect a reaction. You've had a bad experience and your body and your emotions need to react, to get it out of your system.

Let other people help you. Don't go it alone. Don't withdraw. You need friends and helpers at a time like this.

Lean on God. At times you may wonder if he's there, and all sorts of doubts and questions and even angry reactions may arise in your mind. Don't worry about these; in fact, the best thing to do with them is to tell God about them and give them over to him to sort out. You are going through a dark valley (Ps. 23:4), and though you can't see him, he is still there with you. Pray when you can; if you can't, get others to pray extra for you. God understands where you are at.

Face up to what has happened. Talk about it to your friends or a counsellor. Don't try and pretend nothing has happened.

Allow yourself to express how you feel. Verbalize the shock and the pain. Cry.

Don't worry if you experience distressing symptoms. After traumas, people often suffer physical pain, mood swings, lethargy, nightmares, a bout of illness, or eating or sleeping problems. This is the shock coming out, and is perfectly normal.

Don't be surprised if you find yourself feeling anger. This anger is a basic reaction to the bad thing that has happened to you, and is in itself healthy and good – it is right to be angry about something that is evil. But be careful; because we're human we tend to direct our feelings of anger at other people, or even at ourselves or God. If you find yourself doing this, get help from a minister or a counsellor (see **anger**).

If you have strong feelings of guilt for what has happened, talk these through with your minister or Christian counsellor.

Accept that you are likely to experience a range of fears. After a road accident, for example, you are likely to be fearful of driving. You may be afraid of other people's reaction to you. You may also be fearful that the pain of your emotional reaction will last for ever, and you will never become 'normal' again. Equally, you may develop irrational fears, which are themselves frightening because you can't understand them. Accept that these fears are part of your reaction, and will not last for ever. If they do persist, or are particularly hard to cope with, get help from a counsellor.

Hold on to hope. Though you may never be the same as before the disaster, you will in time come through the pain and the process of reacting to it.

Be determined that even this experience will not ultimately be a destructive one in your life. Rather, with God's help you will learn things through it that are positive and that will help you to grow as a person.

See also **anger**, **fear**, **guilt**, **suffering**.

UNANSWERED PRAYER

Although there are few specific biblical examples of requests to God receiving the answer 'No' (Jesus in Gethsemane, Luke 22:42, and Paul's thorn in the flesh, 2 Cor. 12:8–9, are the two outstanding ones), we can safely assume 'unanswered' prayer has always been a feature of the experience of the people of God. We can be sure, for example, that the citizens of Jerusalem cried to God for deliverance when their city was besieged, or that the disciples prayed fervently that Jesus would be rescued from the cross; but God let his people go into captivity, and Jesus died.

Sadly, some people have an understanding of prayer that seems to ignore this feature, at times almost seeming to say that we have the right to demand anything from God in prayer and that he is required to give it to us. It is not hard to imagine the chaos and tragedies that would result if this were really so; we can be grateful that God has so ordained things that the decision as to what will actually happen is not ours, but his.

But the fact remains that many people find unanswered prayer difficult to cope with. Their problems may be on a number of levels, or may be a combination of factors:

- There is a basic disappointment. We set our hearts on something. We ask for it. And we don't get it.
- There may be frustration and anger. 'Why don't you give me what I want?'
- The experience of unanswered prayer may 'destroy' faith. 'If God's like that, I don't want to believe in him any more.' (See **loss of faith**.)
- There is the theological issue of the verses in the Bible which, taken in isolation, seem to say that all we have to do is ask, and we'll get what we want.
- There is the further theological issue that God in his love will always give us the best. We feel we know what is best for us, and ask for it – and don't get it.

Helping those who are struggling with unanswered prayer

Show understanding, sympathy and love. Though intellectual and theological answers have their place, most people's problems with unanswered prayer are basically emotional – feelings of disappointment, hurt and so on. These emotions are best countered by the love and grace of God, experienced, if necessary, through us.

Help them to focus on God rather than on the issue they've prayed for or their reaction to the unanswered prayer. Gently remind them of his love and wisdom and faithfulness. Help them to have a big vision of the greatness of God, and the mystery of his purposes; his ways and plans are far beyond our thoughts (Is. 55:8–9). Encourage them to take their reaction to him, and to seek his strength and grace in their disappointment.

If necessary, get them to talk about their disappointment and even anger about the unanswered prayer. Help them to deal with it creatively; if necessary encourage them to talk it through with a minister or counsellor.

Help them to have a biblical understanding of prayer. Stress that prayer is not a way of forcing God to do what we want. However vehemently we pray, or with however much faith, God still makes the final choice – and he always chooses what is ultimately for the best. We are not able to see that truth at the time, but it is essential for us to leave that final decision to him, as Jesus did in the Garden of Gethsemane (Luke 22:42), and be willing to accept it, even if we do not want it and cannot understand it. It may be helpful to point out that the cross was a shattering example of unanswered prayer for the disciples; doubtless they had prayed fervently that somehow Jesus should be rescued. But in God's purposes the cross was not only essential, it was the most beautiful and loving thing he had ever done.

Point out that prayer is not just a matter of asking for things; it is given primarily to bring us into the presence of God and to help us to stay there, walking with him day by day, experiencing his grace and strength for each situation.

Point out that God not only hears all our prayers, but is committed to giving the very best response to each of them. This best response, of course, is what he in his wisdom knows is best, not what we in our limited understanding think is best.

It may also be necessary to explain that in any prayer situation God may choose to answer our prayer immediately, or he may choose to answer it partially, or he may answer it in a way we do not expect, or the answer may be delayed.

It may be right to encourage them to follow Paul's example, where he seems to have prayed very strongly on three occasions over a specific issue, and then left the outcome with God, confident that his grace would be sufficient whatever happened (2 Cor. 12:8–10; see **suffering**).

Encourage them to keep praying, in particular making sure their prayers are more than just asking for what they want. Emphasize that no prayer is ever wasted, even if God responds to it in a very unexpected way. It may be helpful to encourage them to pray with a wise Christian friend or group of friends, who will be able to enrich their praying.

Help them to reach the point where they are able to say they are willing to accept whatever God may decide is best for their lives, even if it is contrary to what they would like or have asked for.

Some Bible passages relevant to unanswered prayer

'My thoughts are not your thoughts,
    neither are your ways my ways,'
                declares the LORD.
'As the heavens are higher than the earth,
    so are my ways higher than your ways
    and my thoughts than your thoughts …
… my word … will accomplish what I desire
    and achieve the purpose for which I sent it.
You will go out in joy
    and be led forth in peace …
This will be for the LORD's renown,
    for an everlasting sign
    which will not be destroyed' (Is. 55:8–9, 11–13).

[Jesus] knelt down and prayed. 'Father, if you are willing, take this cup from me; yet not my will, but yours be done.' An angel from heaven appeared to him and strengthened him. And being in anguish, he prayed more earnestly, and his sweat was like drops of blood falling to the ground (Luke 22:41–44).

Paul and his companions travelled throughout the region of Phrygia and Galatia, having been kept by the Holy Spirit from preaching the word in the province of Asia. When they came to the border of Mysia, they tried to enter Bithynia, but the Spirit of Jesus would not allow them to. So they passed by Mysia and went down to Troas. During the night Paul had a vision of a man of Macedonia standing and begging him, 'Come over to Macedonia and help us.' After Paul had seen the vision, we got ready at once to leave for Macedonia, concluding that God had called us to preach the gospel to them (Acts 16:6–10).

We know that in all things God works for the good of those

who love him, who have been called according to his purpose (Rom. 8:28).

... there was given me a thorn in the flesh, a messenger of Satan, to torment me. Three times I pleaded with the Lord to take it away from me. But he said to me, 'My grace is sufficient for you, for my power is made perfect in weakness.' Therefore I will boast all the more gladly about my weaknesses, so that Christ's power may rest on me. That is why, for Christ's sake, I delight in weaknesses, in insults, in hardships, in persecutions, in difficulties. For when I am weak, then I am strong (2 Cor. 12:7–11).

UNEMPLOYMENT

Redundancy and unemployment bring with them a cluster of problems, financial, family, personal and social. Most people who lose their jobs go through something like a bereavement process. Having lost the clear daily structure and sense of purpose that a job gives, they are particularly prone to suffer from insecurity and low self-image.

There is often a common pattern to people's reaction to being unemployed, though factors such as personal attitude, age, finance and support can make a great deal of difference, and the pattern is by no means a rigid one. The loss of work generally causes a period of shock, which may include a sense of unreality ('This can't be happening to me') and denial that there is any problem. Following this comes a comparatively optimistic period, characterized by activity and confidence that the spell of unemployment will be short. But if no job is found, this can change to a period of discouragement and despair, which after a time may lead to apathetic acceptance and resignation. Clearly, being in either of the last two stages will lessen the chances of getting a job, so it is important for the unemployed person to maintain hope and momentum, both personally and in the search for work.

Helping those who are unemployed

Make sure everything you say and do shows acceptance, respect and affirmation. Avoid anything that might seem condemning or patronizing. Very few people are unemployed because they don't want to work. Sadly, some long-term unemployed people become so discouraged and so lacking in self-esteem that they give up trying to find work. But these need extra understanding and encouragement, not criticism and condemnation.

Remember that many people gain their sense of self-worth from the job they do, so those without work will need extra love and affirmation, and continuous encouragement to find self-worth in their relationship to God and others, and in what they are able to be and do.

Keep an eye open for particular reactions such as anger, loss of confidence, loss of self-respect, and so on. Many people find the period about six months into unemployment the hardest time. Provide help and encourage them to seek counselling before things get too serious.

Remember that in a family situation the other family members will be under stress. Keep an eye on them, and make sure they seek help if problems arise.

Help those who are unemployed to maintain hope, and to sustain the motivation to remain active. Share the pain of job application rejections with them, but help them maintain the determination to keep looking for work. Help them with their decision-making, but don't make decisions for them. Be patient; there will be mood swings and dark periods; but they need you to remain a dependable source of support and encouragement.

What could I say?

Unemployment situations vary greatly, but you may find it helpful to make some of these suggestions.

Make use of all the help you can get. Accept that redundancy and unemployment can give rise to significant personal and emotional problems, quite apart from the practical issues like loss of income, and that you may have to go through these. To do this you will need all the help you can get. Whatever you do, don't try and cope on your own. Allow family and friends to help and support you. Get others to pray for you. Find a counsellor or understanding friend with whom you can talk about your reactions and feelings. Join a local support group for the unemployed.

Keep an eye open for the reactions that are common among unemployed people. Most common among these are anger and depression; do what you can to deal with them as soon as they begin to appear. Be aware that there will be an extra strain on your family; watch for signs of tension and deal with them before they get too big.

Pace yourself. Combine a hope that the period of unemployment will be short with a realism that accepts it may not be.

Keep yourself occupied. Never do nothing. Draw up a list of jobs to do round the house. Do the garden for the old lady down the road. Give a couple of mornings a week to the church office or to Mencap. Offer to help in the local charity shop. Join the staff of a playgroup. Do voluntary work in your local school. Take on a new ministry in the church. Take up new hobbies. Grow vegetables. Join a local club. Develop new domestic skills. Do a project on local history, or birds in your local park. Run, swim, walk, keep fit. Offer your skills to your neighbours. Work out your family tree. Every week, plan and do something new that you've never done before.

Structure your day and your week. Aimlessness will quickly lead to boredom and despair. Follow as clear a structure as you had when you were working.

Use the opportunity to learn new skills. Take advantage of retraining schemes. Do a course in your local college.

Take it that God is giving you a 'sabbatical' from work so that you can do something special for him. It may be some special service, or it may be giving a lot of time to prayer, or study of the Bible.

Take the opportunity to reflect. Give yourself time to do some serious thinking about your career, your values, your goals, your family, your priorities, the principles that are controlling your life, and your relationship to God. Work out and put into practice any necessary adjustments.

Use the opportunity to develop a simpler lifestyle, and to have more understanding of the less fortunate in the world.

Make a point of maintaining and developing your relationships with friends and family. Fight the tendency to withdraw; God is giving you extra time to spend with them. If you have lost many of your friendships because they were work-related, make every effort to develop new friendships to replace them. Get alongside lonely people. Widen your circle of friends at church and in the community.

If you have financial problems, get help before they become acute. Replan your budget. Write to your mortgage provider. Talk to the Citizens Advice Bureau. Make sure you are getting any state benefits available.

Make full use of schemes and centres for the unemployed run by the government and churches and voluntary organizations.

Get advice over letter-writing skills, composing a CV, filling out job applications, and interview techniques.

Remember, unemployment is a challenge, not a disaster. However unpleasant the experience, be determined you will learn and grow through it as a person and as a Christian.

See also **bereavement**.

A helpful book

P. Curran, *A Way Forward* (CWR)

VIOLENCE

Violence is the deliberate use of force against a victim, usually resulting in physical injury. In a broader sense it covers threatening or restricting activity, such as shouting, intimidating, or denying legitimate freedom. It appears in many forms in our society, including road rage, mugging, rape, and school or workplace bullying. But its most frequent location is in the home.

Most violence is by men against women or by adults against children, but perpetrators of violence may be children or women. A recent *Panorama* programme claimed that 11% of all women engage in acts of violence.

Quite apart from the seriousness of physical injury or psychological damage, violence is unacceptable because it treats people as objects, and thus expresses the opposite of the Christian concept of human relationships which have at their heart respect, care and love for others.

In a culture where the media increasingly portrays violence as acceptable and positively entertaining, we need to remember that it is a serious criminal activity. The common tendency for the perpetrator and sometimes the victim to minimize the seriousness of the violence needs to be resisted. Although some perpetrators struggle with their violent tendencies and feel remorse after an outbreak, most will try and convince themselves and others that they have not got a problem. For the victims, the shock of violence is often followed by a sense of unreality ('This can't be happening to me'), and so to denial that anything serious has happened. There can also be a sense of shame in the victim, who wants to hush the violence up.

There are a number of specific factors that tend to promote or exacerbate violence. Alcohol is the biggest. Others include personal frustration, inability to control sexual needs, a history of being a victim of violence, anger, stress, and various forms of inadequacy or impotence.

Since violence is a criminal activity, it is our duty to report it to the police or the Social Services.

What could I say to the victims of violence?

Do something. Get help. Don't keep it secret or say there is nothing that can be done. Don't be intimidated. Violence is a criminal activity, and it damages not just the victim but the perpetrator. It must be stopped. If you are being bullied at school, tell the head teacher or your parents or the school counsellor. If you are suffering marital violence, contact your minister or a marriage guidance organization. If you've been attacked, tell the police.

Don't minimize the crime that has been committed against you by blaming yourself. Even if you are partly to blame (and most victims are not), for example by allowing a row to develop, the responsibility for the violent action rests wholly with the perpetrator.

Take specific steps to avoid a recurrence. This could be a temporary marital separation, or avoiding certain streets at night. Sadly, some victims of violence almost encourage further violence by putting themselves in vulnerable positions; don't do this.

Talk to someone about how you feel. Find someone you can trust, such as a counsellor, and be honest about your feelings, reactions, fears and the like.

Don't bottle up any anger you may feel. Instead, deal with it constructively.

Resist the pressure to react to violence with violence. Many perpetrators of violence were themselves once victims; battered wives may take it out on the children. Be determined that this will not happen. Break the pattern. Commit yourself, with God's help, to a non-violent response in every situation.

Hold on to hope. Even if you are being victimized again and again, with the help of God and others you will find a way out.

Keep praying. Pray for the person who has used violence against you (Matt. 5:44). Ask God to use even this experience to do something beautiful in your life. Ask others to pray for you. If appropriate, ask your church leaders to arrange a special time of prayer ministry for you, in which you specifically bring the pain and the hurt to God for his healing.

Accept that your experience may affect your self-confidence for a time and make you apprehensive. When you feel able, with the help of a friend or a counsellor, begin to work at dealing with your fear and restoring your self-confidence.

What could I say to a violent person?

Admit that you have a serious problem and need help. This is not a negative step, but the first positive step that will lead to the solving of your problems and to increasing wholeness.

Get help. See a minister or a counsellor who will be able to spend time with you, and will help you to understand yourself and your needs and what has to be done about them.

Check out the situations in which you are prone to be violent, and do everything you can to avoid them. Learn to recognize the signs that you are beginning to lose control, and take immediate drastic action.

Give up alcohol. Ninety-two per cent of crimes of violence occur after a person has been drinking.

Check to see if there are factors that underlie your violence. These could be things such as marriage problems, the need to get your own way, or addiction to violent films. Get professional help in dealing with these.

With the help of your counsellor, try and discover any roots of violence in your past. Were you the victim of violence? Are there past hurts or frustrations or bottled-up anger?

Find ways of dealing with your anger, stress, frustration and the like without resorting to violence. Develop a healthier lifestyle; take more exercise. Get some help in developing better communication skills; disagreements do not have to become rows and end in violence.

Admit the sin of your violence to God. With the help of your minister or a Christian counsellor, seek his forgiveness and healing. Daily ask the Holy Spirit to control you and give you his fruit of self-control (Gal. 5:23). Study how Jesus coped with difficulties, opposition, provocation and so on. Model your response on his.

Admit the damage you have done to other people's lives by your violence. Accept that it was your fault and not theirs, even if you feel they may have provoked you. In the course of time, when you have made real progress in dealing with your violence, tell them how sorry you are for what you have done, and do anything you can to provide reparation.

See also **anger, communication, conflict, fear, stress.**

A useful book

H. L. Conway, *Domestic Violence* (Lion)

A support organization

Victim Support, Cranmer House, 39 Brixton Road, London
SW9 6DZ. 020 7735 9166. www.victimsupport.com

WORK ISSUES

For many people their job takes up nearly a quarter of their time, or a third of their waking hours. It is their source of income, of status, and of a sense of achievement and fulfilment. It may also be the basis of their social life.

Patterns of work are varied and constantly changing. There are still some jobs that are relatively secure and 'for life'. But for most people there is little prospect that their job will continue unchanged and secure. Social change, technological development, market-place competition, mergers and takeovers, the demands of productivity and so on all threaten the stability of jobs and careers. Adaptability, retraining, keeping ahead of the game, and the ability to cope with high demands and pressures and stay on top have all become essential. Promises of decreasing working hours have been fulfilled for some, but many, especially those in managerial and professional jobs, are finding themselves having to work longer hours to complete their work and hold on to their job.

The Bible describes God as a worker. He creates and upholds the universe and is involved in it. Jesus described his own ministry as the work his Father had given him to do (John 9:4; 17:4). Work, with its attendant skills and rewards, is a gift from God to humankind made in his own image (Gen. 1:26; 2:15), enabling men and women to share in his creativity and activity, and to take responsibility for the world around them and their own well-being.

The Bible does not set 'secular' work over against Christian service. All work is Christian service (Col. 3:23–24, 17), done specifically for the Lord, as an act of worship. It is also to be seen as service for others, an expression of our love and self-giving. Paid work (1 Tim. 5:18) and unpaid 'voluntary' work (Acts 20:33–35) are both evident in the New Testament.

There is another area in which the Bible counters contemporary thinking. For many in our society, work is the source of their significance. It gives life meaning; it is the basis of their sense of self-worth. They define who they are by the job they do. This can even continue after retirement: 'He's a retired bank manager.' Loss of work for such people is thus disastrous, not just because of the loss of income, but because it takes away the very meaning of their lives. Further, this view leads to a strongly discriminatory attitude: someone who is a bank manager is seen as considerably more important that someone who does an unskilled manual job.

The Bible rejects this attitude. Work is not the basis for our value or worth. These arise from our relationship to God, not from what we do. In that our relationships in the Christian community express our relationship to God, our worth or value also arises from our place as part of the body of Christ. This is not to say there is no source of value in work. Like everything we do, it does give us a sense of self-worth. It is right to feel a sense of achievement and fulfilment in what we are able to do; we are sharing God's pleasure at seeing what he had made and recognizing that it was very good. But this is not the primary source of our value. Someone who, perhaps through a disability, is never able to do what our society calls 'work', can still have an awareness of true worth in the family of God.

In most churches, probably only a minority are in paid employment. But this doesn't mean that the issue of work is irrelevant to the majority. Many of them will be involved in voluntary work of one sort or another; and all should be concerned for those who serve God in the market-place and be aware of the stresses and pressures they face so that they are able to give them appropriate encouragement and support.

Helping those in paid secular employment

If necessary, encourage them to break down any barrier that exists in their mind between their 'secular' work and their 'Christian' life and service. Help them to understand and apply the New Testament teaching that everything we do is to be done in the name of Jesus Christ, and for him as Lord. To help them in this you might make the following suggestions:

- Specifically give your job, your work situation, your career, your relationship with your work colleagues and the like over to God. Recognize it as a task he has given. Tell him that from now on you will do it for him, not for the boss, or for money, or whatever. You might choose to make this act of dedication of your work to God a public thing, in the presence of other Christians, and with their prayer support.
- Think through your work and try and view it as Jesus would view it if he was here today. In particular, seek to see it as a means of service, and so of expressing love, to others. Clearly, this will be easier in some jobs than in others. But even if you are doing something that is not directly related to helping people, it should be possible to think of ways in which it ultimately does so. Should this not be possible – for instance, if you are involved in making weapons of mass destruction – you perhaps ought to consider looking for another job.
- Make your job a matter of regular prayer. Get others to pray for you and with you about it and about issues that arise. Pray while at your job; get into the habit of sending up quick prayers each time you start a new piece of work, or begin a new conversation with a colleague or client. Pray for your boss, the company, and those you work with. In particular, bring to God the problem areas, the stresses, the immoral practices and so on.
- Where possible, get together with other Christians in your place of work to encourage and support each other and to pray together for the workplace.

Help them to develop a wholesome balance between time spent at work, and that spent with family and friends, in leisure pursuits, church activities and so on. Help them to resist the temptation to allow the earning of money to become the dominant feature of their lives. Stress the significance of the Bible's teaching on rest and the Sabbath principle.

Where they are under particular stress, show awareness and understanding. Help them to face it and deal with it (see **stress**).

Where appropriate, encourage them to lay down some of their church responsibilities for the time being.

Help them to develop a positive attitude to any job insecurity they may have to face. Encourage them to put their trust in God and his faithfulness. Help them to look on life as an exciting journey of faith, rather than a long-term sitting in one small corner.

Encourage others in the local group or church fellowship to demonstrate concern and support for individuals in their work situation. Provide opportunities for issues to be discussed and prayed over.

Where people are faced with ethical issues in their jobs, be slow to give definitive advice. These issues are often very complex, and a straightforward application of a Christian principle, such as 'You should always tell the whole truth and nothing but the truth', may be unrealistic and unhelpful. In some situations it may be possible to find someone else in the church who has faced the same problem and whose experience can be of help, though even there we need to be aware that what applies in one situation does not necessarily apply in another. There may be value in talking through the issue in a house group or the like, but perhaps the main value here is in helping others to be aware of the complexity of this kind of issue, rather than getting them to solve it. Help those concerned to identify the Christian principles that have a bearing on the issue (often there will be several principles, at times conflicting). Pray over the issues with them, and support them as they make up their mind how to apply these principles in the specific situation.

Similarly, it is rarely possible to give clear advice over issues of career development and change of job. Your role is more likely to be that of a listener and facilitator – helping them to express and think through all the issues involved.

Support and pray for them as they live out their Christian lives before their colleagues, and witness to their faith and seek to bring others to Jesus.

Stand with and support those who are the victims of workplace injustice or discrimination. The tendency to fight for our rights is almost universal, and there will be times when it is acceptable to do so in the name of justice. However, there is a considerable amount of teaching in the New Testament about turning the other cheek, submitting to injustice, and following the example of Jesus in remaining silent when treated unjustly (Matt. 5:38–41; 1 Cor. 6:7; 1 Pet. 2:18–23), and on occasion this may be the right course. Again, it is for the individual to make the final decision, backed by the support and prayer and concern of fellow-Christians.

Helping those in paid Christian work

Christian workers are free from many of the stresses of those involved in secular work, but it is worth bearing in mind that there are other pressures that they have to face. These can include things like high demands and expectations from those they are seeking to serve, the stress of bearing other people's burdens, a feeling of isolation, and the sense that their job is never done. Like all workers, they need encouraging and supporting, both by prayer and in word and action.

Remember that in many cases the income of Christian workers is inadequate or uncertain or both. This can give rise to particular stresses and anxieties, as, for example, they watch their children being deprived of things other Christians take for granted. Show understanding and love, and where possible take the opportunity to help.

A useful book

P. Curran, *All the Hours God Sends?* (IVP)

Two Christian organizations that specialize in work issues

Centre for Marketplace Theology, PO Box 18175, London EC1M 6AU. 020 8942 9128.
London Institute for Contemporary Christianity, St Peter's Church, Vere Street, London W1M 9HP. 020 7399 955.
www.licc.org.uk

A NOTE ON RESOURCES

Some resources are listed at the end of some of the articles. These are mostly limited to the UK and are by no means exhaustive. Sadly, books go out of print fairly quickly, and details of helping organizations change from time to time. Even so, there is a huge range of resources that we can tap into when trying to help people with their problems. Here are some suggestions for finding them.

The *internet* is now one of the major resources for contacting specialist caring and advice organizations, wherever you are in the world. There are websites for everything; some skill is needed to find just the thing you want, but it is always worth trying.

Your *doctor's surgery or medical centre* will have access to details of many specialist helping organizations locally and nationally. Just about every disease or medical condition has its support group for victims and carers.

Most *Social Services offices* will have a Voluntary Services Officer or the equivalent, who will know about the voluntary resources in your area.

Another place to try is the local *phone book* or *Yellow Pages* or its equivalent. (In the latter, try 'Charitable and voluntary organisations'; 'Counselling and advice'; 'Disability – information and services'.) 'Helplines' and the like may be listed at the front, or in the body of the directory. Even if a specific issue is not listed, try contacting a related organization. For example, my local phone book doesn't mention Alzheimer's, but it gives two helplines under 'Older people'.

Local *Citizens Advice Bureaux* and *local libraries* will either have information or be able to tell you where to get it.

For specifically *Christian organizations* consult *The UK Christian Handbook* (ask for it at your library) or your national equivalent. Denominational local or national offices often have specialist sections that will either offer help or say where to get it. Local 'networking' often yields results. Browsing in a Christian bookshop can be very valuable. Again, even if you don't find exactly the book you need, you may pick up useful information: for example, from a 'Further reading' section, or by checking through publishers' catalogues.

CARE (Christian Action Research and Education) is a particularly useful resource, especially for the UK, but also internationally: 53 Romney Street, London SW1P 3RF. 020 7233 0455. www.care.org.uk. They have three helplines: 0800 028 2228 (pregnancy crisis and post-abortion), 0845 762 6536 (respite care, counselling referral), 0845 601 1134 (childcare issues).

Another UK Christian resource, specializing in marriage, parenting, stress, debt, work pressures and caring for elderly relatives is The Christian Family Network: www.cfnetwork.co.uk.

INDEX

Bold type indicates an article or feature on the subject.